Vsevolod Pudovkin

Published and Forthcoming in KINO: The Russian Cinema Series
Series Editor: Richard Taylor

Film Propaganda: Soviet Russia and Nazi Germany (second, revised edition)
Richard Taylor

Forward Soviet! History and Non-fiction Film in the USSR
Graham Roberts

Real Images: Soviet Cinema and the Thaw
Josephine Woll

Cinema and Soviet Society: From the Revolution to the Death of Stalin
Peter Kenez

Vsevolod Pudovkin: Classic Films of the Soviet Avant-Garde
Amy Sargeant

Savage Junctures: Images and Ideas in Eisenstein s Films
Anne Nesbet

KINOfiles film companions:

The Battleship Potemkin
Richard Taylor

Bed and Sofa
Julian Graffy

Burnt by the Sun
Birgit Beumers

The Cranes are Flying
Josephine Woll

Ivan the Terrible
Joan Neuberger

Little Vera
Frank Beardow

The Man with the Movie Camera
Graham Roberts

Mirror
Natasha Synessios

Repentance
Josephine Woll and Denise Youngblood

The Sacrifice
Christine Åkesson

VSEVOLOD PUDOVKIN

Classic Films of the Soviet Avant-Garde

AMY SARGEANT

I.B.Tauris *Publishers*
LONDON • NEW YORK

Published in 2000 by I.B.Tauris & Co Ltd
6 Salem Road, London W2 4BU
175 Fifth Avenue, New York NY 10010
www.ibtauris.com

In the United States of America and in Canada distributed by
St Martins Press, 175 Fifth Avenue, New York NY 10010

ISBN 1-86064-455-4

A full CIP record for this book is available from the British Library
A full CIP record for this book is available from the Library of Congress

Library of Congress catalog card: available

Typeset in Monotype Calisto by the Midlands Book Typesetting Company, Loughborough, Leicestershire
Printed and bound in Great Britain by MPG Books Ltd, Bodmin, Cornwall

Contents

Introduction vii

Acknowledgements xxxii

Abbreviations xxxiii

Illustrations xxxiv

KINO: The Russian Cinema Series General Editor's Preface xxxvi

1 The old regime and the new: from *Hammer and Sickle* to *Chess Fever* 1

2 Russian Physiology and Pudovkin's *The Mechanics of the Brain (the Behaviour of Animals and Man*) 29

3 *The Mother* and the return of the actor 55

4 *The End of St. Petersburg* 81

5 *Storm over Asia* 111

6 *A Simple Case* and *The Deserter*: the sound film and sound film acting 139

7 The Eisenstein/Pudovkin Controversy 168

Bibliography 193

Index 205

Introduction

Vsevolod Illarionovich Pudovkin has fared comparatively and curiously badly in the annals of Soviet film history, in spite of the fame and reputation enjoyed by his major works of the 1920s and early 1930s, at home and abroad.

In spite of his artistic status but also, paradoxically, as a consequence of this popular success: as early as 1928 the avant-garde in Russia was accusing Pudovkin of betraying the principles which it had entrusted to him and of descending to outright commercialism; in the West, the indictment that Pudovkin had disappointed the hopes previously invested in him came later. According to Babitsky and Rimberg, 'Kuleshov never relinquished his artistic credo and always opposed the idea that the cinema should serve a narrow propaganda function, whereas Pudovkin devoted his great talent wholly to the service of the Party'.[1] Indeed, Pudovkin was judged and found wanting not only in particular films but also by the supposedly retrogressive trend which they announced to critics attached to a notion of a Soviet state productive of work that could be readily identified as revolutionary both in form and content. Winifred Ellerman (writing in the 1920s in Britain), Léon Moussinac (in France) and Vlada Petrić (reporting, in retrospect, American opinion of a similar date), recount that what was most valued artistically in Soviet film screened abroad was its divergence from the home-grown product, even to the extent that silent and black and white films from Russia were preferred by art-house audiences well into the 1930s.[2] Eugene Lyons, an American in Moscow, commented in 1935 that:

> There is little question that Russia is in advance of Hollywood and most other places in the theory of film art, in strikingly original and

effective photography – above all, in making pictures socially significant rather than merely amusing and ornamental. But the general level of its picture output has been steadily declining instead of rising.[3]

At one stage Pudovkin's work appeared to embrace a new and promising trend, distinct from the mainstream Hollywood product; later it failed to satisfy the expectation that it would continue to change and failed to mark progress by differentiating itself clearly from precedent or in relation to whatever was happening elsewhere. Pudovkin's practice and especially his writing became increasingly conservative.

Pudovkin's oeuvre has similarly proved unwieldy and unrewarding to film historians determined to map consistent traces of current work and thinking in past practice and theory. This arguably modernist position tends also to estimate the available evidence in so far as it can be deemed to match, herald or approach current modes. Strangely, as the supposed Russian Griffith (an appellation suggested already by Eisenstein and a comparison made by Piotrovsky) Pudovkin has also been placed by his theoretical technique alongside the dominant Hollywood tradition, and then has equally been found not to sit comfortably in the place allotted to him. Certainly, much of Pudovkin's writing in the 1920s invites such a classification, and certainly his concern with clarity and economy of means is highly reminiscent of American technical manuals of the teens.[4] Noël Burch has astutely observed a number of points at which this is contradicted in Pudovkin's concurrent film practice. Raymond Williams and Michael Orrom hint at a favourable and fruitful way of regarding this divergence, I think, when they conclude that inconsistencies in the spatial editing pattern 'appear to have been used deliberately'.[5] It is the deliberateness with which such patterns are interrupted, the licence that Pudovkin allows himself and the particular choices that he makes in each individual case which continue to warrant his being considered experimental. Fundamentally, it seems to me, he is searching in each film to achieve a particular effect, to which end he may attempt something new or may resort to the tried and trusted (as codified in 1926 in *Kinostsenarii* and *Kinorezhisser i kinomaterial*); at best, Pudovkin's means are economical and purposeful.

Pudovkin himself has proved equally exasperating. Georges Sadoul's accusation of naiveté, made at a safe distance in time and space from

Stalin's dictatorship, is presumably prompted not only by his opinion of Pudovkin's collaboration with the regime, in his production of compliant films in which Sadoul found little artistic merit. Pudovkin acted also as something of an ambassador for his country; the artistic esteem in which the classic work of the 1920s stood later was opportunistically recognised by the Soviet authorities as endorsing Pudovkin's respectability and stature as their spokesman abroad, and he duly participated in peace congresses and cultural missions on their behalf. The British scientist Waddington met Pudovkin in 1951 and was amazed at his spirited defence of the biologist Lysenko, who was then regarded in the West as thoroughly disreputable and a charlatan.[6] Ironically, although Pudovkin throughout the years voiced publicly his belief in artistic freedom, he was also quick to recognise and to establish himself in a politically expedient position. Certainly, Pudovkin was prepared to repudiate his previous preoccupations, formed in response to a discarded agenda, to denounce himself and the work of erstwhile colleagues. Pudovkin was consistently politically compliant, but the politics of the Soviet Union shifted such that communist and socialist correspondents in the West (such as Sadoul) found that their sympathies lay increasingly with those dissidents whose voices were silenced rather than with those who continued to work for the Soviet state.

The lack of ease with which Pudovkin can be accommodated may account for the partiality of treatment that his work has received: any sustained investigation on either front can but acknowledge the theoretically dissatisfying vicissitudes of the writing and the qualitative unevenness of the films. Monographs by Barthélémy Amengual, Stefano Masi and Guido Aristarco devote themselves to the exemplary works of Pudovkin's heroic period (*The Mother*, *The End of St. Petersburg* and *Storm over Asia*) as do Karaganov and Glagoleva.[7] Iezuitov's biography of 1937 provides a good discussion of the work thus far and is the basis for Mariamov's 1951 publication, the prevailing tone of which is amply given by the 1954 German translation *Pudowkin: Kampf und Vollendung* [Pudovkin: Struggle and Achievement].[8] Peter Dart (*Pudovkin s Films and Film Theory*, 1974) acknowledges Pudovkin's earlier apprenticeship with Vladimir Gardin but says nothing of the work itself, appends a translation from the later writings but gives little space to the later films. There are occasional references to both periods in the reminiscences collected together by Jean and Luda Schnitzer (*Poudovkine*, 1968), by Nina

Glagoleva (*Slovo o Pudovkine*, 1968) and by Tatiana Zapasnik and Adi Petrovich (*O sebe i svoikh fil makh,* 1975 and *Pudovkin: v vospominaniiakh sovremennikov*, 1989).

My research has drawn upon these secondary materials, in addition to Pudovkin's own writings in books and journals. It is based upon material in VGIK (the State School of Cinematography), in Gosfilmofond, in the Muzei Kino, in RGALI (the Russian State Archive for Arts and Literature) and in the State Library (formerly Lenin Library, Moscow). The journals consulted actively endeavoured to construct debates around particular themes: discussion of *The Mechanics of the Brain*, in *Sovetskoe kino* 1, is accompanied by items concerning similar scientific subjects; *Sovetskoe kino* 7, collects together reviews of Barnet's *Moscow in October*, Shub's *Ten Years*, Eisenstein's *October* and Pudovkin's *The End of St. Petersburg*. But, in contrast to Eisenstein, Pudovkin was increasingly unwilling to commit himself to a distinct theoretical position. In addition I have consulted various memoirs and articles written by his colleagues (Baranovskaia, Inkizhinov, Zarkhi and especially Golovnia) and Eisenstein's account of their differences of opinion. Much of Pudovkin's writing is theoretically not well considered. Pudovkin, unlike Eisenstein, seemingly was not a good apologist for his own work, nor is he comfortable with theoretical writing for its own sake. Pudovkin participates in current debates but rarely, unlike Eisenstein, initiates them himself. Pudovkin's contribution resides more in his films than in the commentary offered alongside them or in any theoretical explanation or interpretation volunteered. Regarding Pudovkin's writing as a whole it does not command the overall cohesion or articulation or intellectual scope of that of Eisenstein and has failed to attract similar extensive and rigorously probing subsequent engagement. Furthermore, Eisenstein can more readily be seen to adhere to avant-garde principles, consistently re-formulating a theory of montage, that which 1920s theory had estimated as the quintessence of film art. In contrast, Pudovkin becomes increasingly concerned with the art of acting, that which 1920s theory firmly consigned to the theatrical film-making of the past. However, it is my belief that his apparent renunciation, in theory, of avant-garde tenets was already presaged in his working practice. For Pudovkin, theory and theorising occupied a much less significant place in his practice and procedure than they did for Eisenstein; Pudovkin was more inclined to be pragmatic and utilitarian,

Eisenstein (even while denouncing it as idle indulgence in others) was given to idealistic speculation.

I am making a deliberate and pointed distinction here between Pudovkin's 'writings' and what may purport to be his 'theory' at any given time. One of the purposes of the following project is to investigate whether the writing does indeed ever constitute theory and, more generally, in the pursuit of this project, to question what criteria are thereby applied. I am concerned broadly with the place of Soviet cinema (Soviet and cinema) in a particular intellectual tradition and secondly with Pudovkin's immediate context, as both film-maker and commentator. The second chapter discusses *The Mechanics of the Brain* and the status of physiology before and after the Revolution. Discussion of *Storm over Asia* (*The Heir to Genghis Khan*) marks the extension to film of a scientistic philosophy. The final chapter endeavours to summarise the bases of the supposed controversy between Eisenstein and Pudovkin, setting this in a climate of heated polemicising and questioning their respective use of scientific examplars.

Pudovkin in Context

Until comparatively recently, Soviet cinema has been broached as a clearly defined 'school', conducted by a small number of monolithic directors, politically committed to the Revolution, producing canonical masterworks exemplifying well-honed tomes of written theory. Eisenstein and Pudovkin have been yoked together as 'revolutionary' film-makers by dint of their historical coincidence, at the expense of further discussion of the disagreements documented by Eisenstein himself (see chapter eight, below) and by well-informed contemporaries (such as Meyerhold) and by later biographers (such as Marie Seton).[9] Nor has there been much negotiation of the particular relevance of the term 'revolutionary'. Grierson reiterates the familiar comparison of Pudovkin with Griffith, saying that, stylistically, he was no revolutionary at all.[10] Peter Kenez doubts the suitability of the appelation, given their adherence to and conformity with the aspirations of the new regime;[11] Renato Poggioli doubts that such an association can ever be more than provisional:

> ... every avant-garde movement, in one of its phases at least, aspires to realise ... the ideal of 'tabula rasa' which spilled over from the

> individual and artistic level to that of the collective life. There is the reason why the coinciding of the ideology of a given avant-garde movement and a given political party is only fleeting and contingent ... identification of artistic revolution with social revolution is now no more than rhetorical ... Sometimes it may, though ephemeral, be sincere, a sentimental illusion ... more often we are dealing with an extremist pose or fashion.[12]

This complacent, generalising, commonplace Western view of a Soviet avant-garde, as Brandon Taylor observes, extends across a range of artistic activity:

> The revival of modernism in Britain and America in post-war years ... coincided with a hardening of attitudes towards the Soviet Union and posture of downright dismissal towards 'official' Soviet culture of the authoritarian years of Stalin's rule after 1932 ... until recently European and American scholars produced a flood of publications devoted to Soviet abstraction and 'modernism', linked to utopian interpretations of the events of 1917.[13]

Boris Groys, from whom I am adopting the apparent oxymoron 'Classic Avant-Garde', offers a polemically revisionist thesis, countering the received wisdom of a Great Break in all Russian culture marked by the rise of Stalin:

> The myth of the innocent avant-garde rests upon the view that totalitarian art of the 1930s and 1940s is a simple return to the past, a purely regressive reaction to the new art that was unintelligible to the masses ... I argue that the relevant distinctions arose not because the avant-garde project was abandoned but because it underwent a radicalisation that the avant-garde itself was unable to accomplish.[14]

But certainly, artists themselves (notably Mayakovsky) found a direct correlation between the vanguardism advocated by Lenin for the correct conduct of the revolution and the self-proclaiming avant-garde in art.[15] Poggioli notes the tendency of modern art to 'express the avant-garde as its own extreme or supreme moment',[16] but again finds the assumption of an automatic connection between political and artistic activity not only facile but doomed to disappointment: '... the hypothesis (really only an analogy or a symbol) that aesthetic radicalism and social radicalism, revolutionaries in politics, are allied, which empirically seems valid, is theoretically and historically erroneous'.[17] The sentimental view here characterised tends also I would suggest, to seek analogies between film and concurrent 'fine' art practice rather than anything more common in its appeal, although distinctions are somewhat blurred by the fascination of certain high-art forms of the 1920s with popular culture (circus, jazz, cinema itself) and the genuine intentions of academically trained artists to serve the proletariat through popular and readily accessible material (posters, industrial design, textiles, photography and so forth).[18]

In the past decade there has been more exposure and discussion of pre-Revolutionary cinema, for its own sake and as a means of countering what Ian Christie has identified as 'the still prevalent view that Soviet cinema was borne ex-nihilo with the Revolution'.[19] There has also been a number of complementary studies, resurrecting for a modern audience the popular cinema of the 1920s and its continuity with its pre-Revolutionary precursors, especially acknowledging the long service in the industry of certain personnel (such as Protazanov and Gardin)[20]. (see chapter one, below) These necessarily confront the embarrassment of the avant-gardists that such state-sponsored films as Eisenstein's *The Battleship Potemkin* [Bronenosets Potemkin, 1925] had been, at time of release, unpopular with the proletariat for whose benefit they were intended and proved, as even contemporary foreign supporters observed, more popular abroad than with domestic audiences.[21] These films were nevertheless advertised as having enjoyed enormous popularity as an enticement to future attendance.[22] Indeed, the course of state policy in the film industry in the 1920s is explicable only in terms of its admitting the failure of such films as *Potemkin* to do good box office and compete successfully with the imported product. For instance, *The Battleship Potemkin* was replaced within days of release in Moscow by Fairbanks' *Robin Hood*.[23] Cinema playbills of the NEP period (1921–1925) list an extraordinary range of films being shown alongside one another. In 1928, Viktor Shklovsky voices a view by then generally and expediently acknowledged (see chapter six, below):

> We still entertain the notion of the spectator as something contained and yet universal. We are surprised when mounted police are required to disperse the queues for Harry Piel; when the peasants of

> Novosibirsk spent the night in town to see *Peasant Women of Ryazan*. We are surprised by the financial collapse of *The Mother* and *The End of St. Petersburg* and by the total success of a *Queen of Spades* made ten years ago.[24]

Conversely, Soviet silent films continued to be popular with foreign art-house audiences well into the sound period, perhaps slightly because of their 'revolutionary' aura. The films of Eisenstein and Pudovkin were dealt with differently, and differently abroad according to particular censors' sensitivities.[25]

Pudovkin is not conveniently contained by any of these given parameters. While no less a figure than the critic Galvano della Volpe would declare Pudovkin his 'aesthetic paradigm in cinema', Pudovkin's *The Mother* was nevertheless not as unimpressive commercially as Shklovsky alleges.[26] Richard Taylor suggests that the press reviews of *The Battleship Potemkin* and *The Mother* indicate the qualities in his work which equipped Pudovkin all the better to survive under Stalin.[27] Pudovkin was increasingly isolated by the avant-gardists even amongst his contemporaries, possibly lending substance to Moussinac's 1928 analogical classification: 'Eisenstein, Pudovkin, Vertov ... one could say, for the sake of discussion, that on the same line of activity Eisenstein finds himself in the centre, Pudovkin on the right and Vertov on the left'.[28] Iutkevich says that even with *Storm over Asia* contempt for his perceived abandonment and betrayal of 'pure' cinema was being expressed (see also chapter five, below):

> Pudovkin was definitely rejected and excommunicated by ... a group of theoreticians, partisans of montage cinema, 'grand' and 'pure'. *Storm over Asia* was considered as regressive, contrary to the general direction of cinema, submissive to its subject and to mere chances of fortune, and other reprehensible things ... there was a conspiracy of silence around this film.[29]

Many of Pudovkin's contemporaries were ostracised, even eventually driven into exile by Stalin's rise to power and the concomitant restrictions on artistic freedom: even Boris Groys admits as much. Accusations of formalism and modernism were then to become a code 'for a high intellectual level not suitable for propaganda purposes'.[30] Pudovkin survived, continuing to direct films almost to the last.

Pudovkin's writings: Western approaches

Writing to Ralph Parker in 1958, Ivor Montagu says that '*Film Technique* and *Film Acting* in the English-speaking world have been reprinted again and again ... because they have been the only simple materials on deep fundamentals available. There is just as much interest in them, as basic classics, as ever'.[31] Even in the 1980s, Ivor Montagu continued to argue for the 'value to the present generation' of his translations of Pudovkin.[32] According to Paul E. Burns, writing in 1981, 'Pudovkin's present reputation primarily derives from his theoretical writings, which are straightforward and accessible'.[33] If this claim is to be accepted, it seems worth enquiring in what form his writings were received in the West, to what extent this corresponds to their original publication and whether the vicissitudes of his career as a director are consistently represented in print.

Pudovkin's first article, 'Time in Cinematography', was written while he was with the Kuleshov workshop and appeared in *Kino* in February 1923 (see chapter one, below).[34] Mostly, Pudovkin applied himself to subjects which were of popular concern and which were commonly addressed elsewhere. In 1926 he published in Moscow *The Film Director and Film Material* [Kinorezhisser i kinomaterial] and also *The Film Scenario* [Kinostsenarii]. Both very slim, very small volumes contributed to a 'popular science' series of some twenty titles, including also Turkin's *The Cinema Actor* and Gavriushin's *I Want to Work in Cinema*; forthcoming attractions included a couple of items by Osip Brik, also a *History of Cinema* and *Cinema City and the Work of the Film Studio in America*. Neither of Pudovkin's 1926 publications were illustrated or referenced. Ivor Montagu translated and amalgamated them under the title *Film Technique*. Pudovkin gave the project his blessing:

> Your proposal to translate my book into English pleased me greatly. I consider it of the utmost urgency to draw together ideas, in order that cinema workers of all countries may stand with one another in close alliance. Not many important and interesting thoughts emerge during the course of work, just for want of such a union. In so far as my book demonstrates the main theoretical principles I will look forward especially to the appearance of the book in English.[35]

Throughout the 1920s, Pudovkin gave academy lectures at home and abroad and produced articles for newspapers and periodicals: *Kino*; *Sovetskoe kino*; *Kino-gazeta*; *Sovetskii ekran*; *Kino-zhurnal ARK*; *Kino i kul tura*. A selection of these were incorporated into the 1935 and later editions of *Film Technique* and, as a matter of courtesy, Montagu continued to send Pudovkin a share of the royalties.[36]

By the early 1930s, Pudovkin's writings for domestic and foreign consumption accommodate the shift in emphasis urged by the state. Articles in *Experimental Cinema* denounce the preoccupation of Soviet directors in earlier years with montage at the expense of all else, notably plot and character development.[37] In 1934, Pudovkin's *The Actor in Film* [Akter v fil'me] was published in Leningrad with an introduction by Iezuitov (see chapter six, below). Pudovkin is praised for his warmth and sincerity towards people and to the cause of the working class. Iezuitov, remembering his first encounter with Pudovkin in *The Mother*, hotly contests accusations from the intelligentsia, expressed in scholarly journals, that Pudovkin's films serve a bourgeois ideology, are merely schematic and lacking in dialectic.[38] The book's illustrations include Pudovkin in his roles in Kuleshov's *The Death Ray* [Luch smerti, 1925] and Otsep's *The Living Corpse* [Zhivoi trup, 1929], of Nikolai Batalov and Vera Baranovskaia in *The Mother* and Valeri Inkizhinov in *Storm over Asia*.[39] Pudovkin cautioned Montagu before he embarked upon the translation:

> I must warn you that this book has been done peculiarly. It has not been written but dictated, therefore I am very much afraid that it lacks the requisite continuity and line. Some questions have been set in the beginning and not solved, simply because I had forgotten about them towards the end of my speech ... at all cost when publishing the book make mention that it has not been WRITTEN BUT TAKEN DOWN from my speeches in the Academy ... write to me about all the unclarities which you will come across when translating (e.g. you probably do not know what the meaning of the 'rehearsal period of Kuleshov' is etc.). I shall send you at once the necessary amplifications and explanations. If a special foreword is necessary for the English edition I shall also write this.[40]

There is little new personal development in Pudovkin's later writing, nor does he make an innovative contribution to a general debate (see chapter seven, below). Much he seemingly arrives at second-hand: for instance, writing in *Iskusstvo kino* in 1938, Pudovkin acknowledges the usefulness of Rudolph Bode's system of gymnastics (which Eisenstein had discussed in 1924 and included in his curriculum) and of Delsarte (familiar to all erstwhile pupils of Gardin and Kuleshov and, similarly, a film school staple).[41] (see chapter one, below) His later articles tend to harp upon a single, safe theme: 'Realism, Naturalism and Stanislavsky's "System"', ['Realizm, naturalizm i "sistema" Stanislavskogo', 1939]; 'Stanislavsky's Idea and Cinema' ['Idei Stanislavskogo i kino', 1948]; an introduction to Aleinikov's book *The Paths of Soviet Cinema and the Moscow Art Theatre* [Puti sovetskogo kino i MKhAT, 1946] and 'The Actor's Work in Cinema and Stanislavsky's "System"' ['Rabota aktera v kino i "sistema" Stanislavskogo', 1952].[42] Pudovkin continued to publish articles into the 1940s and 1950s, allowing his name to be attached to proselytising state publications intent upon the promotion of current Soviet film practice elsewhere and the denunciation of bourgeois formalism. In *Soviet Films: Principal Stages of Development* (1951), he declares that:

> ... the first works of Kuleshov idealised American detective films with their empty and only superficial dynamics ... FEKS ... expected to produce cinema actors and films which first of all would strike spectators by the unusualness of their affected form. Young Eisenstein produced ... *The Strike* filled with mere formal tricks. Instead of showing a serious and important stage in the history of the Russian labour movement, the formalistic freaks of the author led spectators away from real life, confused and sometimes distorted the link of the film with actual historical reality.[43]

Meanwhile, Ivor Montagu's original translation of *Film Technique and Film Acting* was pirated and published without his permission in the United States. The USSR was not party to international copyright agreements, making it possible for material to be taken without consent. Montagu intended a new edition as a counter-attack, to which Pudovkin provisionally agreed; he could have proceeded in the absence of Pudovkin's authorisation but felt 'morally bound not to do so'.

> Pudovkin is very interested to bring out an edition but only in the following form. With a new critical preface by himself or by himself

> and myself jointly; possibly adding an essay he has written on the history of Soviet film and ... delivered as a speech a short while ago; and possibly the iconography brought up to date ... It is my feeling, though, that he will not get down to the critical preface and notes side of the work until he is pressed.[44]

In subsequent years, Montagu and Herbert Marshall continued to badger Pudovkin into producing the new material, which was in turn repeatedly promised. Montagu's despatch of 27 June 1952 runs as follows:

> Dear Vsevolod Illarionovich
> I am writing to send you what has almost become an annually repeated letter of reproach.
> You promised me some time ago that you would write a new preface for the famous work 'Pudovkin on Film Technique', written to apply to silent days, placing it in perspective; and you said that until you had written this preface you did not wish it to be reprinted.
> When last we met I told you, and it is still the case, that there is great interest in this book all over the world. This is not because people are under any illusion that the book is the last word on film art as it is understood today, or in its realist application, but as a classic of silent cinema and therefore part of the complete storehouse of culture with which all intending students should make themselves familiar.
> I am constantly being pressed to allow a reprint and up to now have always had to refuse because waiting for the preface which you promised. The result is that the Americans, after vainly trying to get our permission, have already stolen the book and published their own reprint without any benefit to us and destroyed part of the market for any revised authorised edition which we might eventually publish.
> This cannot be helped, but I am reminded of the situation by the fact that I have today received a request from Japan to be allowed to publish a translation and have once again to give the reply that this cannot be allowed ... But is it not possible for you to turn out even if only just a little brief introduction, that will enable us to take control of all these proposals once again? Our failure to do so does not act as

> a dam to the flood of editions, only diverts them into unauthorised forms . . .[45]

Eventually, in 1955, a new selection of Pudovkin's writings was published posthumously in the Soviet Union and Ivor Montagu asked for advice as to its potential merit in translation.[46] His old friend Sergei Nolbandov was not encouraging:

> Here is my general opinion. Frankly I was disappointed. There is nothing new or exciting from a film technique point of view. A great deal is polemical, on the defensive, public self-criticism which sounds a little false and is in a way rather unpleasant. So is the self-justification. The style is rather turgid and pompous, studded with 'educated long words' and often loaded with pious political orthodoxy. This was of course absent in Pudovkin's earlier work. In many instances you will find political statements in the approved manner . . . 'Towards the Communist Target' – high faluting and pompous; 'How I became a film director' – which unfortunately tells very little of 'how' – I would recommend a foreword . . . On the whole I do not feel that any of this material, except Pudovkin's radically changed views on 'typage' and professional acting (versus the Stanislavsky system) and his more interesting and developed theories of montage would add any lustre to the old edition. There is a general aura of fossilisation over the whole thing. It may be that his elephantine style and heavy humour just get me down. I was rather bored.[47]

The edition under discussion was out of print by 1960. Currently, the most complete collections of Pudovkin's writings are available only in Russian: *The Collected Works* [Sobranie sochinenii, 1974–1977] edited by Karaganov with Zapasnik and Petrovich; the second volume of this, *About Myself and My Films* [O sebe i svoikh fil'makh, 1975], edited by Zapasnik and Petrovich, is partly available in German as *Time in Close-Up* [Die Zeit in Grossaufnahme, 1983].

For leftist film-makers and artists of the 1920s, producing works of theory was a required corollary to practice. More crucially, theory was required in order that things could be made and made effective (see chapter eight, below). Mayakovsky stated the ground rules of his own practice, more craft perhaps than art:

> Poetry is a manufacture. A very difficult, very complex kind, but a manufacture.
> Instruction in poetical work doesn't consist in the study of already fixed and delimited models of poetical works, but a study of the procedures of manufacture, a study that helps us to make new things.[48]

Through their writings they entered into fierce debate with one another (for instance, the damning by Mayakovsky in *Kino* and by others of Eisenstein's depiction of Lenin in *October*) and with commentators abroad. The journals construct debates around particular themes. Discussion of *The Mechanics of the Brain* in *Sovetskoe kino* 1 is accompanied by items concerning similar scientific subjects (see chapter two, below); *Sovetskoe kino* 7 collects together reviews of Barnet's *Moscow in October*, Shub's *Ten Years*, Eisenstein's *October* and Pudovkin's *The End of St. Petersburg*. Petrov's *What the Cinema Actor Needs to Know* (1926) and likewise Pudovkin's *The Actor in Film* (1934) address themselves to the need to familiarise oneself with the whole collective film-making process. Kuleshov dedicates his *The Art of the Cinema* (1929) to cinema audiences, executives and film-makers, seeking to engender a discussion between these parties and to engage a larger public in the issues raised.[49] Pudovkin speaks of the need for a popular audience to be schooled in film-watching as it is becoming in literature. However, even in the journal articles, Pudovkin's early writing adopts a measured form and lacks the predominant political thrust and angry polemicising which characterises the self-styled manifestos of the period. He never presumes for himself or for his practice an exclusive prerogative on correctness:

> The film is yet young and the wealth of its methods is not yet extensive; for this reason it is possible to indicate temporary limitations without necessarily attributing to them the permanence and inflexibility of laws.
> Everything said here regarding simple methods of taking shots has certainly only information value. What particular method of shooting is to be used, only his own taste and his own finer feelings can tell the scenarist. Here are no rules; the field for new invention and combination is wide.[50]

Pudovkin's writing is tempered and qualified by the recognition of the potential in film yet to be discovered: Dziga Vertov sets the tone against which I am casting Pudovkin:

> WE call ourselves Cine-Eyes as distinct from cinematographers: that flock of junk-dealers who do rather well peddling their rags ... WE declare the old films, the romantic, the theatricalised etc., to be leprous.[51]

This haranguing of the reader was not confined to film criticism. 'Everyone who feels himself capable of doing so', jibes Zamiatin, 'is required to compose treatises, epic poems, manifestos, odes or other compositions dealing with the beauty and grandeur of One State'.[52] However, privileged by its comparative youth, its popular and transnational appeal and its documentary attachment to contemporary events as they happened, film was credited with particular effect and impetus.

Much of early film theory, in Soviet Russia and elsewhere, is concerned with establishing the equal status of film with the ancient arts (Caciotto, Canudo, Arnheim, Harms, Lindsay et. al.) and also with delineating its distinct parameters. Although Kuleshov, Pudovkin and Eisenstein elect to practise montage differently, true to type as a Soviet 'school', in the 1920s at least, they agree that editing is the technique by which film distinguishes itself. Pudovkin stresses also the nature of its material base, the substance which the artist/director handles and crafts in the editing process:

> ... the active raw material for the film director is those pieces of celluloid on which, from various view points, the separate movements have been shot.[53]

This emphasis on the materiality of film and its origins in photography placed its claims qua art in an arguable position, amply articulated by the various polemicising factions. The cameraman Vladimir Nilsen reports the unanimity with which the congress of 'Russian Artists and Amateurs of Art' in 1894 disqualified photography's artistic ambitions: 'Photography may serve as a simple substitute but not as an independent means of artistic creation'.[54] Photography was rejected as a merely mechanical record. Pudovkin implicitly responds to the extension of this dismissal to film. In *The Film Director and Film Material*, he stresses the distance in the relationship between the fabricated product (the film) and its various subjects in nature, the happening of real events in real space and real time: 'To show something as everyone sees it is to have accomplished nothing'.[55] Pudovkin prioritises editing as the process of synthesis and transformation of material required in order that film should attain accreditation as art, but also acknowledges that the most basic element of film, the individual camera set-up, is fundamentally analytical, selective and estranged from natural perception:

> Normal human vision can embrace a little less than 180° of surrounding space ... the field of the lens is considerably less ... already the director begins to leave behind the normal apprehension of real space ... picks out from it only a part ... Not only does the small view angle set bounds to the space in which the action develops both in height and in width but ... the depth of the space picked out is also limited.[56]

In this straightforward acknowledgement of the formal implications for film imposed by the camera's technical properties, Pudovkin at once marks himself out from the cultish commentaries of many of his contemporaries. The camera and camera lens appear as a frequent motif on film posters, often superimposed on a bespectacled or naked eye (for instance, the posters by Rodchenko and the Stenberg brothers for Vertov, and the Stenbergs' poster for Ruttmann's *Berlin* [Germany, 1927].[57] Anatoli Golovnia, Pudovkin's cameraman, was photographed framed by a lens for Lily Brik's *Eye of Glass* [1929]. 'I am the Cine-Eye', proclaimed Vertov:

> I am the mechanical eye. I the machine show you the world as only I can see it. I emancipate myself henceforth and forever from human immobility. I am in constant motion. I approach objects and move away from them I creep up to them I clamber over them I move alongside the muzzle of a running horse. I tear into a crowd at full tilt I flee before fleeing soldiers I turn over on my back I rise with aeroplanes I fall and rise with falling and rising bodies ... Freed from any obligation to 16–17 frames a second, freed from any restraints of time and space I juxtapose any points in the universe regardless of where I fixed them. My path leads

> towards the creation of a fresh perception of the world. I can thus decipher a world that you do not know.[58]

The recurrence of the image asserts the primacy of the camera as an instrument of vision itself, but also asserts the camera-derived image as the product of a machine, and, as such. an object of veneration. Vertov, like Mayakovsky, urged that material be drawn from the street, constantly mobile and constantly changing.[59] Vertov argued that, by recording life as it was, by making films of fact rather than of constructed fiction, he was closer to an authentic view of the world and that this authenticity constituted an art more appropriate to a revolutionary society. Indeed, Vertov was with extraordinary alacrity and facility simply turning the old academicians' objection to photography on its head: the mechanical, documentary functions which had hitherto denied its artistic status were now pronounced its crowning glory.

Pudovkin's films: Western approaches

Devotees of Pudovkin's films, as of his writing from the Heroic Age of Soviet Cinema, have, for the most part, disparaged his later work for its want of inventiveness and the apparent willingness to comply with an orthodox cultural and ideological agenda. However, the spirit with which Pudovkin launched himself into the early experiments with montage and 'close-ups in time' is not entirely lost: the French critic Pierre Billard was sufficiently generous to find something worthwhile amidst the routine dreams of tractors in *The Harvest* [Vozvrashchenie Vasiliia Bortnikova, 1952], praising it for its adventurous use of colour.[60] During the war, *Suvorov* (1941) was praised in some unlikely quarters in the Allied Nations, for its portrayal of an historic Russian victory against Austria.[61] *Nakhimov* won Pudovkin a prize at the 1947 Venice Festival for his direction of crowd scenes. Meanwhile, Georges Sadoul, like Nolbandov, accuses Pudovkin of naiveté, intending, I think, his style and temperament and his complicity with the state.[62] Dmitri and Vladimir Shlapentokh say that Pudovkin was sufficiently astute to supply Dukelsky, head of Soviet cinema from 1938, 'with new "evidence" of the criminal activity of the previous leadership. At the same time, as a good friend, he tried to exploit this discussion in favour of his colleagues by suggesting that they were also victims of "enemies of the people" who controlled cinematography. In this way he was able to protect both himself and his friends';[63] but the Shlapentokhs hold Pudovkin significantly accountable, though certainly not alone, in the denunciation under Stalin of himself and former colleagues. It is beyond the scope of the present enquiry to attempt to estimate the sincerity of Pudovkin's service after the so-called Great Break, or, for that matter, to question his original adherence to the ideological and cultural ideals of the 1920s. Gabrilovich probably comes near to a truth by which I, at least, am persuaded: 'In order to understand so many of the puzzles, secrets and absurdities of our complicated life, it is necessary to comprehend most of all, the real significance of fear'. Gabrilovich places himself, along with Eisenstein, amongst those who managed to glorify reality 'but with various reservations and innuendoes'. Eisenstein, for instance, sought an 'expert' opinion from Stalin as to the exact length of Ivan the Terrible's beard.[64] Nor was Pudovkin, although managing to continue to work, exempt from criticism from officials and onetime colleagues: Rotha, writing in 1951, reports the criticisms levelled at Eisenstein, Pudovkin, Vertov and Dovzhenko 'for the pursuit of barren intellectualism';[65] certainly there was much wrangling with the censors over *The Deserter* and the actor Mikhail Bleiman says that he well remembers Pudovkin pleading his case 'in the blue room'.[66] *Life is Very Good* was drastically re-worked; *Suvorov* was the subject of a letter to the director from Stalin himself and was publically vilified[67] (see chapter six, below).

Pudovkin's *The Actor in Film* and the journal articles of the early 1930s appear already to endorse what had by then become official doctrine. It may be that Pudovkin was prepared to compromise the previous theoretical principles in order to survive but I should like to suggest that the ease with which he seemingly acclimatised himself to a revival of 'psychologism' in film was equally presaged in his direction in the 1920s of *The Mother* and *Storm over Asia* and in his performance in *The Living Corpse*: that is to say, the writing expressed a practice in which he already felt comfortable. In his portrayal of the unloved and unloving husband Theodore, Pudovkin adopts a minimalist style: the slow lowering and raising of the eyes as a gesture of resignation; the merest hint of a shrug of the shoulders to indicate the tedium and indifference with which he now meets the world and accepts the sole prospect for his own redemption.

Peter Dart's monograph, *Pudovkin s Films and Film Theory* (1974), takes it for granted that the selected writings of Pudovkin under consideration constitute a work of theory. There is no discussion of what might be usefully deemed a film theory nor yet what might be construed as theory per se. Given that Pudovkin is frequently tagged 'the Russian Griffith', there lacks any consideration on Dart's part that Pudovkin's chief purpose may have been no more than to codify and lend testimony to techniques which he judged had proved themselves already efficacious elsewhere. Pudovkin's *The Film Scenario* and *The Film Director and Film Material* appeared shortly after the premier of *The Mother*; *The Actor in Film* appeared after the much delayed completion of *A Simple Case (Life is Very Good)* and *The Deserter* and refers also to the performance in *The Living Corpse*. Both Pudovkin and Eisenstein quote practical work in which they have been engaged in order to illustrate and clarify the argument presented. Pudovkin frequently refers to his experiences on set with Doller, Golovnia, Baranovskaia, Batalov, Inkizhinov, Zarkhi and others. He is willing to share credit and says that ideas could be volunteered by any one of them, to be taken up by the group. Indeed I venture to suggest that, for the most part, Pudovkin's writing would be better represented as a collection of workshop 'receipts'. In comparison to Eisenstein, Pudovkin's output of theoretical material was not large, and unlike Eisenstein, he seemed to lack the temperament (or the stomach) for theoretical writing for its own sake (see chapter eight, below). While Pudovkin later balked at Montagu's request for new material, perhaps restrained by a reluctance to fall foul unwittingly of the authorities, and confined himself to the repetition of safe and pious platitudes, Eisenstein continued ever to elaborate and revise the theoretical basis of films he would not live to realise; Eisenstein seemingly enjoyed theoretical endeavour as a distinct enterprise.

In conclusion to his 1974 thesis, Peter Dart conveniently invokes Bazin's preference for depth of field and the expansive, uninterrupted spaciousness of full-focussed shots as more cinematic than the fragmented analysis necessary for montage; he draws from Bazin the moral that such means are inherently less intentional on the part of the director, more democratically involving of the spectator. Dart sets up Bazin in opposition to the Soviet 'school', whose filmic methods he then facilely suggests are concomitant in their marked intentionality with a dictatorship over the film audience and the wider public. 'According to Bazin', says Dart, 'montage as used by Kuleshov,

Eisenstein or Pudovkin, "did not give us the event, it alluded to it"'.[68] However I find the assumption made by Dart of a direct correlation between methods and political context ('Pudovkin's film theory is', he declares, 'well-suited to the ends of socialist-realism') unconvincing both as a general thesis and in the particular circumstances of Soviet film in the 1920s and early 1930s. Also I find the suggestion that Bazin was himself hostile to, or unappreciative of, early Soviet achievements in film misplaced and erroneous. Bazin distinguishes between two broad and opposing trends:

> ... those directors who put their faith in the image and those who put their faith in reality. By 'image' I here mean, very broadly speaking, everything that the representation on the screen adds to the object there represented. This is a complex inheritance but it can be reduced essentially to two categories: those that relate to the plastics of the image and those that relate to the resources of montage, which, after all, is simply the ordering of images in time.[69]

Bazin praises the image of the stone lions (while wrongly accrediting this to *The End of St. Petersburg*) as 'a symbol of the aroused masses' and lauds Eisenstein: 'Maybe it does not really matter if Russian painting is second rate providing Russia gives us first rate cinema. Eisenstein is her Tintoretto'.[70] But Bazin generally values the development of a cinema of reality, marked by a number of formal traits:

> Well-used, shooting in depth is not just a more economical, but a simpler, and at the same time a more subtle way of getting the most out of a scene. In addition to affecting the structure of film language, it also affects the relationships of the minds of the spectators to the image, and in consequence it influences the interpretation of the spectacle ... in general terms:
>
> 1) ... depth of focus brings the spectator in closer relation with the image than he is with the reality. Therefore it is correct to say that, independently of the contents of the image, its structure is more realistic;
>
> 2) ... it implies, consequently, both a more active mental attitude on the part of the spectator and a more positive contribution on his part to the action in progress. While analytical montage only calls for him to follow his guide, to let his attention follow along

> smoothly with that of the director who will choose what he should see, here he is called upon to exercise at least a minimum of personal choice. It is from his attention and his will that the meaning of the image in part derives.
> 3) From the two preceding propositions, which belong to the realm of psychology, there follows a third which may be described as metaphysical. In analysing reality, montage presupposes of its very nature the unity of meaning of the dramatic event. Some other form of analysis is undoubtedly possible but then it would be another film. In short, montage by its very nature rules out ambiguity of expression. Kuleshov's experiment proves this 'per absurdum' in giving on each occasion a precise meaning to the expression on a face, the ambiguity of which alone makes the three successively exclusive expressions possible.[71]

When Bazin proceeds to a discussion of the particular cinema which he values most highly (the Italian School of the Liberation), he again posits a notion of reality in which he requires the director to place his faith: 'Is not neo-realism primarily a kind of humanism and only secondarily a style of film-making? Then as to the style itself, is it not essentially a form of self-effacement before reality?'; 'I am prepared to see the fundamental humanism of the current Italian films as their chief merit. They offer an opportunity to savour, before time finally runs out on us, a revolutionary flavour in which terror has yet no part'.[72] However, in as much as Bazin's predisposition for reality over image inclines him towards a particular subject matter as direct source, he finds the true precursor of *Paisà*, as a film and as an event, in the Soviet 'school' and especially in *The Battleship Potemkin*:

> Was it not from the outset their search for realism that characterised the Russian films of Eisenstein, Pudovkin and Dovzhenko as revolutionary both in art and politics, in contrast to the expressionist aestheticism of the German films and Hollywood's mawkish star worship?[73]

Bazin's view of the affinity between Pudovkin and neo-realism is apparently endorsed by the Italians themselves. Zavattini comments: 'Pudovkin for us, is not only a great director, Pudovkin for us *is* cinematography'; Umberto Barbaro adds: 'Pudovkin's creative work brings together, into an harmonious and unified whole, a profoundly humane perception of humanity, both theoretically and artistically'.[74]

Consequently, it may be not just a reappraisal of Pudovkin that is now required, but also an examination of the received canon in which he has habitually found himself placed.

Notes

[1] Paul Babitsky and John Rimberg, *The Soviet Film Industry*, New York 1955, p. 122

[2] see Winifred Ellerman (Bryher), *Film Problems of Soviet Russia*, Territet 1928; Léon Moussinac, *Le Cinéma soviétique*, Paris 1929; Vlada Petrić, 'Soviet Revolutionary Films in the U.S.A.', Ph.D., N.Y. U, 1973

[3] Eugene Lyons, *Modern Moscow*, London 1935, p. 252

[4] see, for instance, Epes Winthrop Sargent, *The Technique of the Photoplay*, New York 1913; H. A. Phillips, *The Photodrama*, New York 1914; Frederick A. Talbot, *Moving Pictures*, London 1912

[5] Raymond Williams and Michael Orrom, *Preface to Film*, London 1954, p. 70

[6] C. H. Waddington report, *Sight and Sound*, 17.68 (1951), p. 159

[7] Barthélémy Amengual, *V.I. Poudovkine*, Lyon 1968; Stefano Masi, *V.I. Pudovkin*, Florence 1985; Guido Aristarco, 'Teoria di Pudovkin', *Bianco e Nero* 9.5 (1948); Nina Glagoleva, *Mat* , Moscow 1975

[8] N. Iezuitov, *Pudovkin: Puti tvorchestva*, Moscow 1937; A. Mariamov, *Pudovkin*, Moscow 1951 and *Pudowkin: Kampf und Vollendung*, Berlin 1954

[9] Marie Seton, *Eisenstein,* London 1952, p. 92: Eisenstein and Pudovkin would stay up late into the night arguing; 'each bought a dog and gave the poor beast the name of his rival. Pudovkin taught his dog, Eisenstein, to beg for titbits, while Eisenstein shouted at his dog, Pudovkin, to make it obey him'; see also RGALI 2060/1/161, letter from Marie Seton to Pudovkin 8 September 1949: 'Do you remember how I insisted that [Eisenstein] was a wonderful person and you were skeptical . . ..'

[10] Forsyth Hardy, ed. *Grierson on Documentary* [1946], London 1979, pp. 24: 'Do not believe it if people tell you we have only to go to the Russians for our guide. The Russians are naturally on the same job as ourselves and more deliberately and with less patience of the reactionary and sentimental Poets-in-Blazers who take the honours of art in our own country. But, looking at the core of the problem, what in fact have they given us? Pudovkin is only Griffith in Revolutionary garb with the sensation of a Revolutionary victory by arms to balance the Ride of the Klansmen and the other fake climaxes of Griffithian cinema'.

[11] Peter Kenez, *Cinema and Soviet Society*, Cambridge 1992, p. 51

[12] Renato Poggioli, *The Theory of the Avant-Garde*, Cambridge MA 1968, p.96

[13] Brandon Taylor, *Art and Literature under the Bolsheviks* II, London 1992, p.xvi

[14] Boris Groys, *The Total Art of Stalinism*, Princeton 1992, p. 8; see also 'The Birth of Socialist Realism from the Spirit of the Russian Avant-Garde', Hans Günther, ed. *The Culture of the Stalin Period*, London 1990

[15] V.I. Lenin, 'Dogmatism and "Freedom of Criticism"', *What is to be Done?* [1902], trans. Robert Service, Harmondsworth 1988, p. 92

[16] Poggioli, p. 81

[17] Poggioli, p. 95; see also Daniel Herwitz, 'Constructivism's Utopian Game with Theory', *Making Theory/Constructing Art*, Chicago 1993

[18] see Camilla Gray, *The Russian Experiment in Art*, London 1986, also *Paris-Moscou*, Paris 1979 and *Berlin-Moskva/Moskau-Berlin*, Berlin 1995

[19] the IAMHIST conference 'Russian and Soviet Cinema: Continuity and Change' (see *Historical Journal of Film, Radio and Television,* 2.2 [1991]), the publication of Yuri Tsivian and Paolo Cherchi Usai, *Silent Witnesses*, London 1986, Yuri Tsivian, *Early Cinema in Russia and its Cultural Reception*, London 1994 and Denise J. Youngblood, *The Magic Mirror: Moviemaking in Russia 1908-1918*, Madison 1999, as also the BFI video series 'Russian Pioneers', have gone some way towards correcting this misapprehension

[20] Ian Christie and Julian Graffy, *Protazanov*, London 1993

[21] Winifred Ellerman (Bryher), p. 30

[22] Kristin Thompson, 'Government Policies and Practical Necessities', Anna Lawton, ed. *The Red Screen*, London 1992 and Denise J. Youngblood, *Movies for the Masses*, Cambridge 1992

[23] Valéric Posener, 'Comment Douglas Fairbanks et Igor Illinski se disputèrent à cause de Mary Pickford', François Albera, *Vers une théorie de l acteur*, Lausanne 1990, p. 70

[24] Viktor Shklovskii, 'K voprosu ob izuchenii zritelia', *Sovetskii ekran* 50, 11 December 1928, p. 6; he is referring to *The Siren*, starring Harry Piel, Olga Preobrazhenskaia's 1927 *Peasant Women of Riazan* (notorious for representing country life and the peasantry as if the revolution had not taken place) and Protazanov's 1916 adaptation of Pushkin's *The Queen of Spades*

[25] for instance, the films of both Eisenstein and Pudovkin were barred from public screens in Britain and prompted parliamentary questions; in the Netherlands, Ansje van Beusekom tells me, Pudovkin's humanitarian appeal was considered more insidiously subversive and potentially dangerous than Eisenstein's overt propagandising; (for reception in the Netherlands, see also Paul Overy, *De Stijl*, London 1991, p.33)

[26] qu. Stefano Masi, *V.I.Pudovkin*, Florence 1985, p. 127

[27] Richard Taylor, *Film Propaganda: Soviet Russia and Nazi Germany*, Cambridge 1979, p. 90

[28] Moussinac, p. 147

[29] Iutkevich, interviewed by Luda and Jean Schnitzer, *Poudovkine*, Paris 1966, p. 159

[30] Dmitri and Vladimir Shlapentokh, *Soviet Cinematography*, New York 1993, p. 28

[31] IMC/BFI/SM item 101

[32] IMC/BFI/SM item 97

[33] Paul E. Burns, 'Pudovkin', *Journal of Popular Film and Television* 19.2 (1981) p. 70

[34] Pudovkin, 'Vremia v kinematografe', *SS* I, pp. 87-89

[35] IMC/BFI/SM item 89, letter from Pudovkin, 7 December 1928

[36] IMC/BFI/SM item 101, letter from Montagu to his solicitor, 14 July 1954

[37] Pudovkin, 'Film Direction and Film Manuscript', *Experimental Cinema* 1.1 and 1.2 (1930)

[38] Nikolai Iezuitov, *Pudovkin*, Moscow 1937, pp. 3–4

[39] these illustrations appear also in the memorial edition of *Film Technique and Film Acting*, London 1968

[40] IMC/BFI/SM item 92, letter to Montagu, 10 January 1935

[41] Pudovkin. 'O vnutrennem i vneshnem v vospitanii aktera', *Iskusstvo kino* 7, 1938, tr. Richard Taylor, *The Film Factory*, London 1988, p.394; Eisenstein, *Selected Works* I, p. 57

[42] for all these, see Pudovkin, ss, 1975-77

[43] Pudovkin, Aleksandrov, Pirev, *Soviet Films: Principal Stages of Development*, Bombay 1951, p. 6; the Shlapentokhs, *Soviet Cinematography*, New York 1993, cast Pyr'ev as an arch-chauvinist

[44] IMC/BFI/SM item 101, letter 25 September 1949

[45] IMC/BFI/SM item 101; see also RGALI 2060/1/150, letter 23 September 1951

[46] Pudovkin, ed. A. Groshev, *Izbrannye stat i*, Moscow 1955

[47] IMC/BFI/SM item 101

[48] Vladimir Maiakovskii, *How are Verses Made?*, tr. G.M. Hyde, Bristol 1990, p. 88; Maiakovskii continues:

> Innovation, innovation in materials and devices, is a sine qua non of every poetical composition ... To understand the social command accurately, a poet must be in the middle of things and events. A knowledge of theoretical economics, a knowledge of the realities of everyday life, an immersion in the scientific study of history are for the poet, in the very fundamentals of his work, more important than scholarly textbooks by idealist professors who worship the past.

[49] Lev Kuleshov, 'The Art of the Cinema', in Ronald Levaco, ed. *Kuleshov on Film*, London 1974, p. 42

[50] Pudovkin, 'Stsenarii: tema' and 'Priemy obrabotki materiala: montazh stroiashchii', *Kinostsenarii*, *SS* I, pp. 56 and 69

[51] *FF*, p. 69, from *Kino-Fot* 1, 25–31, 1922

[52] Evgenii Zamiatin, *We*, tr, C. Brown, Harmondsworth 1993, p. 3

[53] Pudovkin,'Metod kino', *Kinorezhisser i kinomaterial*, *SS* I, p. 97

[54] Vladimir Nilsen, *Cinema as a Graphic Art*, London 1936, p. 140; see also David Elliott, *Photography in Russia 1840-1940*, London 1992, p. 51, re the use of paintings as models for early photographs.

[55] Pudovkin, 'Material kino', *Kinorezhisser i kinomaterial*, *SS* I, p. 100

[56] Pudovkin, 'Rezhisser i operator: operator i apparat', *Kinorezhisser i kinomaterial*, *SS* I, p. 123

[57] see Mildred Constantine, *Revolutionary Soviet Film Posters*, London 1974 and Susan Pack, *Film Posters of the Russian Avant-Garde*, Berlin 1995

[58] *FF*, p. 93, originally *Lef* 3 (1923); Vertov here identifies himself with an apparatus seemingly detached from an operator; elsewhere in the film journals there are features devoted to intrepid cameramen (including Kaufman) creeping, clambering, rising and falling with camera

[59] Maikovskii, *How are Verses Made?*, p. 88

[60] Pierre Billard in *Cahiers du Cinéma* 55.1, 1954 qu. in Jean and Luda Schnitzer, *Poudovkine*, Paris 1966, p. 169; on *Vasilii Bortnikov*, Pudovkin's adaptation of Nikoleva's novel *Harvest*, see Vance Kepley Jr, 'Pudovkin, Socialist Realism and the Classical Hollywood Style' in the *Journal of Film and Video* 47.4, 1995-96, pp. 3–16

[61] in 1944, Ivor Montagu supplied Pudovkin with research material from the Victoria and Albert Museum and elsewhere for *Nakhimov* and sent him the appreciative British reviews

(including one from *The Lady*, no less) for *Suvorov*; RGALI 2060/1/151, letter 28 February 1944: '*Suvorov* everyone here liked very much ... You have made in this film ... an historical classic which really does what all such classics succeed in doing, that is creating a reality so vivid that it even replaces history itself in the imagination of the beholder. One cannot read about Suvorov, after seeing the film, without seeing in every line of his doings and battles the characters depicted on the screen'; see also Pudovkin's letter to Montagu, *SS* III, p. 276.

[62] Georges Sadoul, *Recherches soviétiques: Cinéma*, Paris 1956, pref.; significantly, this remark is made after Stalin's death at a time when the Left in France is undergoing its own de-Stalinisation

[63] Dmitri and Vladimir Shlapentokh, *Soviet Cinematography*, New York 1993, p. 28

[64] Shlapentokhs, p. 24

[65] Paul Rotha, *The Film Till Now*, London 1951, p. 566

[66] Jean and Luda Schnitzer, *Poudovkine*, Paris 1966, p. 176 and Tatiana Zapasnik and Adi Petrovich, *Pudovkin v vospominaniiakh sovremennikov*, Moscow 1989, p. 214

[67] Shlapentokhs, p. 57; see also Babitsky and Rimberg., *The Soviet Film Industry*, New York 1955 and Leyda, *Kino*, London 1960

[68] Peter Dart, *Pudovkin s Films and Film Theory*, New York 1974, p. 155: Bazin here speaks of Kuleshov, Eisenstein and Gance and not of Pudovkin (see *Qu est-ce-que-le cinéma?* I, Paris 1958, p. 133). Dart concludes, p. 156, that 'Pudovkin's film theory is well-suited to the ends of socialist realism'. To the contrary, the period of 'socialist realism' under Stalin's control saw a rejection of the type of montage which Dart associates with 'intentionality'. Consequently I am suspicious of Dart's reading of Bazin and of his understanding of periodic changes in Soviet film and in Pudovkin's contribution.

[69] André Bazin, *What is Cinema?* I, tr Gray, Berkeley 1967, p. 24

[70] Bazin, *What is Cinema?* I, p. 12

[71] Bazin, *What is Cinema?* I, p. 35

[72] Bazin, *What is Cinema?* I, p. 29 and II, p. 21

[73] Bazin, *What is Cinema?* II, p. 16

[74] Nina Glagoleva, *Slovo o Pudovkine*, Moscow 1968, p. 3; see also Mark Zak, *Rasskaz o Pudovkine*, Moscow 1970

Acknowledgements

The following work is based upon a doctoral thesis, 'Pudovkin and Pavlov's Dog', written under the supervision of Professor Ted Braun. Both the doctorate and additional archival research was funded by the British Academy. In addition I should like to thank Maddy Mitchell and Colin O'Neill, from the Department of Film and Television (University of Bristol) and, for her patience with an often recalcitrant pupil, Dorinda Offord, Department of Russian (University of Bristol). I am grateful to the late Dr. Robin Evans and to Dr. Catherine Cooke (University of Cambridge) for firing an interest in research and in things Russian. Rashit Iangirov, Vance Kepley Jr. and Ian Christie were encouraging from the outset. Naum Kleiman and his staff at the Muzei Kino, Svetlana Artamonova of the Russian State Library, Valeri Bosenko and the staff at Gosfilmofond, the staff at RGALI, and Tatiana Storchak, Natasha Ushkakova and Sasha Ikonnikov at VGIK were all helpful too. I am grateful to Katia Khokhlova for allowing me access to the family archive and to Valérie Posener. Enormous thanks are due to Richard Taylor for inviting me to contribute to this series: a more supportative, attentive and generous editor one really cannot imagine.

Abbrevations

RGALI	Russian State Archive of Art and Literature
VGIK	State Institute of Cinematography
IM/BFI/SM	Ivor Montagu Collection, British Film Institute Special Materials
FF	Richard Taylor and Ian Christie, eds. *The Film Factory*, London 1988
IFF	Richard Taylor and Ian Christie, eds. *Inside the Film Factory*, London 1991
SS	A. Karaganov with T. Zapasnik and A. Petrovich, eds. *Sobranie sochinenii*, Moscow, volume I 1974, volume II 1975, volume III 1976

List of Illustrations

Back cover: Pudovkin photographed in *Proletarskoe kino*, Moscow 1925, p. 9

Front cover: Borisov and Zhukov poster for Otsep's *The Living Corpse*, 1929; Pudovkin in the role of Fedia

Chapter one: The old regime and the new
Fedia (Pudovkin) and the Gypsy in *The Living Corpse* 10
Zhban's finger crooking (*The Extraordinary Adventures of Mr. West . . .*) 12
Mr. West (*The Extraordinary Adventures of Mr. West . . .*) 15
Gardin shot patterns, à la Delsarte 16
Mr. Trotsky (*The Extraordinary Adventures of Mr. West . . .*) 19

Chapter two: *The Mechanics of the Brain*
the unconditioned reflex in a newly born baby 41
white coated lab. technicians 46

Chapter three: *The Mother*
Pudovkin as a police officer 68

Chapter four: *The End of St. Petersburg*
the church and autocracy (the statue of Nicholas II) 90
St. Petersburg's shaking foundations 94
the Petrograd side housing blocks 99

Chapter five: *Storm over Asia*
Deni poster, 1918 120
Valerii Inkhizhinov as Bair, the Mongolian trapper 125

Chapter six: *A Simple Case* and *The Deserter*
Mashenka 145
the hero returns to his first wife 147
a policeman conducting traffic 154
Fritz defies the tanks 154

Chapter seven: The Eisenstein/Pudovkin controversy
Timoshenko's diagrammatic rendition of Kuleshov 187

KINO: The Russian Cinema Series General Editor's Preface

Cinema has been the predominant popular art form of the first half of the twentieth century, at least in Europe and North America. Nowhere was this more apparent than in the former Soviet Union, where Lenin's remark that 'of all the arts, for us cinema is the most important' became a cliché and where cinema attendances were until recently still among the highest in the world. In the age of mass politics Soviet cinema developed from a fragile but effective tool to gain support among the overwhelmingly illiterate peasant masses in the civil war that followed the October 1917 Revolution, through a welter of experimentation, into a mass weapon of propaganda through entertainment that shaped the public image of the Soviet Union – both at home and abroad and for both elite and mass audiences – and latterly into an instrument to expose the weaknesses of the past and present in the twin processes of *glasnost* and *perestroika*. Now the national cinemas of the successor republics to the old USSR are encountering the same bewildering array of problems, from the trivial to the terminal, as are all the other ex-Soviet institutions.

Cinema's central position in Russian and Soviet cultural history and its unique combination of mass medium, art form and entertainment industry, have made it a continuing battlefield for conflicts of broader ideological and artistic significance, not only for Russia and the Soviet Union but also for the world outside. The debates that raged in the 1920s about the relative revolutionary merits of documentary as opposed to fiction film, of cinema as opposed to theatre or painting, or of the proper role of cinema in the forging of postRevolutionary Soviet culture and the shaping of the new Soviet man, have their echoes in current discussions about the role of cinema *vis-à-vis* other art forms in effecting the cultural and psychological revolution in human consciousness necessitated by the processes of economic and political transformation of the former Soviet Union into modern democratic and industrial societies and states governed by the rulc of law. Cinema's central position has also made it a vital instrument for scrutinizing the blank pages of Russian and Soviet history and enabling the present generation to come to terms with its own past.

This series of books intends to examine Russian and Soviet films in the context of Russian and Soviet cinema, and Russian and Soviet cinema in the context of the political and cultural history of Russia, the Soviet Union and the world at large. Within that framework the series, drawing its authors from both East and West, aims to cover a wide variety of topics and to employ a broad range of methodological approaches and presentational formats. Inevitably this will involve ploughing once again over old ground in order to re-examine received opinions but it principally means increasing the breadth and depth of our knowledge, finding new answers to old questions and, above all, raising new questions for further inquiry and new areas for further research.

The continuing aim of the series is to situate Russian and Soviet cinema in their proper historical and aesthetic context, both as a major cultural force in Russian history and Soviet politics and as a crucible for experimentation that is of central significance to the development of world cinema culture. Books in the series strive to combine the best of scholarship, past, present and future, with a style of writing that is accessible to a broad readership, whether that readership's primary interest lies in cinema or in Russian and Soviet political history.

Richard Taylor
Swansea, Wales

1. The old regime and the new: from *Hammer and Sickle* to *Chess Fever*

In his 1951 essay 'How I Became a Film Director', Pudovkin outlines a basic autobiography: he was born in Penza in 1893 and in his youth his interests included painting, music and theatre.[1] In 1910 he entered Moscow University to study physical chemistry then in 1914 volunteered for service in the artillery. His enthusiasm for cinema, he says elsewhere, dates from his first encounter with Griffith's *Intolerance* [USA, 1916] in 1920. This same year, Pudovkin was introduced to Vladimir Gardin by the actress and later director Olga Preobrazhenskaia. Gardin recalls how Lodia [Pudovkin], from the start, was animated by questions of film process and technique, just at the time when he himself was attempting to formulate a preliminary theory of film montage, and especially of rhythm.[2] Pudovkin became a student of the first state film school, a pupil of the old regime (Gardin) and the new (Kuleshov).[3] During this time he worked on Perestiani's 1920 agit-film *In the Days of Struggle* [V dni borbi], in which he played the part of a commandant in the Red Army and on which he collaborated with Feofan Shipulinsky.

Neither in this late essay nor in his major writings of the '20s does Pudovkin have much to say about his apprenticeship with Gardin, although he does mention in passing the films on which they worked together: *The Iron Heel* [Zheleznaia piatka, 1919], in which Preobrazhenskaia acted; *Sickle and Hammer* [Serp i molot, 1921], in which Pudovkin again acted and worked as assistant director of Shipulinsky's scenario; *Locksmith and Chancellor* [Slesar' i kantsler, 1923], co-written with Gardin and with Preobrazhenskaia as assistant director and

Hunger... Hunger... Hunger [Golod ... golod ... golod, 1921] on which he and Gardin shared responsibility for the scenario and its direction. Here Pudovkin met Eisenstein's future cameraman, Eduard Tisse; Natan Zarkhi, Pudovkin's scenarist for *The Mother*, *The End of St. Petersburg* and, in part, for *Victory* [Pobeda, 1938], also wrote the scenario for Gardin's 1924 *The Golobins Estate* [Osobniak Golubinykh].[4] Although Pudovkin tends to underplay the the influence of Gardin on his work, *Hammer and Sickle* is notable for the parallel editing in the final reel (Pudovkin, as the husband, returning home as his wife fights off an attempted rape, the husband arriving in the nick of time and hitting her attacker with an axe), especially in comparison with the end sequences of *The Mother*, as in the war parade in *The End of St. Petersburg*, the little girl, the mother and the old man return to the village alone; as in *The Mechanics of the Brain*, a mask is used to draw attention to a particular element within a larger frame. But in 1922, Pudovkin joined Kuleshov's workshop and it is this experience to which *The Film Scenario* and *The Film Director and Film Material* more often refer.

Iezuitov, writing in 1940, claims that Gardin (himself a theatre-trained actor) endorsed the practice of Stanislavsky:

> Heralding a new psychology and physiology, Gardin pursued a course of strict experiment, confirming the teaching of Konstantin Stanislavsky. 'Supporting the emotion (the dominant) during the spoken reaction ... there is the modulation of the given characteristic emotional colouring, the symbolic given condition of the hero, which does not shade the meaning of his words but nevertheless relegates them into second place'[5]

Certainly, it was not opportune for Pudovkin to associate himself in the early 1920s with a tendency then regarded as regressive. Later, of course, Pudovkin proclaimed that Stanislavskian principles were most fully realised in cinema.

In later years it then became expedient for Pudovkin to denounce the early work of Kuleshov as '[idealising] American detective films with their empty and only superficial dynamics'. Even in the mid '20s, in the spirit of healthy debate, he complains of the pacing of *The Extraordinary Adventures of Mr. West in the Land of the Bolsheviks* [Neobychainiye prikliucheniia Mistera Vesta v strane bol'shevikov, 1924]: 'the dynamically saturated earlier reels are easy to look at and grip the spectator with ever-increasing excitement. But, after the end of the third reel, where the cowboy's adventures came to an unexpected end, the spectator experiences a natural reaction, and the continuation, in spite of the excellent directorial treatment, is watched with much diminished interest'.[6] However, for the most part, Pudovkin is full of praise for his mentor, even after his return to work with conventional actors. In 1929 Pudovkin appeared as a fakir in Kuleshov's film *The Gay Canary* and jointly prefaced Kuleshov's book *The Art of the Cinema*: 'We made films; Kuleshov made Cinema'.[7] Certainly Kuleshov sought to distance himself from the old cinema of Gardin, especially his Film d'Art literary adaptations (see chapter three, below). He sought to legitimise a theory of montage on the basis of his original observations of audience reactions and an appeal to popularity with an exemplary statistical mean: 'The public in cheaper theatres, less eductated, much rougher and more spontaneous, was not as neurotic and therefore reacted much more directly to the effect of action and entertainment on the screen'.[8] He noticed that American films affected audiences most and therefore adopted these as an object of study. It was remarked that it was action within and between frames which conspicuously characterised American cinema. It was action also which most markedly distinguished this cinema from the static staging of pre-Revolutionary cinema. Official interest in the cinema, as an industry, extended to the collection and collation of statistics of film reception and receipts, as an instrument of instruction (comparable with radio) and to the monitoring in model conditions of the effects of various films directed at children. In its very first issue, *Sovetskoe kino* exhorted personnel to respond to the needs of the countryside.[9] In spite of Kuleshov's optimistic appeal to public preference it was readily demonstrable popular disaffection for much of the avant-garde product which prompted changes in official policy.[10]

Kuleshov's self-confessed but somewhat ironic enthusiasm for things American is evinced also in the collection of archetypal poses which appear to quote from a general precedent: for instance, Khokhlova and Pudovkin 'doing' the 'We'll build a new tomorrow' shot; Khokhlova and Pudovkin, framed by the iris as a sunset, 'doing' the 'happy ever after' shot, Khokhlova smiling broadly, leaning back with her arms bent but tilted forwards, the backs of her hands perched on her waist. Frequently the attitudes are reminiscent of a 'photo roman' or a comic strip: there is a 'detective' figure in a trilby and herringbone coat with upright collar, dark glasses with a polo-necked jumper pulled up to the ears. There is a sense of these serving as a catalogue (akin to Delsarte's inventory), assembled and rehearsed for future reference.

An enthusiasm for the metaphorical and utopian notion of a scientific laboratory in which the new society was to be developed was heralded in 1920s nomenclature: Kuleshov worked in a workshop (equating the activity with manual labour), frequently termed his laboratory.[11] This romanticising of science is evident also in such films as Protazanov's *Aelita* and Kuleshov's *The Death Ray* and *Engineer Prait s Project*. The image he hopes to evoke is of a team collectively dedicating their experimental endeavour towards a common, social good. Kuleshov lists as experiments the various preparatory episodes, tasks and exercises undertaken by the group, sometimes later incorporated into a finished film. The laboratory also worked as a collective in a real sense, sharing and exchanging responsibilities. As part of the collective, Pudovkin worked as designer, scenarist, assistant director and actor-model [naturshchik]. In his 1924 article for *Kinogazeta*, 'On the method of work on *The Death Ray*', Pudovkin tells how Kuleshov devised a particular procedure of rehearsal, with the intention of economising on time. Generally, he says, in Russia and in the West, it proves unaccaptable to rehearse every detail, even every sequence, with the result that scenes are constrained by production costs and one is obliged to compromise. Scenes involving groups of people were carefully choreographed in advance, standing Pudovkin in good stead for his later work on the workers' demonstrations in *The Mother* and *The Deserter*, even on the epic *Admiral Nakhimov*. Kuleshov delegated to four experienced workshop assistants to work on a single scene or model with the other members of the collective.[12] Certainly, it seems from photographs in the Kuleshov archive that Pudovkin once rehearsed the part of Mr. West (subsequently taken by Podobed), complete with Harold Lloyd's trademark round spectacles, although eventually appearing as Zhban.[13] Such a practice, one might suggest, distances itself from the absolute identification of an individual with a specific character (see chapter six, below, for comparison).

Pudovkin and the Kuleshov Experiment

Léon Moussinac, in *Le Cinéma soviétique* (1928), says that abstract experimental cinema as it was known in Paris and Berlin (Richter,

Eggeling, Delluc, Dulac *et al.*) was not considered relevant by Soviet film-makers to the practical urgencies and necessities of the Revolution. Indeed, much of Kuleshov's experimentation was prompted by mundane constraint as much as by a fervent spirit of enquiry. Kuleshov made 'films on paper' in the absence of stock. He blocked and performed a 'film without film' in which actors' movements before a fixed camera, and the duration of those movements, corresponded exactly to their envisaged fixing on film.[14] Kuleshov suggested that this would avoid the waste of re-takes and of cutting between multiple camera positions and that it would also encourage the sponsorship of films by giving potential financiers a very clear idea of the final product to which they were being invited to commit themselves. However, Pudovkin remarks on the very limited applicability of the procedure, its failure to match the demands of scenarios covering a variety of locations and a large cast. It was confined to orthogonal framing. Sometimes, Kuleshov's experiments serve no purpose other than to summarise current procedure and to demonstrate the adequacy of the 'new' medium to realise phenomena evinced in other forms elsewhere. Kuleshov nevertheless declares the phenomena themselves to be uniquely novel in cinema. By means of the engagement of imagination, as much as by editorial intervention, montage renders film a creative and not merely an imitative art. The assemblage of depictions of features from a number of women to render an impression of a unitary ideal is at least as old as Zeuxis. Kuleshov and Zeuxis follow a similar procedure, deviating from the mere imitation of nature, the difference is that Zeuxis organises his parts into a simultaneous objective whole whereas Kuleshov offers them successively.[15]

The over-emphasis in the 1920s on montage, later to be censured, was surely prompted in no small part by this compunction to affirm artistic status for film. However, even in the 1920s Pudovkin seems to deal in the theoretical currency without being consistently tied to it in practice. Whereas Kuleshov can tend towards the apprehension of fragmentation as the end product in the spectator, Pudovkin is often more intent upon accomplishing summation and synthesis. The constituent shots of Kuleshov's experiments seem static and self-contained: for instance, the 1921 sequence in which Khokhlova and a man meet; a close-up of a handshake; she points; he looks. But such experiments were deliberately staged to test a particular hypothesis and are not extracted from a larger scenario. The conclusion I think, is twofold:

that a conceptual event can be broken down (differentiated) into a logical sequence *and* that the concept can be constructed (integrated) from individual pieces shot in isolation. For Eisenstein, the concept often does not arise before this integration, there is no previous referent (see chapter seven, below). Bazin narrowly construes the concept as a pro-filmic event to which montage can only allude, and requires that the differentiation process be effaced by a subsequent integration. In the interests of economy, Kuleshov endeavoured to find the minimum number of shots in which the integration can be effected; for Kuleshov this minimum is the optimum. Minima were necessitated by strict economic constraints; but the notion of economy was also scientistically and aesthetically appealing.[16] The proof of Kuleshov's hypothetical 'created geography' and 'created woman' resides in the necessary synthesis being effected in the spectator's imagination, the synthesis which Pudovkin says ought to be actively assisted by movement forging a transition from, for example, a long shot cut to a close-up.[17]

It is to Pudovkin, as Kuleshov's assistant, that subsequent film theorists have turned for an account of the most famous of the experiments and the supposed derivation of the Kuleshov 'effect'. Sometimes the experiment is described incorrectly, sometimes it is incorrectly ascribed to Pudovkin himself.[18] Generally, the 'effect' is quoted as tacitly proven, as if the experiment itself was impervious or no longer worthy of interrogation. Ironically, directors to whom use of the 'effect' (as a cinematic device) is credited have sometimes denied knowledge of the experiment (Bresson, for instance).[19] Here follows Pudovkin's account, delivered in a lecture in London in 1929:

> Kuleshov and I made an interesting experiment. We took from some film or other several close-ups of the well-known Russian actor, Mozzhukhin [Mosjoukine]. We chose close-ups which were static and which did not express any feeling at all: quiet close-ups. We joined these close-ups, which were all similar, with other bits of film in three different combinations. In the first combination the close-up of Mozzhukhin was immediately followed by a shot of a plate of soup standing on a table. It was obvious and certain that Mozzhukhin was looking at this soup. In the second combination the face of Mozzhukhin was joined to shots showing a coffin in which lay a dead woman. In the third the close-up was followed by

> a shot of a little girl playing with a funny toy bear. When we showed the three combinations to an audience which had not been let into the secret the result was terrific. The public raved about the acting of the artist. They pointed out the heavy pensiveness of his mood over the forgotten soup, were touched and moved by the deep sorrow with which he looked on the dead woman, and admired the light, happy smile with which he surveyed the girl at play. But we knew that in all three cases the face was exactly the same.[20]

Pudovkin left the workshop in 1925 to direct his own material. In *The Art of Cinema* Kuleshov provides an account at variance with that of his assistant. It could be the account of an entirely separate encounter:

> We had an argument about whether montage could have some effect on the actor's display of emotions. There were those who asserted that this factor could not be altered by montage. We had a dispute with a certain famous actor to whom we said:
>
>> Imagine this scene: a man, sitting in jail for a long time, is starving because he is not given anything to eat; he is brought a plate of soup, is delighted by it and gulps it down. Imagine another scene: a man in jail is given food, fed well, full to capacity but he longs for his freedom, for the sight of birds, the sunlight, houses, clouds. A door is opened for him. He is led out onto the street and he sees birds, clouds, sunlight and houses and is extremely pleased by the sight. And so, we asked the actor: will the face reacting to the soup and the face reacting to the sun appear the same on film or not? We were answered disdainfully: it is clear to anyone that the reaction to the soup and the reaction to freedom will be totally different. Then we shot these two sequences and regardless of how I transposed those shots and how they were examined, no one was able to perceive any difference in the face of this actor, in spite of the fact that his performance in each shot was absolutely different. With correct montage, even if one takes the performance of an actor directed at something quite different, it will still reach the viewer in the way intended by the editor because the viewer himself will complete the sequence and see that which is suggested to him by montage.

Kuleshov goes on to describe a scene from Razumny's *Brigade Commander Ivanov* [Kombrig Ivanov, 1923]:

> I saw this scene I think, in a film by Razumny: a priest's house, with a portrait of Nicholas II hanging on the wall; the village is taken by the Red Army, the frightened priest turns the portrait over and on the reverse side of the portrait is the smiling face of Lenin. However, this is a familiar portrait, a portrait in which Lenin is *not* smiling. But that spot in the film was so funny and it was so uproariously received by the public, that I, myself, scrutinising the portrait several times, saw the portrait of Lenin as smiling! ... The montage was so edited that we involuntarily imbued a serious face with a changed expression characteristic of that playful moment. In other words, the work of the actor was altered by means of montage. In this way, montage had a colossal influence on the effect of the material. It became apparent that it was possible to change the actor's work, his movements, his very behaviour, in either one direction or another, through montage.[21]

The claim that these experiments conclusively prove anything seems to me highly spurious. Even Pudovkin offers the disclaimer that 'the combination of various pieces in one or another order is not sufficient' and suggests that different lengths of film in combination yield different phenomenological and emotional effects on the spectator. The experiments are unsatisfactory by any scientific criteria and seemingly produce results which, if not entirely contradictory, are at least not simultaneously sustainable.

Pudovkin urged caution upon those who would seek to extrapolate a general theory from isolated examples of Kuleshov's studio practice, however interesting they may be in themselves. 'What is theory? It is experience codified ... Pavlov conducted thousands of experiments minutely controlled and studied'.[22] Amongst the characteristics of Pavlov's research which rendered it an exemplary model to his fellow scientists were the length of time for which his team worked with particular subjects, the detailed and independent analysis of individual idiosyncracies (allowing a single aberrant instance to jettison a hitherto established theory) and insistence on the exact definition of terms (see chapter two, below). Set against this paradigm, the Kuleshov experiment (or experiments). make a poor showing. To how many people did Kuleshov show the film or films and how was the audience constituted? As Yuri Tsivian observes, the notion of the experiment casts its audience as an uninitiated tabula rasa, but the most basic conventions of story reading, that is to say, an established customary handling of pictorial or written text, predisposes the spectator to project one image forwards on to the next: amongst Kuleshov's contemporaries, Eikhenbaum and Shipulinsky were not alone in making such an observation. Tsivian suggests that classic conventions of shot/reverse shot editing were by the 1920s thoroughly naturalised in the Soviet audience.[23] Similarly familiar was the facial close-up as used by D. W. Griffith, as a prelude to the exhibition of the object contemplated. A desire to read a causal relationship between images may proscribe the option of finding a contiguous pairing void of meaning. Surely, the desire of the spectator to make sense of the 'new woman' assembly (the body of Nata Vachnadze with the face of Alexandra Khokhlova) and the priority inherently given to a particular interpretation are equally operative as the fact of temporal linkage of the parts. Elsewhere, Pudovkin noted that juxtapositions were susceptible of different interpretations according to the ordering of the sequence.[24] Béla Balázs says that the face in close-up has a peculiar effect on the viewer, who sees it as pure physiognomy, abstracted from a spatial context.[25]

The use of the famous actor raises additional objections. Mozzhukhin was well known and lauded in the pre-war cinema for his 'full' style, his formidable gaze and mesmerising intensity, the concentrated static internalisation of emotion. 'The stare works in reverse, offering a window into the protagonist's (usually) tortured psyche ... the audience is invited to imagine what has gone before and within: a sign of subjectivity'.[26] This seems remote from the use of blank models, in themselves supposedly of no significance, mannequins on which the director by choice or necessity hangs a chosen meaning by the conjunction with external material. This, however, is the sense in which the experiment is commonly invoked. Pudovkin himself contrived such a passively psychologised performance in Otsep's *The Living Corpse*, where it makes a stark contrast with the animated expressiveness of his 'gypsy' co-star, Nata Vachnadze. In spite of Kuleshov's contention that 'in either one direction or another' it was possible to change the actor's work, as the accounts stand they appear to demonstrate distinct phenomena: 1) subject to his own qualification, Pudovkin shows that a particular facial arrangement of the actor Mozzhukhin in close-up was

Fedia (Pudovkin) and the . . .

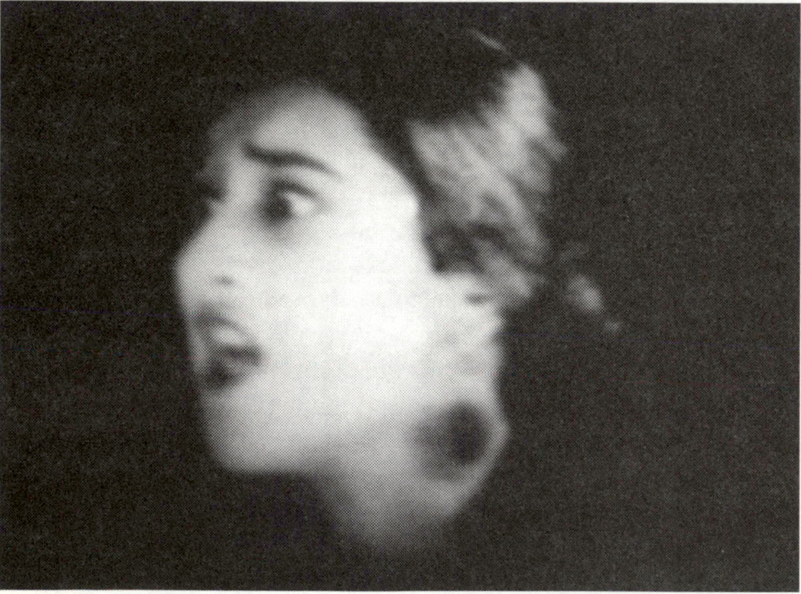

Gypsy in *The Living Corpse*

retrospectively perceived and interpreted differently according to the different proceeding images; 2) Kuleshov says that the effect of editing particular images can overrule an actor's effective performance, included as an image in that sequence (endorsing his claim elsewhere that, in cinema, the editor held the prerogative); 3) Kuleshov says the general ambiance of a sequence, which he does not attach to any particular object or image in that sequence, was able to invade his perception of a particular image; he seems to interpret the picture of Lenin as acting in the sequence as if it were a picture of an actor, an objective equation of actor as 'filmic material' which, also, he makes elsewhere. The single common conclusion here seems to be that images in film are not viewed objectively, in isolation. Such apprehensions are not unique to film. Darwin too had observed in his 1872 *Expression of the Emotions in Man and Animals*, that '. . . if from the nature of the circumstances we expect to see any expression, we readily imagine its presence'.[27]

Kuleshov and the training of the model actor

There is broad agreement between Gardin, Kuleshov and Pudovkin that an actor's training in the new society should differ appreciably from that under the old. Kuleshov and Pudovkin maintain that film, specifically, requires different skills. The new actor needs must work on himself before he embarks upon his role, even if the example as to what constitutes this work will differ according to the school in which he is trained. There is agreement on the preparatory training of the body as the tool of the actor.

Under Kuleshov, the actor's mastery of his body is a positive attribute; indeed, its acquisition is a fundamental task which precedes any role. This can be set against a broader urge towards physical fitness and expertise as necessary skills of the 'new man' and 'new woman' in the building of Soviet society. Marchand and Weinstein, reporting in 1927, include acrobatics in the curriculum of the Leningrad Film School and Trauberg's directors' course, reprted by Moussinac, included such one-to-one sports as fencing and boxing.[28] Such sports, traditional to stage training, enhance deportment and balance and sharpen reflexes. Kuleshov and Inkizhinov boast of Barnet's talents in the workshop being nurtured by his previous training as a boxer; Chistiakov, who worked frequently with Pudovkin, similarly came to the workshop from athletics (see chapters three, four, five, six). The workshop archive includes photographs of Inkizhinov rehearsing with Barnet, with Khokhlova and with Barnet and Pudovkin.

The circus was admired as a display of physical skill and agility in its performers as much as in its formal organisation, as a succession of such 'turns'. Such journals as *Kino, teatr, sport* (1923) endeavoured to cover all these activities equally, as spectacle. Members of Kuleshov's workshop performed their own stunts: he gives an account of a hazardous four-storey leap by Pudovkin.[29] Under Kuleshov, physical malleability is required of the actor in order that he can with ease undertake any move set by the director. For Kuleshov (theoretically) the actor is not an artist; the actor is subservient to the creative prerogative of the director (single or collective) assembling the montage pieces and thereby to the requirement of 'optimal organisation' of shot for quick and easy apprehension by the cinema audience; the actor is no more and no less than a moving 'shot sign', equivalent in communicative status to the prop 'curiosity'. A character can, indeed, be reduced to an essential sign, an isolated typical gesture (for instance, Zhban's finger-crooking in *Mr. West*). Khokhlova, as the Princess, is photographed sitting, hands separate and lifted and parallel to the picture plane,

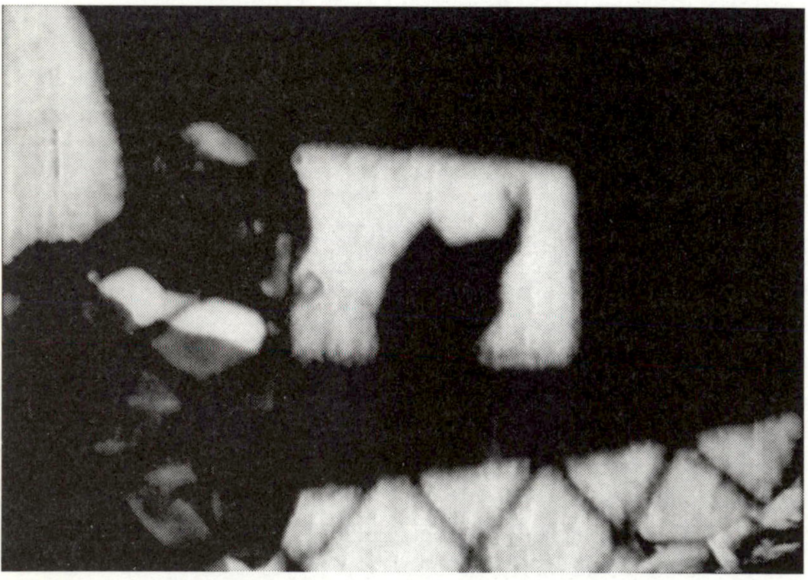

Zhban's finger crooking (*The Extraordinary Adventures of Mr. West ...*)

fingers splayed; Podobed, as Mr. West, stands with his arms bent, hands lifted but dropped limply at the wrist (almost like the paws of a begging dog anticipating a reward). The photographs of antagonistic pairs of attitudes, posed on the roof against white sky, seem intent upon demonstrating and delineating the shapes adopted with utmost clarity, as much as adding to dramatic tension. The shot is framed, the action is blocked and the workshop actor's body is trained to achieve graphic clarity, simplicity and economy of expression.[30] In 1926, Pudovkin reiterates the lesson learnt from his erstwhile master: 'the ... requirement, conditioned by the basic character itself of filmic spectacle, will probably exist forever: the necessity for clarity'.[31]

There is much in Kuleshov's exposition which is reminiscent of Meyerhold's exercises in biomechanics. Indeed, the personnel of both collectives at one time worked in adjacent studios. Meyerhold similarly differentiates exercises involving actors by themselves ('drawing the bow') and together ('the leap onto the chest') into a series of basic moves. However, there seems to be a fundamental discrepancy between Kuleshov and Meyerhold as to the relationship between the actor's ability to sign bodily a particular emotion effectively to an audience and the concomitant sensation of that emotion. Kuleshov, with Eisenstein, insisted that 'the work of film actors be so constructed that it comprises the sum of organic movement with "reliving" held to a minimum', appearing to hold with Diderot that the actor does not personally experience that which he conveys externally.[32] Stanislavsky held that 'reliving' the rediscovery of emotion within the memory of his own experience, was crucial to the actor's art. The actor was to summon forth his memory to pre-empt convention (see chapter six, below). According to Meyerhold, there existed a reciprocal and reflexive relation between the physical exercise and the psychological state, as though the experience which caused an expression equally could be effected in the actor in the undertaking of the prescribed posture.[33] There are sources for the system in Taylorism, in William James, in Pavlov and even in Darwin, especially in the composition of the reflex: as sensation (initial withdrawal, refusal of action); cerebration; tendency to action. 'Meyerhold was able to ... [cause the actor] to automatically experience an entire gamut of emotions due to a constantly changing arrangement of his musclature. This would also enable the actor to precisely establish the relationship between his physical appearance and his own inner nervous feelings'.[34]

In *The Art of Cinema*, Kuleshov wrote that he preferred the movements of the real life stevedore loading sacks to those of any actor (Kamerny, Meyerholdian or Moscow Art Theatre).[35] It was something of a contemporary commonplace to celebrate in manual labour an aesthetic as much as a social value. The repetition of a given activity reduces the movement to an essential and typical standard denominator, to the least expenditure of physical effort required to accomplish the task.[36] The paring of human energy fits the individual into the general industrial equation, minimising time and motion maximises productivity. 'The Table of Hours, it turns each one of us . . . into a six-wheeled epic hero . . .', crows Zamiatin. 'No doubt about it, that Taylor was *the* genius of antiquity'.[37] Gastev, Taylor's prominent and zealous Soviet acolyte, used photography in his laboratory to analyse the component parts of simple tasks (for instance, swinging a hammer). Any task, says Kuleshov, in terms derived from Taylor, can be rendered as a labour process.[38] Huntley Carter's 1924 survey of Soviet theatre and cinema is fancifully illustrated with stylised paper-cut figures, supposedly demonstrating 'Taylorised Gesture', with the size of angle annotated between body and limb. In practice it seems that Meyerhold's biomechanical exercises were subject to individual variation and re-interpretation.[39]

Kuleshov employs a relativity of performance styles to comic effect in *Mr. West.* To suggest, as does Lindley Hanlon, that Kuleshov's group *over*act, is to miss the point.[40] Mr. West himself is played as an ingénu, with child-like mannerisms like dropped-jaw gawping. His naiveté is underscored by his inability to recognise in the ostentatious pretence of Zhban, the Princess and their cronies, the falsity of their story. Assuming that Mr. West sees what the audience sees simultaneously, one is amused that he could be so readily duped by the frenetic lip-biting and popping eye-balls of the Princess (played by the famously odd Alexandra Khokhlova), yet one appreciates also that Mr. West's credulity when confronted by 'The Barbarian horde' has been anticipated in his reading of the inflamatory catalogue of Soviet types.[41] At the end of the film, Mr. West encounters the real Soviets: Trotsky, the Red Army and the 'leather-jacketed officer with the Mauser at his hip'.[42] A similar contrast of style is employed to comic effect in Pudovkin's *Chess Fever* [Shakhmatnaia goriachka, 1925] and to dramatic effect in *The Living Corpse.*

In the training schedule, the 'labour processes' correspond to unit

Mr. West (*The Extraordinary Adventures of Mr. West . . .*)

tasks (sitting down at a table, opening a door). Only in the third year of Trauberg's curriculum were students allowed to progress to composite tasks and complete scenes.[43] For Kuleshov, the typical action is arrived at through improvisation, as though pre-thought spontaneity can short-cut the unthinking evolution of the stevedore's sack-lugging. This is preferred to inherited convention, but once the typical action is settled upon in rehearsal its repetition in performance is fixed. For Stanislavsky, on the other hand, it was a function of the living actor that he be free to act spontaneously. Mikhail Iampolsky has made much of the influence of the French stage theoretician Delsarte on pre- and post-Revolutionary directors, quoting Anna Zemtsova (aka Anna Lee) in an article testifying to a close familiarity with his writings as translated by Count Volkonsky.[44] Delsartism is listed as a subject of study at the Leningrad school and was familiar to Eisenstein. Gardin illustrates how Delsarte's catalogue of facial pattern can be translated to specific shots.[45] Kuleshov insists that Delsarte's usefulness does not extend beyond 'an inventory of the possible changes in the human mechanism' and that it cannot be regarded as a method of acting.[46] In practice, one of the most wonderful things about the wonderfully odd Khokhlova is her ability to strike a succession of distinct expressions and poses:

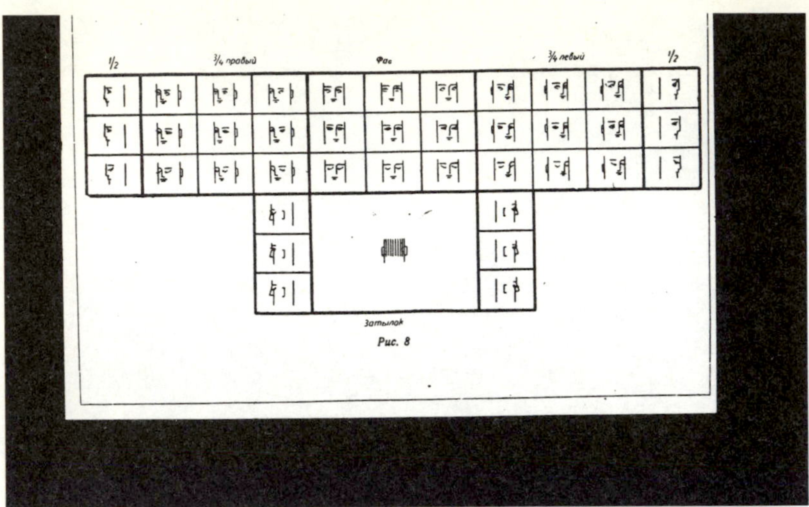

Gardin shot patterns, à la Delsarte

witness, for instance, her performance in *Mr. West*, *By the Law* and *The Female Journalist*. But Kuleshov inherits none of Delsarte's cabalism, nor his manic tripartite classifications (constitutional, passional and habitual gestures; Thought, Sensation, Emotion; Goodness, Beauty, Truth) nor his attachment to classical notions of beauty at the expense of the authentic expression of emotion.

Pudovkin and Kuleshov are also broadly in agreement in their rejection of the theatrical staging popular under the ancien régime. They hold in contempt the artificiality of its painted back-cloths and its exhaustive clutter of knick-knackery. Kuleshov stresses the careful selection of objects, but this concern is directed less towards the stage business enacted by an individual than towards the fast and clear signification to the audience of character or setting within a general schema. Sometimes, as in the female journalist's office or the 'prison' cell in which Mr. West is incarcerated, the setting is indicated by cast shadows. A workshop photograph for *The Death Ray* shows Khokhlova sitting bolt upright in bed with her arms lifted in surrender; a gunman stands at the foot of the bed but he casts a clear shadow on the wall directly above her. Here again, the minimum required to achieve the desired effect is to be preferred.

Kuleshov cites such prop 'curiosities' as the coat hanger in a vase and glass elephant supplied by Rodchenko for *The Female Journalist*; in *Mr. West* the same table seemingly appears on several occasions, variously accompanied by a low-slung washing line with washing (Zhban's garret) or a telephone and post-card size stars and stripes (the American Embassy); the sets for *Engineer Prait s Project* are similarly pared down and spartan, the backgrounds deliberately and graphically flattened. Kuleshov praises the example of the 'new' theatre to foreground or oversize significant objects, and sometimes uses paint or cloth to deliberately minimise or diffuse variation in a background in order to clearly delineate and to focus attention on the object proper.[47] Sometimes the preparatory story boards show the use of frames within the frame (doorways, archways, spaces between buildings) as a means of concentrating attention. In 'The Method of Work on *The Death Ray*', Pudovkin speaks of the workshop searching for cheap materials with which to cover large surfaces and of their rejection of carpets and decorative prints (the old system) in favour of grey paper. Pudovkin sets Lebedev's desk in *The End of St. Petersburg* far back from the camera, the conspicuous expanse of polished parquet flooring in the foreground and the offices beyond conveying a sense of the industrialist's extensive command over property. With the advent of montage and the close-up cutaway, props and settings acquire a significance equivalent to that of performers: literally and metaphorically they can be made to figure as largely in the imagination. It is in this sense that, for Eisenstein, the dispute between actor and non-actor becomes pointless and that, for Arnheim, the stage prop can be said to perform as an actor.[48] Kuleshov, and especially Pudovkin, recognise that, with the advent of cinema, expression is no longer signified by the actor alone, the emotion can be conveyed and stirred by montage of a number of elements between and within shots as much as by an actor's performance.

In practice, Kuleshov did not work with stevedores but with a close group of professionals: Pudovkin, Fogel, Barnet, Podobed, Khokhlova. Pudovkin worked again with Fogel on *Chess Fever*, with Barnet on *Storm over Asia* and with Barnet and Podobed on *The Living Corpse*. However, Kuleshov chooses not to make much of their familiarity with one another as a basis for sound collective work: their shared interests are represented theoretically as professional rather than personal. In practice, Pudovkin worked as a director with actors from a variety of backgrounds (Batalov had been used by Protazanov for *Aelita*; Baranovskaia came from MKhAT, Inkizhinov came via the Kuleshov workshop and, from 1916, tutor in biomechanics with Meyerhold). However, Pudovkin says that his own training left him feeling ill-equipped initially to create the necessary rapport with artists themselves trained with Stanislavsky. Endorsing Baranovskaia's reservations, he later claims that he discovered the System through his acquaintance with these artists as an effective means of establishing trust between themselves:

> On what could one base this confidence? ... I still looked at actors from a formalist point of view, entirely externally ... How could I reach the intelligence and the heart of those whom I had to direct, whom I had to direct, whom I had to guide in the creation of characters which still existed only in my imagination. How to find a common language?[49]

Pudovkin says that the idea of 'recollected emotion' was born in him in his creative work with these actors. He advocates Stanislavsky as a means of drawing the reality of the everyday and ordinary into the artificial construction of the film and filming practice. Pudovkin invokes spontaneity or the quasi-subconcious as a route to an act which will prove effective and affecting on screen:

> In the film *Storm over Asia* I wanted to have a crowd of Mongols looking with rapture on a precious fur. I engaged a Chinese conjuror and photographed the faces of the Mongols watching him ... Once I spent endless time and effort trying to obtain a good natured smile ... when I photographed [a mongol's] face smiling at a joke I made, he had been firmly convinced that the shooting was over.[50]

Chess Fever and filmic syntax

In the midst of the trials and tribulations of making *The Mechanics of the Brain*, Pudovkin and Nikolai Shpikovsky directed the short comedy *Chess Fever*.[51] This follows the example of the use of footage of Kalinin in *Give to the Poor, Take from the Rich* (1924) and *Mr. West*'s incorporation of Trotsky and the Red Army parade, where Kuleshov niftily employs binoculars to legitimise the shift in scale. Like Komarov's *The Kiss of Mary Pickford* [Potselui Meri Pikford, 1927], constructed from sequences documenting the actual visit to Moscow of Pickford and Fairbanks in 1926, in *Chess Fever*, location

Mr. Trotsky (*The Extraordinary Adventures of Mr. West ...*)

footage of the 1925 Moscow Chess tournament is edited into the story, showing the participants Capablanca, Grüfeld, Torré, Spielman and others.[52] 'Every photograph of the masters', says the reviewer in *Sovetskoe kino*, 'shows us a moment in the course of play'. Capablanca, occasionally looking nervously to camera, was persuaded to appear in the film as a performing 'type' (the 'type', that is, of Capablanca himself), alongside Anna Zemtsova. 'By the editing together of the pictures he meets the heroine, befriends her and initiates her enthusiasm for Chess'. *Sovetskoe kino* was appreciative of this highly profitable and successful film, which in Moscow and Leningrad equalled the best foreign hits:

> The general enthusiasm for Chess is making itself felt in cinema ... The comedy is pieced together as a parody of a newspaper story ... ordinary everyday matches acquire exaggerated scale: caricatures of the policeman, the cabman, of the chemist, the public at the tournament and others are wittily portrayed ... There is much humorous incident, much movement, the material forwarded pointedly by the serial story form.[53]

In addition, it seems to me, the film serves as something of a satire on pre-Revolutionary films which took Chess as a theme or motif: I am thinking of *The Game of Life* [Shakhmaty zhizni] (a star vehicle for the stupendous Vera Kholodnaia) and *The Game of Love* [Shakhmaty liubvi] (an exotic comedy), even the play on words, *The Shah and the Mother to the King* [Shakh i mat' koroliu], 'an amazing picture'.[54] The presence of the veteran director Iakov Protazanov (as the chemist) and of Konstantin Eggert (as the sinister Chess-shop owner) in 'caricature' cameo roles in *Chess Fever*, further points to such an intention on the part of Shpikovsky and Pudovkin.

However, my main concern here is the extent to which the film uses the 'results' of the Kuleshov experiments to render a number of visual gags, precisely relying for their effect on the tacit acceptance by the viewer of 'naturalised' conventions of editing. As Shipulinsky, too, remarked in 1919:

> The procedure of viewing and perceiving film works on the principle of exchanging images which appear for a moment on screen and are immediately associated with those which have just disappeared so that the viewer's imagination is the very factor which gives new meaning to the moving objects on the screen.[55]

Although Pudovkin speaks hypothetically in *The Film Scenario* (1926) of the correspondence of the editing of shots with the 'natural' [estestvennyi] 'transference of attention of an imaginary observer (who, in the end, is represented by the spectator)',[56] Pudovkin is aware, along with Eikhenbaum, and indeed Bazin, that the means whereby such a natural transference is effected in cinema is no more than an artifice, a style or convention and that other means equally lie at the disposal of the director:

> Once we begin to speak about film styles and about shot composition, that much-talked-about 'naturalism' can be seen to represent only one of many possible styles, a style which is in no way less conventional than the others ... naturalism in cinema is no less conventional than literary or theatrical naturalism.[57]

In *Chess Fever*, Pudovkin makes an entertaining play on such a convention, the hypothesis of creative geography tested by Kuleshov. After the establishing shots of the Moscow tournament, in which competitors are shown facing each other either side of the board, we are introduced to another scene by a series of close-ups: a jacket sleeved hand moves the white pieces; from the opposite direction, a hand in a shirt cuff moves the black; the camera pulls back to reveal Fogel, as Galadrev, playing one piece then moving to the other side to play the next. Later, this hapless husband to be goes to his fiancée, Verochka, to beg her forgiveness for forgetting the hour of their wedding. Zemtsova turns away from him, angrily casting the cloth which she has held to her fevered brow into her lap, but slowly, in close up, we see her face change: her eyes lift heavenwards and she smiles. Then we are returned to a midshot and Fogel, on his knees at her feet, is playing Chess with a miniature set of pieces on a checked handkerchief on the floor.

It seems to me that this playfulness of Pudovkin, his mastery of received method such that he can make light of it, heralds the subsequent experiments of *The Mother*, *The End of St. Petersburg* and *Storm over Asia*. Arnheim, Orrom, Kepley and Burch note Pudovkin's deviation from syntactical rules governing the spatial and temporal orientation of the film spectator, some of which Pudovkin appears to endorse himself provisionally in *The Film Scenario* and *The Film Director and Film Material*; Dart says that this damages the required spectatorial 'identification' with the film.[58] In practice, while Pudovkin adheres consistently and rigorously to a certain set of working procedures, formal construction is governed by expedience and a particular context within the film. Pudovkin wills a particular interpretation of an image by its position in a sequence; images may be introduced in an apparently narrative sequence which grounds them in the diegesis, then are subsequently interspersed as individual frames in later montage sequences in which they figure metaphorically, as a momentary tendentious reminder of a larger synthesis (the 'supra artistic concept', perhaps). A shot of a factory worker, collapsed from exhaustion, is established early in *The End of St. Petersburg* and then recurs; a soldier dying agonisingly slowly in the mud of the trenches is cut successsively into the stock-market sequence, the frenetic activity as prices rise ('both sides are satisfied'); the single silhouette of St. Isaac's dome is used to locate parallel action in St. Petersburg alongside the trenches. Pudovkin creates a unique realm which does not of necessity refer to a context of real space and time; the film provides its own context in which a particular image is crucial. Pudovkin's images, certainly before *Storm*, are rarely simply decorative. As Tarkovsky says: 'The straightforward narrative cannot contain the pressure of ideas awakened by the story, the necessity arises to work not in the prosaic, plot-centred form but in the "compositional" poetic form'.[59]

Mayakovsky declares that, for the poet, the creation of neologisms is no less than obligatory and that syntactical rules exist to be broken: 'A poet is a person who creates these very rules ... A mathematician is a man who establishes, enlarges and develops mathematical rules, a man who introduces new concepts into mathematical knowledge'[60] (see chapter seven, below). But Mayakovsky is equally dismissive of the 'free' verse and of art for art's sake:

> I make this stipulation: establishing rules is not in itself the aim of poetry, otherwise the poet turns into a scholastic exercising his powers in formulating rules for non-existent or useless things and propositions ... A proposition which demands formulation demands rules, is thrust upon us by life. Methods of formulation, the aim of rules, are defined by factors of class and the needs of our struggle.[61]

The deviation of Pudovkin's practice from standard logical syntax (to which he adheres closely in *The Mechanics of the Brain*) is in some measure exonerable as (or even demonstrative of) poetic licence:

> The film is yet young and the wealth of its methods is not yet extensive; for this reason it is possible to indicate temporary limitations without necessarily attributing to them the permanence and inflexibility of laws.
>
> Everything said here regarding simple methods of taking shots has certainly only information value. What particular method of shooting is to be used, only his own taste and his own finer feelings can tell the scenarist. Here are no rules; the field for new invention and combination is wide.[62]

In *The End of St. Petersburg* and *The Mother*, and less successfully in *A Simple Case*, Pudovkin rhythmically repeats images in order to underscore a particular meaning quite apart from the immediately contiguous diegetic context; these shots are not routinely interpolated into a standard pattern of editing, rather the particular rhythm and syntax of the film is constructed out of them.

1920s film theory declared its own formulations of the relationship between the spectator and the director, between the screen and the camera. An attempt was made to incorporate formal positions concerned with the peculiar material and apparatus of film with the perceptual and conceptual effect upon the spectator. Kuleshov posits a formal equation in which the supposed experience of the viewer informs the the direction of the scene (see chapter seven, below). For Kuleshov, the frame retains its substantive presence: 'Imagine the screen as a blank white rectangle to be filled . . .'.[63] Kuleshov hypothesises a geometric grid, 'a pyramid with its apex resting on the camera', along the axes of which the performed action is organised for optimum figurative clarity. This equation serves separate scenes rather than the transitions. Kuleshov says little of what is is conceptually constructive in the formal conjunction of these pieces. Theoretically, Eisenstein lays most emphasis on his own editing of the film as the moment at which it begins to exist and as that procedure in which the greatest and most decisive effect is achieved on the spectator. Eikhenbaum and Eisenstein argue that meaning is made in the computation or 'equilibration' of neural fragments and that montage correspondingly imitates this process, that the formal mechanism maps onto the conceptual, activity occurs in juxtaposition (see chapter six, below).

Pudovkin too asserts the construction of identity between spectatorship and the making of the film. The process begins for him with the camera angle, his basic unit. Mechanically, the shot is less important for Pudovkin as a photographic record than as a means of selecting and isolating material (frame, focal length, length of shot, angle of camera and angle of vision): THE CAMERA COMPELS THE SPECTATOR TO SEE AS THE DIRECTOR WISHES.[64] Theoretically, Pudovkin aligns the act of viewing a projected film with his imagining and direction of scenes, already thematically dictated by his scenario. The scenario is pragmatically subdivided in accordance with the length of reels currently available and the customary number of reels per feature. Shutko, writing in 1927, nicely appreciates this as standard practice rather than decisively formulated:

> . . . it is sometimes amusing to read of the idle experiments of

> certain theorists who try to time such cinematic masterpieces as *The Tobacco Girl from Seville* or *The Spanish Dancer* and who discover an amazing regularity: each act lasts 11–12 minutes. Their theoretical brains are already ticking over, a cinematurgic 'law' for the construction of a section of a film is ready to be born but it transpires that this is all the result of the more or less constant length of each reel and nothing else.[65]

Pudovkin uses diegetic movement in a single frame juxtaposed with movement in the adjacent frame to ease logical or emotional coherence to the succession of the fragments and uses montage movement to aid the apprehension of his theme: in both direction of the parts and the whole he observes his 'psychological law', 'guiding the spectator' (see chapter two, below). Theoretically, Pudovkin allows little room for ambiguity or divergence between himself and his audience, 'despotically leading' his audience.

However, direction is for Pudovkin not an entirely unilateral process. The director, he suggests, anticipates a potential viewer's shift of attention from one point of a supposed pro-filmic event to another, both in space and in time. The director's 'despotism' resides in his presuming the expectation which he then obligingly satisfies. This shift, he suggests, is ordained by the sequence in which attention would be attracted were an event to be witnessed naturally. Here, however, Pudovkin invites criticism, using as examples citations from scenarios already conventionally, actively ordered into such a sequence. But when Dart and Arnheim complain of inconsistency in practice (sometimes there is no such referent pro-filmic event or an apparently natural sequence is disrupted) they fall foul of a similar presumption, criticising Pudovkin for contravening a convention which is an accessory of the art, no more than provisional, usual but not natural in the sense of essential to the medium, no more than occasionally expedient, even if in practice this becomes a generally favoured option (see chapter seven, below). The convention of identifying the camera with a participatory role in the event is, for Pudovkin, subordinate to the task of effecting in the spectator a particular theme. A common sense analogy with literature seems useful here; Pudovkin takes the liberty which is allowed the author, sometimes narrating action, sometimes reporting dialogue, but in both capacities adopting a thematic point of view.

Notes

1 Pudovkin, 'Kak ia stal rezhisserom', *SS* II, p.33; Pudovkin's early sketchbook, reproduced by Tatiana Zapasnik in *Die Zeit in Grossaufnahme*, is now held by the Muzei Kino, Moscow. Not unusually for an 18 year old boy, Pudovkin was keen on drawing horses (but could not do fetlocks) and large women in flimsy blouses; his portrait/caricature sketches are the most interesting items

2 V. R. Gardin, *Vospominaniia,* Moscow 1949, p. 192; Gardin in his memoirs outlines the courses which he taught and proposed for the new State School of Cinematography; Gardin maintained that montage should not replace the portrayal of character psychology (a position to which Soviet cinema in general returned in the 1930s)

3 Gardin was irked to find himself ousted by the upstart Kuleshov and was adamant that his was the first proposal for the systematic teaching of film: see *Vospominaniia,* p.196

4 see RGALI 2003/1/36; 37; 38; 46, 47, 48, 49, 50.

5 Nikolai Iezuitov, *Gardin XL let*, Moscow 1940; p. 41; compare Pudovkin's 1938 'O vnutrennem i vneshem v vospitanii aktera'

6 Pudovkin, 'Siuzhetnoe oformlenie temy', *Kinostsenarii*, *SS* I, p. 60

7 Pudovkin, Obolenskii, Komarov, Fogel', 'Predislovie k knige L. Kuleshova "Iskusstvo kino"', *SS* II, p. 358; even in 1934, Pudovkin valued the training provided by Kuleshov's schooling: *Akter v fil me*, *SS* I, pp. 236–237

8 Ronald Levaco, ed. *Kuleshov on Film*, Berkeley 1974, p. 45

9 'Kino i derevnia' *Sovetskoe kino* 1, February 1926, pp. 14–15; this discussion of cinema can be compared with the articles of Petrov, Katsigras and others on the uses of radio in the countryside; see also Taylor and Christie, eds. *The Film Factory*, pp. 299–305.

10 Viktor Shklovskii, 'K voprosu ob izuchenii zritelia' *Sovetskii ekran* 50, 11 December 1928, p. 6

11 see Richard Stites, *Revolutionary Dreams*, Cambridge 1989 for a discussion of the distance between science fantasy and reality; also Loren Graham, ed. *Science and the Soviet Social Order*, London 1990

12 Pudovkin, 'O metodakh raboty "Lucha smerti"', *SS* II, p. 41; Anatolii Golovnia worked as Levitskii's assistant on *The Death Ray*

13 RGALI 2679/1/162

14 Léon Moussinac, *Le Cinéma soviétique*, Paris 1928, p. 181

15 Panofsky gives sources for this story in *Idea*, New York 1968, p. 15

16 see Mikhail Iampolskii, 'Kuleshov's Experiments and the New Anthropology of the Actor', *IFF*, p. 45 for details of the allocation of film stock for THE experiment itself

17 Pudovkin, 'Organizatsiia "sluchainogo" materiala', *Kinorezhisser i kinomaterial*, *SS* I, pp. 108–109

18 see, for instance, Hitchcock's reference in James Naremore, *Acting in the Cinema*, p. 240 and the apparently mangled version given by Brunius in

Roger Manvell, ed. *Experiment in the Film*, London 1949, p. 62

19 Lindley Hanlon, *Fragments: Bresson s Film Style*, London 1986, p. 213

20 Pudovkin, 'Naturshchik vmesto aktera', *SS* I, p. 182

21 Levaco, p. 54 and Lev Kuleshov, *Selected Works*, tr. Dmitri Agrachev and Nina Belenkaia, Moscow 1987, p. 138; the Razumny film was distributed abroad as *The Beauty and the Bolshevik*.

22 Golovnia interview, Jean and Luda Schnitzer, *Cinema in Revolution*, tr. D. Robinson, London 1973, p. 144

23 Yuri Tsivian, 'Some Historical Footnotes to the Kuleshov Experiment' [1986] Thomas Elsaesser, ed. *Space Frame Narrative*, London 1990, pp. 249–251

24 Pudovkin, 'Montazh stroiashchii', *Kinostsenarii*, *SS* I, p. 71

25 Béla Balázs, *Theory of the Film*, London 1952, p. 61

26 Ian Christie and Julian Graffy, *Protazanov*, London 1993, p. 20; see also V. S. Lukhachev, *Istoriia kino v Rossii 1896–1913*, Leningrad 1927, p. 171 for a wonderful (and I suspect touched-up) picture of Mozzhukin's mesmerising stare.

27 Charles Darwin, *The Expression of the Emotions in Man and Animals* [1872], Chicago 1965, p. 12

28 Moussinac, p. 127; René Marchand and Pierre Weinstein, *Le Cinéma*, Paris 1927, p. 159

29 Levaco, p. 173; see also James Riordan, *Sport in Soviet Society*, Cambridge 1977, on the shift from physical culture in the '20s to competitive sport in the '30s

30 Levaco, p. 58

31 Pudovkin, 'Tema', *Kinostsenarii*, *SS* I, p. 57

32 Levaco, ed. p. 100; on the connections of film with Meyerhold's practice see Osip Brik's article and the illustrations of Igor Il'inskii in *The Forest* in 'Kino v teatre Meierkhol'da', *Sovetskii ekran* 20, 18 May 1926, pp. 6–7

33 Béatrice Picon-Vallin, *Meyerhold*, Paris 1990, p. 109

34 Mel Gordon, 'Meyerhold's Biomechanics', *Drama Review* 18.3 (1974) p. 77

35 Levaco, p. 99

36 current research into repetitive strain injury (notably on fishing trawlers, the closest instance I could find to stevedores) suggests that Kuleshov's confidence was misplaced

37 Evgenii Zamiatin, *We*, tr. C. Brown, Harmonsworth 1993, pp. 13 and 34; see also F. W. Taylor, *The Principles of Scientific Management* [1911], New York 1947, p. 79, for instructions on how best to lay bricks; Taylor's example is not as good as it seems as softening the mortar could well mar the stability of the wall . . .

38 Levaco, p. 56

39 Huntley Carter, *The New Theatre and Cinema of Soviet Russia*, London 1924, p. 277; see also proceedings of 1995 CPR 'Past Masters' conference and Jörg Bochow, *Das Theater Meyerholds und die Biomechanik*, Berlin 1997

40 Hanlon, p. 213: '[Kuleshov's] films include very exaggerated performances'
41 see 'However odd, Khokhlova!', Eisenstein, *Selected Works* I, ed. Richard Taylor, London 1988, p. 71
42 for the recurrence of this figure as a new Soviet type see Geoffrey Hosking, *A History of the Soviet Union*, London 1990, p. 86; it also appears as a puppet in Sevzapkino's *N+N+N* (1924); the Museum of the Revolution on Tverskaia in Moscow has a good display of the actual article
43 Moussinac, p. 128; see also Viktor Shklovskii, 'O rozhdenii i zhizni "FEKSov" ' [1928], *Za sorok let*, Moscow 1965
44 *IFF*, p. 33; see also François Albera, ed. *Vers une théorie de l acteur*, Lausanne 1990 and, for the continuing use by Khokhlova of Delsarte in actor training, Vlada Petrić, 'A subtextual reading of Kuleshov's satire "The Extraordinary Adventures of Mr West in the Land of the Bolshevik" ' in Andrew Horton, ed. *Inside Soviet Film Satire*, Cambridge 1993, p. 67. For Volkonskii's thoughts on cinema see 'O russkom ekrane' [1928] reprinted in *Kinovedcheskie zapiski* 13, 1992
45 V. R. Gardin, *Vospominaniia*, Moscow 1949, pp. 201–203
46 Levaco, p. 107
47 Levaco, p. 73
48 Eisenstein, *Selected Works* I, ed. Richard Taylor, London 1988, p. 151; Rudolf Arnheim, *Film as Art*, London 1958, p. 186
49 Pudovkin, 'Rabota aktera v kino i "sistema" Stanislavskogo' [1952], *Izbrannye stat i*, Moscow 1955, p. 217
50 Pudovkin, 'Naturshchik vmesto aktera', *SS* I, p. 183
51 *Sovetskoe kino* 1, February 1926, gives Shpikovskii as scenarist and co-director; Denise J. Youngblood, *Movies for the Masses*, Cambridge 1992, p. 216, suspects that *Chess Fever* is in large part his work
52 see Denise J. Youngblood, 'An ambivalent NEP satire of bourgeois aspirations' in Horton, ed. pp. 48–58
53 *Sovetskoe kino* 1, February 1926, p.13; the article is delightfully designed like a chequerboard, with alternating blocks of text and photographs of the Chess grand masters
54 see *Vestnik kinematografii* 123, 1917 and *Kine-zhurnal* 5-6 p. 110 and 11–16 p. 161, 1917
55 qu. Vlada Petrić, 'Soviet Revolutionary Films in the USA', Ph.D. thesis, New York 1973, p. 95
56 Pudovkin, 'Priemy obrabotki materiala', *Kinostenarii*, *SS* I, p. 70
57 Boris Eikhenbaum, 'Cinema Stylistics', ed. Herbert Eagle, *Russian Formalist Film Theory*, Michigan 1981, p. 67; for a useful discussion of this essay see Paul Willemen, 'Reflections on Eikhenbaum's Concept of Internal Speech in the Cinema', *Looks and Frictions*, Bloomington 1994
58 Peter Dart, *Pudovkin s Films and Film Theory*, New York 1974, p. 110
59 Maya Turovskaya, *Tarkovsky*, London 1989, p. 101
60 Vladimir Maiakovskii, *How are Verses Made?*, tr. G. M. Hyde, Bristol 1990, p. 49
61 Maiakovskii, *How are Verses Made?*, p. 44

62 Pudovkin, 'Tema' and 'Prosteishie spetsial'nye priemy s''emki', *Kinostsenarii*, *SS* I, pp. 56 and 69
63 Levaco, pp. 66 and 110
64 Pudovkin, 'Apparat zastavliaet zritelia videt' tak, kak etogo khochet rezhisser', *Kinorezhisser i kinomaterial*, *SS* I, p. 125
65 Kirill Shutko, preface to Boris Eikhenbaum, ed. *Poetika kino* [1927], Richard Taylor, ed. *Poetics of Cinema*, Oxford 1982, p. 2

2. Russian Physiology and Pudovkin's *The Mechanics of the Brain (The Behaviour of Animals and Man)*

It was not mere chance that the task of filming Pavlov's new laboratory was entrusted by Mezhrabpom-Rus to the relatively inexperienced Pudovkin. Pudovkin trained as a chemist in his youth; supposedly a colleague of Pavlov was sufficiently impressed by Pudovkin's knowledge to offer him a placement.[1] According to his wife, Anna Zemtsova, Pudovkin retained a zealous interest in science and scientific innovation. She depicts him as something of a Renaissance polymath and an eternal adolescent, always interested in things new.[2] He hoped to make a film which would demonstrate and explain a great scientific idea or principle. In retrospect it now seems that he came closer to realising this aim with *The Mechanics of the Brain* [Mekhanika golovnogo mozga (Povedenie zhivotnykh i cheloveka), 1925] than with the Stalinist bio-pics devoted to Great Men of Science (the aviator Zhukovsky) similar in tendency to his Great Men of History series of the same period (General Nakhimov, Admiral Suvorov). Although *The Mechanics of the Brain* includes an establishing shot of Pavlov's Leningrad laboratory, followed by a brief glimpse of academician Pavlov himself, reading in his study, and even occasional accredited quotations, the film is more an exposition of the work than a paean to the man.

Boris Babkin was a pupil of Pavlov who fled the Soviet Union for England then Canada. Corroborating the usual assumption of the pertinence of Pavlov's work, he says that:

> Very soon after the accession of the Bolsheviks to power Pavlov's teachings on conditioned reflexes were recognised by them as affirming that the intellectual life of people can be radically reconstructed and that a proletarian revolution worldwide would create a new human society.[3]

However, this welding of Pavlov to Bolshevik interests occurred in spite of his own protestations and that of scientific research in general. Nor was Pavlov alone; many bourgeois intellectuals remained outside the Party and Lunacharsky stalwartly defended their right to do so.[4] Reflexology was taught also at the Communist Academy, but the inferiority of its work to that of Pavlov's Institute was widely acknowledged.[5] In 1921, Lenin himself had signed a decree safeguarding the work and Pavlov personally. In 1922, he asked Lenin if he could take his work abroad, but was refused permission.[6] In September 1923, after a brief foreign tour, he delivered a public lecture criticising Bolshevism as he saw it and, specifically, Bukharin's *ABC of Communism*. He complained of the likely loss of life consequent on pursuing a programme of world revolution in a world which did not want it; he criticised the idea that 'cultural intellectual production' could be assumed by the proletariat and applied to the furtherance of the class war; he criticised the Party establishment for its intervention in the appointment and expulsion of university staff and criticised Bolshevism in general for being as prejudicial to the advancement of science as the Orthodox Church had been hitherto under Tsarist protection:

> Science and free criticism, these are synonymous ... if you acknowledge that Marxism and communism are not absolute truths, that it is only a theory in which there may be a part of a truth, but in which there is perhaps no truth, then you will look on all life with freedom of view but not with such slavery.[7]

Bukharin took the attack sufficiently seriously to publish a reply. Given the usefulness of Pavlov to the party's agenda and given Bukharin's preference for the superiority of science over the arts, its tone is strangely condescending:

> ... even the sun has spots. These spots have the tendency to increase substantially when specialists of natural science begin to deal with

things which they – I hope that the author of conditional reflexes will forgive me – simply do not know.[8]

Admittedly, late in life, when Bukharin had long since fallen from grace, Pavlov voiced patriotic support for the Soviet state and it may be that he was by then genuinely persuaded of its cause. It may be that he was thereby expressing gratitude for its benevolence towards his laboratory and research, and for the personal privileges extended to himself and his wife in times of hardship.[9] It may be that he was afraid of losing a guarantee of security. Certainly, Pavlov did not retain into the 1930s the high esteem which he had enjoyed previously. In the late 1940s and 1950s he was unequivocably rehabilitated to the ranks of accepted national worthies and, perversely, inexperienced aspirant scientists were discouraged from freely criticising his principal tenets.[10]

Theories of associative learning based on Pavlov's conditioned reflex (the thesis of stimulus-response) were of immediate service to the Soviet programme of mass education. They were subsequently taken up by Watson and Skinner and a whole generation of psychologists in the United States.[11] The suggestion that learning (as the acquisition of habit) was a mechanical process independent of the prescriptions of inheritance was commensurate with an ideology of egalitarianism and with the internationalist thrust of early '20s Soviet policy. The education programme continued throughout the '20s in apparent disregard of Pavlov's later work in typology which obliged him to admit, ultimately, that some dogs were simply born more intelligent than others.[12]

n addition to the specific utility and convenience of Pavlovian physiology to Bolshevism, in the promotion of a revolutionary movement in society an earlier period of Russian history was invoked. Sechenov, to whom Pavlov referred as 'the father of Russian physiology' had been associated (and, like Pavlov, often against his will) with Nihilist subversion and resistance to the metaphysics of Orthodoxy and the Tsarist regime. Daniel P. Todes, in 'From Radicalism to Scientific Convention', suggests that Pavlov's allegiance to Sechenov may even have been over-stated in the official record in order to stress a convenient line of descent.[13] Pavlov and Sechenov were both heralded for their admission of women to their courses; their laboratories were even idealistically construed as social models of collective endeavour. Many adherents of Pavlov were physicians from clinics concerned to treat illness by the best means possible. When his news-sheet, *The Contemporary*, was banned from publishing Sechenov's overtly challenging *Reflexes of the Brain* (1863), Chernyshevsky supported Sechenov in his campaign to have it published elsewhere. By taking its title as its own, Lenin's strategic pamphlet *What is to be Done?* (1902) explicitly acknowledged and honoured the Chernyshevsky novel of 1862, as did articles by Kuleshov dated 1923 and 1930. Sechenov was deemed to be the original for Chernyshevsky's Dr. Kirsanov and also for the medical student Bazarov in Turgenev's *Fathers and Children*:

> 'All men are similar, in soul as well as in body ... It is enough to have one human specimen in order to judge all others ... We know more or less what causes physical ailments; and moral diseases are caused by the wrong sort of education, by all the rubbish people's heads are stuffed with from childhood onwards, in short by the disordered state of society. Reform society and there will be no diseases'.[14]

Herzen's relative 'The Chemist' is a similar social type.[15] Not only was physiology socially practicable and progressive (in medicine, in public health, in education) but by citation of historic precedent, its leading players could be rendered as causally inked to perceived political progress also. The fact that physiology had aroused such strong opposition from the old regime disposed towards its facile characterisation as a fundamentally revolutionary force.[16] *The Mechanics of the Brain* demonstrates at considerable length the experiments with frogs for which Sechenov was famous, as the basis for Pavlov's enquiry into higher nervous activity.

Pavlov's personal importance to the Soviet state was further enhanced by his enormous international standing. In 1904, Pavlov had received a Nobel Prize for his work on the digestive system in dogs. Thereafter, his laboratory attracted students from abroad, including Anrep, who was responsible for the 1927 English translation of the *Lectures*. Pavlovian psychology came to acquire a status equivalent to that of schools developing contemporaneously from beginnings in France, Austria, Germany and America. Pavlov's scientific eminence and respectability, the exemplary facilities with which the state provided him and his colleagues, lent kudos (however spurious) to the Soviet claim to be a modernising, science-led society. While the Soviet state was conscious of its inferiority in so many other areas, in the new science of Physiological Psychology, it could congratulate itself on its excellence. In spite of the Revolution, noted J. B. S. Haldane, the conduct of fine science in Russia continued.[17]

Herbert Spencer's *Principles of Psychology* (1855) was acknowledged by Sechenov to be influential in his own speculations into the activities of reflexes in animal behaviour: Spencer straightforwardly linked biology and socio-cultural evolution. Sechenov equally admired Darwin (both *The Origin of Species* and *The Expression of Emotions in Man and Animals*) for establishing grounds for the proposition that behaviour in humans and animals could be commonly rooted and activated by the instinct to survive. For Pavlov too, Darwin was fundamental: 'Darwin must be counted as founder and instigator of the contemporary comparative study of higher vital phenomena of animals ... the hypothesis of the origin of man from animals gave great impetus to the study of higher phenomena of animal life ... '.[18] However, Sechenov lacked the experimental techniques necessary to test his theories scientifically. Pavlov took this as his immediate task within the discipline of physiology. He confronted the inherited dualistic anxieties (William James' 'leaking joints') as far and only as far as science would allow:

> Pavlov viewed philosophy and science as complementary: the goal of philosophy is to unveil the essence of natural phenomena; the goal of science is to understand the functioning of the mechanisms through which nature works. In examining the human brain ... science is not concerned with the ontological essence of the 'physical' and the 'physiological' but with the functions of the cerebral cortex that are related to specific phases of consciousness ... Pavlov made no effort to reduce all physical phenomena to physiological actions, even though his interest centred on establishing physiological processes underlying given psychological phenomena.[19]

George Bernard Shaw's criticism of Pavlov for denying 'the existence and authority of ... any metaphysical factors in life whatsoever, including purpose, intuition, inspiration and all religious and artistic impulses',[20] is an entertaining tease, but, if taken seriously, unfounded and unfair: Pavlov was simply endeavouring to pursue a scientific line of enquiry as far as it could take him. When the hero of Zamiatin's dystopia *We* is subjected to the Bell (surely intended as a reference to the reflex apparatus) to cure him of his illness (Imagination) he condemns a distortion of Pavlov's work which Pavlov himself would never have defended.[21] However resolutely Pavlov bound himself to the constraints of laboratory practice and resisted the appellation of psychologist he was nonetheless pressed into service. Psychology, seeking to establish its own scientific credentials and to distance itself from introspective psychologising, appropriated his name. At an international conference celebrating a century of psychology in 1985, a speaker invoked 'Wundt, Pavlov and Freud' as its 'great founding triumvirate'.[22]

Scientific films in Russia

Scientific films had been made before the revolution, in Russia and elsewhere. Frederick A. Talbot's *Moving Pictures* (1912) refers to films of microbes, flowers, insects and polyps.[23] Professor Voskresensky, Pudovkin's assistant on *The Mechanics of the Brain*, says that such films enjoyed enormous popularity with Russian audiences and that, before the Revolution, the majority of these films were imported. Voskresensky, like Professor Tikhonov writing in *Kino* in 1922, finds that German films of natural science subjects merit particular mention.[24] Similar films, and films about anatomy and public health and hygiene continued to be made in Russia and distributed in the '20s. For instance, *Sovetskii ekran* includes a discussion of a 'kul'turfil'ma' about the structure of the human eye and the care of eyesight. Other films addressed abortion and promoted the Soviet campaign against alcoholism. Discussion of *The Mechanics* is accompanied by topics of associated interest: *Sovetskoe kino* devotes an article to the attempts of Mezhrabpom-Rus to popularise science. It gives *The Sky and the Earth* and *Alcohol and Health* as films in production and *Problems of Nutrition* (to be directed by Boris Barnet) and *Mother and Child (How to Tell Children the Facts of Life)* as under preparation. *Modern Neuroses* is listed as a film intended for Pudovkin, but this was unfortunately never realised.[25] Articles under the heading 'How to make an educational film' appear, for instance, in *Sovetskoe kino*, including the contribution from Pudovkin, in *Art-ekran* and in *Kino i kul tura.*[26] Elsewhere it was suggested that cinematography could be employed to render Einstein comprehensible to a wider audience and German scientific films imported into Russia included *The Theory of Relativity.*[27]

Scientific films for a general audience were part of the wider Soviet campaign to educate and inform a massive widespread population, a high percentage of which was illiterate.[28] Before the Revolution, cinema-going had been an almost exclusively urban occupation. At Lunacharsky's instigation, the Commissariat of Enlightenment set up specialist film units: Mikhail Romm, trained with the Children's Film Unit, making films and studying audience reception.[29] A designated studio for documentary films, Kult'kino, was established in 1924 but its disbanding in 1926 left Mezhrabpom-Rus the major producer in the field.[30] The Commissariat levied taxes on cinema tickets in order that funds could be re-directed towards the making of educational films, which, together with Mezhrabpom's independent revenues, allowed it to make geographical, topical and scientific documentaries. Under Lenin's cinefication programme such films were carried into the regions, by boat, train and camel, with projectors powered by mobile generators, or were shown in workers' clubs, in schools, hospitals and in factories, as cheaply as possible to make them accessible to all.[31] Sometimes these were shown to the accompaniment of an explanatory lecture. Often the screenings were fraught with practical difficulties: projectors being liable to break down and there being poor knowledge of maintenance; inexperienced projectionists showing films at incorrect speed and films soon becomimg damaged by being exhibited on inadequate equipment.[32] In the major commercial cinemas in the larger towns, a programme often billed a documentary film as the first item, followed by a comedy short then the main feature. Such documentary films were generally released at a loss and no more than ten copies were made. *The Mechanics of the Brain* was unusual for raising a profit.[33]

The Mechanics of the Brain

The title of Pudovkin's 1926 film, *The Mechanics of the Brain (The Behaviour of Man and Animals)*, describes the research with which Pavlov was immediately concerned and his particular physiological contribution to psychology. The first reel shows basic reflexes in animals and reproduces Sechenov's experiments with frogs; the second reel shows the formation of conditioned reflexes in dogs and the training of monkeys to respond to alternate colour stimulii; the third reel shows the effect of damage to various parts of the human brain and the performance of tasks by children at different ages.

Given the routine acknowledgement of the influence of Pavlov's theories on Soviet film practice I find it remarkable that this film has been very largely overlooked.[34] It seems to me that a study of this film is useful as an indication of what was commonly understood of Pavlov's work, as an indication of how the film camera might be employed as an instrument of scientific exposition and as to how Pudovkin constructed and construed a logical scenario adequate to this task.

Moussinac mentions it in passing in *Le Cinéma soviétique* (1928) as exemplary of its kind and Bryher's *Film Problems of Soviet Russia* (1929) provides a fuller description of its content.[35] Leyda's *Kino* (first edition 1960) adds a brief commentary on the difficulties surrounding its production. John Maddison, in his contribution to Manvell's *Experiment in the Film* (1949), regrets that few Soviet science films reach western audiences, but finds *The Mechanics of the Brain* still worthy of attention.[36] Catherine de la Roche (1948) cites a sound film made by Bazykin, *The Physiology and Pathology of Nervous Activity*, which at least stands witness to a continuing interest in familiarising an audience with Pavlov's work, but nothing is said of its predecessor. The cursory reference in Peter Dart's monograph, *Pudovkin's Films and Film Theory* (1974), and his unsubstantiated claim that it 'must be regarded as the best scientific film of the silent period' is, I suggest, lifted directly from Mariamov, as is much else.[37] Mariamov in turn quotes the 1937 appraisal by Iezuitov, but conveys little sense of experiencing the film first-hand: 'In the work on this film Pudovkin could satisfy his enthusiasm and partiality for philosophical analysis: with the aid of his scientific understanding he could reach the very core of his subject'.[38] Paul Rotha claims, possibly extravagantly, that the 'key to Pudovkin's direction lay plainly in *The Mechanics of the Brain*, for it gave an exposition of the methods which he employs for the selection of his visual images, based on an understanding of the working of the human mind'.[39] Anatoli Golovnia is unforthcoming in his *Light in the Art of the Cameraman* [Svet v iskusstve operatora, 1945], but refers to *The Mechanics of the Brain* in his interview with Jean and Luda Schnitzer as the film with which his long-standing partnership with Pudovkin was initiated.[40] At the time, he wrote with understandable exasperation about the technical problems of working with children and animals, and suggested that in future such work be undertaken by specialist personnel; little wonder that the opportunity to film *Chess Fever*, in the midst of these difficulties, was welcomed with glad relief:

> The film was composed from such models as mad men, idiots, paralytics, a woman in childbirth, new-born infants and not new-born ... ordinary dogs and dogs without a brain; dissected frogs and undissected frogs, monkeys, lions, bears, eagles, cows, horses, hippopotami, crocodiles. And all this entire ensemble turns around, fidgets, runs off or separates out, seizes our operator or grasps onto the camera.[41]

To these problems can be added, say Golovnia and Pudovkin, the aggravations of lighting and filming in small spaces with multiple camera positions, the time taken to move from one position to another.[42]

Like *The Mother*, *The End of St. Petersburg* and *Storm over Asia*, *The Mechanics of the Brain* was refused a licence for public screening on release in Britain.[43] However, it was shown privately to the Film Society and to a meeting of the Neurological Section of the Royal Society of Medicine, for which Montagu prepared English subtitles. Unfortunately, the minutes do not record any opinion of the film.[44] Winifred Ellerman (Bryher), committed and gratefully acknowledged supporter of the Soviet film in Britain, extolled the didactic potential of *The Mechanics of the Brain*: 'Surely this could be admitted as a scientific film free of duty, for in the world of research and medicine at least there ought to be no barriers'.[45] Other members of the Film Society found it thoroughly objectionable. Montagu does not relate whether complaints were prompted by the pictorial content (mentally retarded and syphilitic patients; a woman in childbirth) or by the ideological thrust of the titles ('All life, all culture is wholly made up of reflexes ... '; 'The study of conditioned reflexes serves as the basis of materialist understanding of the behaviour of animals and man'). Certainly this pictorial content did not meet the standard criteria of the BBFC.[46] A screening intended for the London Workers' Society consequently necessitated drastic cuts.[47]

I have yet to find any mention of the film in a biography of Pavlov (Cuny, Gray, Joravsky, Vucinich), not even those written by erstwhile students of Pavlov in the Leningrad laboratory in which the film was made (Babkin, Frolov).[48] Pavlov himself, writing in the

1930s of his studies of sleep, recognises the usefulness of film to clinical science, but says nothing of his earlier collaboration with Pudovkin:

> It is a pity that cinematography appeared too late and could not be utilised by us and our physiological laboratories. Had it been as accessible then as it is now, all these phenomena could have been very easily comprehended. We could now demonstrate them to you in the space of fifteen minutes and you would leave us with the deep conviction that inhibition and sleep are one and the same process. But while inhibition is a concentrated process, hypnosis and sleep represent an inhibition which spreads over more or less vast areas.[49]

There is later documentary footage of Pavlov at work in the Leningrad laboratory in the Krasnogorsk archive.

Contradictory reports are to be found in other sources of Pavlov's reaction to the film. Luda and Jean Schnitzer say that he approved the result,[50] whereas Jay Leyda says that he resisted the idea from the outset and draws a comparison with Freud's opposition to Pabst's stylised drama, *Secrets of a Soul* [Geheimnisse einer Seele, Germany 1926].[51] Certainly, the Gosfilmofond copy of Pudovkin's meticulous shot list bears Pavlov's signature. Mariamov and Fefer (regular contributor to *Sovetskii ekran* and *Sovetskoe kino* on matters scientific) say that Pavlov took no part in the filming and that the original scenario was volunteered to Mezhrabpom-Rus, unsolicited, by Voskresenky (himself a follower of Pavlov).[52] Pudovkin says that Pavlov, ever cautious, was originally reluctant to co-operate, fearful that popularisation was tantamount to 'vulgarisation', but that he was eventually reconciled to the project.[53] Pavlov did not care for anything likely to disrupt the work of his laboratory or his account thereof. In the preface to the first Russian edition of the *Lectures*, he records laconically a major interruption to which they were subject:

> Five years ago, when I was confined to my bed for several months on account of a serious fracture of the leg I prepared a general review of all our investigations. Then the Revolution began. This, of course, distracted my attention ... Thus it happened that what I had prepared was never printed.[54]

Pudovkin's task on *The Mechanics of the Brain* was rendered yet more difficult by the fact that in 1925–6 many of Pavlov's discoveries in conditioned and unconditioned reflexes were yet to be published and that he was therefore obliged to work from a collection of notes and addresses, sometimes incoherent or contradictory. From this experience, Pudovkin concludes, those engaged in the making of scientific films needs must be competent scientists themselves and not simply technicians. He praises the work of his assistants on *The Mechanics of the Brain*.[55] More broadly, although physiology had been enormously fashionable in literary circles from the nineteenth century onwards, it also seems worth noting the absence of a tradition popularising eminent work in the field and the absence, perhaps, of a readership for such a genre.[56]

What I have gleaned of Pavlov's methods and principles elsewhere endorses Pudovkin's representation of the reserve with which Pavlov met *The Mechanics of the Brain*. It leads one to suspect that Pavlov would be at least sceptical and more likely downright hostile to the translation of his work to a medium with which he was not familiar and was disposed to consider with distaste. It could well be that Pavlov, the strict and particular physiologist, then regarded film in general as a trivialising medium, inappropriate to serious enquiry. Pavlov was wont to change his mind (and his theories) as new evidence presented itself in experiments: for instance, in the documented disputes with Bekhterev and in his drastic amendment of the hypothetical Hippocratic model originally adopted for his work in typology.[57] Pavlov chose to publish the *Lectures on Conditioned Reflexes* unrevised, close to the form in which they had been delivered, in order that the methodical working through of a problem could remain apparent:

> As a result of continued experimentation some of the deductions and interpretations ... had to be considerably modified. However ... I intentionally allowed the chapters to remain as they left my hands ... incorporating in the later lectures the new material ... In this manner the reader is placed in a position to obtain a much clearer idea of the natural growth of the subject.[58]

The fixing of experiments on film, especially experiments as yet unpublished in more orthodox form, could be construed as presenting as conclusive and irrevocable theory that which in actuality was no more than work in progress. 'Pavlov was critical of results obtained in the laboratory and of theories that might be forwarded regarding them', says Babkin; 'a theory was good if it could connect facts for six months at least'.[59] 'It was ... my habit', says Pavlov himself, 'to lay aside a written article in order to forget it, so that when I re-read it I could the better note its shortcomings'.[60]

Pavlov was always (as was Freud) keen to stress his concern with the normal functioning of the brain, albeit under laboratory conditions, and took care to eliminate external variables which might disrupt the constancy of the controlled model set-up: even a flake of plaster falling from the ceiling or a fly in the room could distract a dog's attention. Pavlov's laboratory (the Tower of Silence) was constructed with a straw-filled moat surrounding it, sand-pugged floors and thick windows to insulate against the irregularity of external noise levels.[61] Pudovkin and Golovnia found that their presence affected the conduct of the experiments, and for the experiments in the paediatric laboratory of Professor Krasnogorsky they took the precaution of building a hide. Shots remain in the final cut in which the child subjects look out to camera.

Pudovkin, although filming actual experiments in the laboratory with dogs and monkeys, also contrived material which would serve to illustrate Pavlov's thesis as he understood it, 'the general underlying principal' in accord with which all the material was organised. The performance of the sea-lion in *The Mechanics of the Brain* was, by Pudovkin's own account, not at all left to its own devices:

> One cannot command an animal to swim in a desired direction or to approach a camera; but at the same time its movement was exactly prescribed in the editing plan with which the construction of the whole picture was bound up.... For the close-up the bait was thrown again and again until the sea-lion leaped onto the right place on the bank and made the necessary turn. Out of thirty takes made, three were chosen and these gave on the screen the desired image of continuous movement. This movement was not organised by direct prescription of the work required but attained by approximate control of chance elements and subsequent strict selection of the material gathered.[62]

Iezuitov and Professor Voskresensky say that in general there is danger in incorporating staged material in science films, as this may provoke

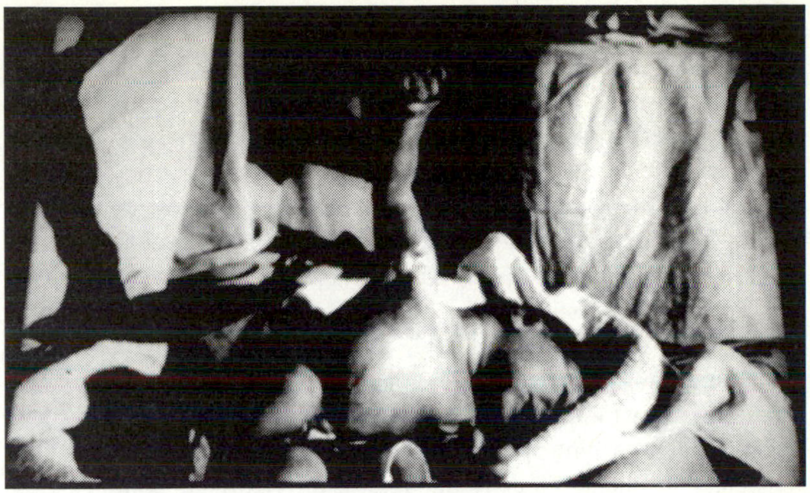

The unconditioned reflex in a newly born baby

incredulity in an audience which may extend to any experimental record with which it is associated.[63]

Another reason for Pavlov's resistance to the initial proposal to present his work may have been the association intended between the bases of nervous activity and behaviour in animals, and developmental psychology in humans. In the new-born child there are unconditioned reflexes: a baby is shown clutching to an adult's finger. In the opening reel of the film an orangoutang and a one year old infant are shown making use of implements (a basic task which the syphilitic patient, shown in the third reel, as a consequence of progressive cerebral paralysis, can no longer perform). The mentally retarded subject is said to have a brain no more developed than that of a fish and, like the one-year-old baby, reacts violently to the removal of food. Later, children of different ages are shown performing more complicated tasks (washing, building with bricks), then solving practical problems (a quoit hung on the wall cannot be reached by a group of children nor can it be reached from a table on which a child stands tiptoe holding up a long stick; thereupon the children decide to put a chair on the table and by standing on the chair the quoit is fetched down). Children play with a toy car and a wendy-house. An older child finds the mechanism which makes the car run. A six-year-old is shown playing with a train. Pavlov is quoted in an intertitle: '. . . between reflexes there has to be a single conditioned reflex, the reflex of purpose – the striving towards the achievement of a certain objective'. Seemingly, Pavlov was satisfied that such parallels were thus far sound.

Pavlov chose the dog as the main subject for experiment because he found it generally amenable; but he also declared the dog a useful insight into the behaviour of man, as a result of their historic and environmental interdependence.[64] It is left to Mikhail Bulgakov, in *The Heart of a Dog* (1925), to draw the absurdly logical conclusion that man and dog are potentially anatomically interchangeable also.[65] Pavlov tacitly cast his work in an evolutionist mould, but was cautious as to undue extrapolation from his results and, conversely, notoriously censorious of 'anthropomorphic' terminology applied to animals in laboratory conditions, exacting fines from defaulting students.[66] While Shaw (amidst much carping at Pavlov's expense) complains of the extra-vernacular character of his language, better informed commentators identify 'the refinement of methodology and scientific nomenclature' as a distinct contribution. 'In a deliberate effort to avoid psychological terminology, Pavlov tied original labels to the concepts that he developed to organise the data obtained from his research'.[67] Outside of the laboratory, Pavlov sometimes indulged himself in what Joravsky and Vucinich term 'holistic' lapses, especially when enthusiastically proclaiming the future potential of physiology to address the world's ills:

> ... now I am deeply and irrevocably convinced that along this path ... will be found the final triumph of the human mind over its uttermost and supreme problem: the knowledge of the laws and mechanism of human nature ... Only science, exact science about human nature itself and the most sincere approach to it by aid of omnipotent scientific method will deliver man from his present gloom and will purge him of his contemporary shame in the sphere of interhuman relations.[68]

Pavlov provocatively hypothesised that even language was no more than a secondary function of higher nervous activity. Bekhterev admonished Pavlov for this tendency to make grandiose prognostications which 'exact science' was hard pressed to warrant:

> Now the question is: do the reduction of the most complex biological activities to such a simple scheme and the supporting of this

> position by expatiating on why, exactly, we Russians have, under the influence of centuries of slavery, lost our volitional busyness, while the Anglo-Saxons, in contrast, have for a long period freely developed their 'aim reflex' – do these afford a solution of the problem in the sense of explaining the given biological Phenomenon? It is scarcely necessary to point out that very little is gained in this way and that the adversaries of the objective method in its application to the investigation of human personality are given a weapon.[69]

However, inside Pavlov's Tower of Silence the laboratory imposed a very precise and strict discipline. Indeed, Pavlov's personal disaffection for popular journals and for the academic conference circuit, his reluctance to engage his scientific practice in a broader cultural context and the preservation of its untainted exclusivity, may have sanctified yet further its credentials as objective authority.[70]

Bekhterev swathed his work in a vast array of philosophical and cultural reference, seemingly subsequently formulating experiments to substantiate the particular position which he had already elected to adopt. Bekhterev's *General Principles of Human Reflexology* (1923) quotes from Wundt, Freud, Münsterberg, du Bois Raymond, Christiansen's *Philosophie der Kunst*, the philologist Potebnia et al; most often it quotes Bekhterev himself.[71] Pavlov confines himself to the citation of other scientists, only where there are specific points of concordance or disagreement: for instance, he acknowledges that Thorndike's experiments in comparative physiology preceded his own by some two or three years but effectively arrived at similar conclusions;[72] he criticises Kretschmer's *Physik und Charakter* (1921) for failing to distinguish between type and character and for reducing all mankind to two clinical pathological types;[73] his numerous objections to Gestalt psychology include its lack of grounding in physiology (it has neglected, he says, to acquaint itself thoroughly with Helmholtz), its rejecting of analysis and the notion of associationism and in turn of the study of behaviour in terms of stimulus-response units, 'not that it dislikes brain mechanics or dynamics; but it believes the brain to work in large patterns, by "closing gaps" ... rather than by the operation of nerve paths linking this and that little centre in the brain'.[74] Bekhterev and Pavlov seem to characterise nicely Karl Popper's distinction between models of deductive and inductive science, with Pavlov laboriously building theory from an accumulation of empirical evidence gathered over considerable time and from a great number of individual examples. Popper draws the distinction in order to cast doubt on the presumed epistemological status of inductive science and to suggest that, in practice, an absolute distinction may not hold fast- but of more immediate concern, it seems to me, is that Pavlov's scientific methodology and Pavlov himself were recognised as highly serviceable to Soviet purposes.[75] Whereas William James, simultaneously attempting to build a psychology on the foundations of natural science, openly confesses that 'here may be no science, only hope of a science', 'metaphysical questions leak through at every joint', Pavlov appears not to trouble to plug the joints but rather to deny the pertinence of the questions.[76] Shaw was not alone in assuming that Pavlov had succeeded in eliminating the notion of 'Soul'; Pavlov himself, in reply to such suggestions, pronounced that declarations of its final demise were somewhat premature.[77] Certain extreme factions of the party were equally eager to leap to this same conclusion:

> Our understanding of the process of cognition does not in the least coincide with the meaning that has been given to these words in all doctrines, except the theory of new biology: for us the words knowledge and cognition signify only physiological reactions without any participation of a psyche i.e. without any participation of non-spatial phenomena.[78]

Techniques of the science film

Pudovkin, in his 1925 article in *Kino-zhurnal ARK* 'Montage in the science film', makes a crucial distinction between the procedures involved in recording experiments, usually intended for a professional scientific audience, and films made for popular consumption. To film a scientific experiment, he says, is to record not only an object but also a dynamic process. But only for the professional audience can this be translated without intervention, in a single unbroken sequence.[79] The former films often require specialist equipment and installations, he says, but says that such films are already being produced in Germany. In such films the camera performs an 'investigative role'.

The camera had, since its invention, served as an item of scientific apparatus and its photographic products had been appreciated as evidence objectively verifying scientific facts. Lisa Cartwright notes

Lumière's 'near-lifelong commitment to medical biology, pharmacology and experimental physiology'.[80] Muybridge and Marey both published their photographic analyses of movement in the 1870s. Darwin's *The Expression of the Emotions in Man and Animals* (1872) reproduces photographs made by Duchenne and uses engravings made from photographs, presumably to show the location of muscles with greater precision. Darwin praises Duchenne for his care and attention.[81] However, the photographic image is here a record of the procedure by which the supposedly typical representation of that emotion was arrived at, rather than a genuine record of emotion spontaneously expressed. The genuineness of the expression (as it relates to a particular emotional state) appears to be taken as given, although no such emotion was experienced at the time the photograph was taken. In Voskresensky's terms, these photographs are staged. Amidst the enthusiasm for the new technique the distinction as to what exactly photography is being employed to corroborate seems to me to be important and relevant to the use of the film *The Mechanics of the Brain* as a record of Pavlov's experiments. The possibility might be suggested that the medium was itself selected to lend additional scientific authority to the material recorded. The notion of Cinema Truth volunteered by Vertov seems pertinent; but, in practice, Pudovkin finds Vertov's directives inadequate to his purpose of constructing a coherent exposition and explanation of Pavlov's work. Pudovkin says that 'specifically filmic means' must be found through which to effect the film-maker's understanding of his subject but that 'the method of Cinema-Truth was rejected' in favour of 'film art's own specific procedures for interpretation: montage'.[82]

The scientific film should not, says Pudovkin, rely on written material interposed between shots (as was current practice), nor on a spoken commentary for its intelligibility. The intertitles in *The Mechanics of the Brain* are well spaced apart, usually short and single frame (with the exception of a longer running quotation from Pavlov), written in bold white type on black, frequently with especially significant words isolated and or underlined or enlarged ('unconditioned and conditioned reflexes serve as the basis of behaviour not only of animals but also of *mankind*'). Pudovkin's intricate, meticulously planned scenario, shows that often at first appearance a title is shown for longer, then again but shorter then for a shorter time again as the audience becomes increasingly familiar with its meaning: the repeated intertitle is used to remind and reaffirm and ensures that slower readers do not miss the point. Sometimes an image or sequence is repeated either side of the relevant written text in order to reiterate the conclusivity of the demonstration: in reel one, when the elephant takes food in his trunk from the hand of his keeper and smartly deposits it in his mouth, the sequence is subsequently broken down into the move hand to trunk, then the intertitle, 'conditioned behaviour in animals is realised by the evolution of the higher regions of the brain', then the move trunk to mouth; in the third reel the children's quoit is shown isolated in close-up as if to identify the precise problem to be solved. Some recognisably similar images or titles are repeated in different instances in order to amplify the general content: the same shot of a one year old infant is used alongside the orangoutang and the syphilitic. 'The scientific film requires a strong idea around which to organise its material', says Pudovkin, 'equivalent to the plot in a feature film'.[83] Frequently there are shots of the mechanical apparatus used to record the results of the experiments, as though with them thereby to endorse: white-coated lab. technicians in their observation chamber; needles jigging along rotating drums of graph paper; a metronome ticking as the monkey negotiates a puzzle; a pressure gauge strapped to the arm of a feeding child.

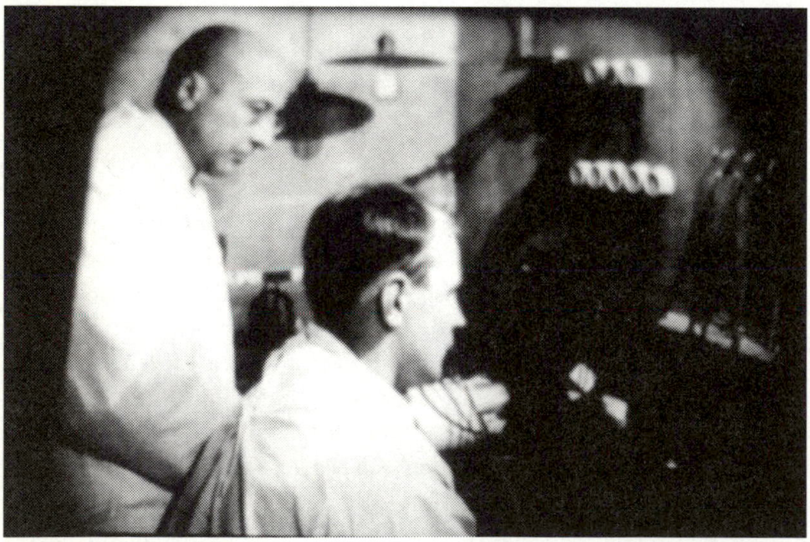

White coated lab. technicians

Titles are also used to end sections decisively and to extend continuity over the interruption between reels. Archive copies of the film match the breaks in the original scenario: 'unconditioned reflexes are innate' (ends reel one); 'What is a conditioned reflex? It's simply demonstrated in the digestion of animals' (begins reel two). Continuity is established between parts of an experiment taken (or staged) as separate shots by maintaining direction of movement, simulating an impression of itself as an unruptured demonstrative and integral whole: an assistant moves in mid-shot camera right to left to remove a phial attached to the cheek of a dog, which has just been fed, harnessed in the stand; the shot is followed by a close-up in which a hand (similarly jacketed) moves camera right to centre to display the contents of the phial. Two similar phials are displayed, the assistant holding them against his dark jacket as background, to compare the quantities of saliva collected from (supposedly) two separate experiments: on the left, the greater quantity of saliva collected from the response to raw meat and, camera right, in response to rusks.

Secretion was in no way essential to the study of reflexes as a whole but had been selected because it offered scope for the consistent verification of the commonest of conditioned reflexes and precise quantitive and qualitative evaluation of stimuli employed.[84] As Darwin observed, 'a hungry man, if tempting food is placed before him, may not show his hunger by any outward gesture, but he cannot check the secretion of saliva'.[85] Mariamov and Iezuitov relate that Pudovkin and his assistants from Kuleshov's workshop found the salivation of the dogs an insufficiently photogenic subject and consequently sought to elicit motor reactions also. This was a procedure favoured by Bekhterev and only occasionally adopted by Pavlov. Animated diagrams, depicting the formation of a conditioned motor reflex, were prepared for *The Mechanics of the Brain* as the second venture of a specialist department of Mezhrabpom-Rus.[86] These were also used by Pudovkin to elucidate the chain of activity and irritation in the leg of a frog and of particular centres of the brain. Other diagrams were used to show which areas of the brain in man governed speech, vision and motor activity. 'The location of the centres in man is similar to their location in higher animals'; after operations, 'in the case of "Clubs" all of the left cerebral hemisphere is removed', 'in the case of "Jamaica" the centre of vision is removed', and co-ordination is lost. An intact dog is shown swiftly negotiating an obstacle course built with chairs.

'The lens of the camera is the eye of the spectator', says Pudovkin, but again he distances himself from the claim of the 'cine-eyes' that material can be simply 'seized from life' [s''emki 'zhizni vrasplokh'].[87]

> It is generally known that the essence of proper montage consists in correctly connecting the attention of the spectator. If I photograph a thing whole, then the spectator will perceive that thing in its entirety, whereas the closer I approach it with the camera, the more the spectator will grasp only selected details. This applies both to the filming of a static object and to the filming of a dynamic process. An observer following a demonstration guides his attention sometimes here, sometimes there, then he pursues some detail, then he occupies himself with the whole. As a result of which the attentive observer secures a clearly delineated impression of the thing. He will endeavour not to disregard any particular characteristic point whatever, nor will he lose sight of them whilst concentrating on the principal features ... It depends on the director whether the spectator becomes a good or a bad observer. It is clear that the shifting here and there of concentration – corresponding to montage – is a strictly regular process. Such laws of observation, which are required for correct understanding, must be fully and completely transferred onto the montage structure[88]

Pudovkin uses close-ups and the closing of the iris to draw attention to particular points, to analyse, to summarise or draw an inference from a whole sequence: the iris closes around the hand feeding the potato to the elephant: it closes around the young boy in the swimming pool, spluttering and shutting his eyes tight against stinging splashes. Pudovkin uses the opening and closing of the iris in the labour sequence to indicate time lapses between contractions.

On completing *The Mechanics of the Brain*, Pudovkin confirmed the principles which he believed fundamental to all film work, 'the imperative for clarity and the careful organisation of camera work in time and space'.[89] His assertions regarding correct planning and cutting were soon to be restated in his 1926 publications, *The Film Scenario* and *The Film Director and Film Material*. In *The Mechanics of the Brain*, Pudovkin produced a montage sufficiently correct (that is to say, coherent, cogent, economical and unambiguous) to satisfy his own purposes and also Pavlov's exacting criteria of empirical exposition. Pudovkin and Pavlov may even be said to be embarked upon a similar project, to map, to trace, to quantify a simple psychical process and, in Pavlov's terms, to claim it for physiology and physics, albeit for a physics which was already becoming out-moded at the time at which he wrote; Pavlov takes Newton for granted as much as he does Darwin: 'Pavlov insisted', says Babkin, 'that the study of the conditioned reflex mechanism permits one to reduce the problem of the activity of the central nervous system to the study of space relations, something psychology is unable to do: "You must be able ... to point ... to where the excitation process was at a given moment and where it has gone".'[90] Pudovkin regards montage as an implement effecting 'the conscious guidance of the spectator'. Pudovkin holds to and constructs (where Pavlov purports to reconstruct) a notional space in which individual elements are cumulatively associated, synthesised and connected.

Pravda reviewed *The Mechanics of the Brain* favourably, finding it to accord with the usual view:

> It destroys totally the myth of the human soul. Without willing it, and even spite of himself, the spectator is irresistibly led to the only possible conclusion: the soul does not exist, the life of the soul, its creation, its inspiration – all this is nothing more than the higher level of a reflex. *The Mechanics of the Brain* is a cultural product of great value, not only for Soviet audiences but also internationally.[91]

Furthermore, in spite of Pavlov's own protestations, this is the meaning which Pudovkin apparently sought to convey. On the day on which he began work on the film, intent upon popularising Pavlov's teaching on the conditioned reflex as the foundation of behaviour in man, Pudovkin wrote:

> It is clear to everyone, how important it is to propagate this idea, corroborated by the materialist world view, that for the present time the notion of 'Soul' is conclusively extinguished.[92]

Notes

1 J. Leyda, *Kino. A History of the Russian and Soviet Film*, London 1960, p. 206: 'Professor Burankov, at the Pavlov Institute, was so impressed by

Pudovkin's concentration and method that he offered him a post as his assistant'.

2 interviewed by Jean and Luda Schnitzer in 1958, *Poudovkine,* Paris 1966, p. 172

3 Boris Babkin, *Pavlov: A Biography,* London, 1951, p. 162; see also R. Fülöp-Miller, *The Mind and Face of Bolshevism,* London 1927, p. 58: 'The fact that Pavlov's "conditioned reflexes" seem to demonstrate the transition from purely physiological automatism to association of ideas and primitive forms of thought, was utilised by the Bolsheviks in the most grotesquely exaggerated way in order to represent that all spirituality whatever, even in its highest forms, art and science, is an expression of mere mechanism, as it were the output of a more or less complicated factory...'

4 David Joravsky, *Soviet Marxism and Natural Science,* London 1961, p. 66 '... an effort was made to win the "bourgeois specialist" in natural science to political sympathy with the regime and, if possible, to ideological agreement with Marxism. But as late as 1928 natural scientists were assured by Lunacharsky that it was their "legitimate right" not to be Marxists'.

5 Joravsky, *Soviet Marxism,* p. 67

6 R. Gregory, *Oxford Companion to the Mind,* Oxford 1987, p. 59

7 transcript made by W. Horsley Gantt of an address given by Pavlov in 1923, *Integrative Physiology and Behavioural Science* 27.3 (1992), p. 271

8 qu. Windholz in 'The Critical Mind and the Arrogance of Power', *Integrative Physiology and Behavioural Science* 28.2 (1993); see also Bukharin in M. Solomon (ed), *Marxism and Art,* Brighton 1979, p. 205. Sheila Fitzpatrick records that, notwithstanding their differences of opinion, Bukharin and Pavlov maintained a respectful friendship: see *Education and Social Mobility in the Soviet Union,* Cambridge 1979, pp. 84 & 273

9 Babkin, p. 152

10 David Joravsky, *Russian Psychology: A Critical History,* Oxford 1989, p.xvi; Loren Graham, *Science and Philosophy in the Soviet Union,* Cambridge 1973, pp. 375-394

11 for differences between Pavlov and the American tradition, and an interesting discussion as to why experimental psychology gained such sway and influence in the USA, see S. Koch and D. E. Leary (eds) *A Century of Psychology as Science,* New York 1985, p. 297

12 see B. M. Teplov, 'Problems in the Study of General Types of Higher Nervous Activity in Man and Animals' in J. A. Gray (ed) *Pavlov s Typology,* Oxford 1964

13 Daniel P. Todes, 'From Radicalsim to Scientific Convention' Ph.D. thesis, Michigan U, 1981, p. 426

14 Turgenev, *Fathers and Sons,* tr. R.Edmonds, Harmondsworth 1979, p. 160; a film adaptation of this was planned during the Civil War, in which Maiakovskii was to play Bazarov

15 Aleksandr Herzen, *Childhood Youth and Exile* [1852], tr. J.D. Duff, Oxford 1980, pp. 90–91

16 see Daniel P. Todes, 'From Radicalism to Scientific Convention'
17 J. B. S. Haldane, *Daedalus, or Science and the Future*, London 1924, p. 8; Haldane was, of course, a Communist sympathiser
18 I. P. Pavlov, *Lectures on Conditioned Reflexes,* tr. Gantt, London 1928, p. 213
19 William James, *Psychology*, London 1892, p. 467; Alexander Vucinich, *Science in Russian Culture*, Stanford 1970, p. 309
20 George Bernard Shaw, *Everybody s Political What s What?,* London 1944, p. 203
21 Evgenii Zamiatin, *We*, [1920–21] tr. C. Brown, Harmondsworth 1993, p. 221
22 S. Rosenzweig in Koch and Leary, *Psychology as Science*
23 F. A. Talbot, *Moving Pictures*, London 1912, pp. 161-169 and 190-197
24 Voskresenskii, 'O nauchnykh fil'makh', *Kino-zhurnal ARK* 9 (1925), p. 12; Tikhonov, 'Kinematograf v nauke', *Kino*, 25 December 1922, pp. 21–22 and 'Kinematografia bol'shoi chastoty', *Kino* , 1 December 1922, pp. 20–21
25 *Sovetskoe kino* 8, 1926, p. 8 'Nauchno-populiarnye'; see also Boris Fefer, 'Mekhanika golovnogo mozga', *Sovetskii ekran* 31 (1926) and *Sovetskoe Kino* 1, 1927; see Nikolai Iezuitov, *Pudovkin; puti tvorchestva*, Moscow 1937, pp. 50-51 and Rashit Iangirov, 'Le cinéma non joué', Valérie Posener, ed. *Le studio Mejrabpom,* Paris 1996, p. 88
26 V. I. Pudovkin, 'Kak delaetsia kul'turfil'ma', *Sovetskoe kino* 1, 1927, pp. 5–7
27 see Rashit Iangirov: ' Le cinéma non joué'; see L. Landry, 'Einstein au cinéma' *Cinéa* 71–72 (1922) p. 12: 'Before indicating the manner in which the theories of Einstein have been represented on screen it is worth remembering ... what is supposedly known of these theories ... One appreciates that the cinematographic illustration of them was extremely difficult'
28 Richard Stites, *Russian Popular Culture*, Cambridge 1992, p. 42
29 Jean and Luda Schnitzer, *Cinema in Revolution*, tr. D. Robinson, London 1973, p. 186
30 Paul Babitsky and John Rimberg, *The Soviet Film Industry,* New York 1955, p. 18
31 see René Marchand and Pierre Weinstein, *Le Cinéma*, Paris 1927; Vance Kepley jr. , Richard Taylor and Ian Christie, eds. *Inside the Film Factory,* London 1991 and Peter Kenez, *Cinema and Soviet Society,* Cambridge 1992
32 see A. Katsigras, *Pravda* 180, 10 April 1924 and Peter Kenez, *Cinema and Soviet Society,* Cambridge 1992, p. 87
33 Iangirov, 'Le cinéma non joué', p. 93
34 see David Bordwell, 'Eisenstein's Epistemological Shift' *Screen* 15.4, 33 & 45: 'Early Soviet Marxism as a whole eagerly embraced Pavlov's reduction of all behaviour to material laws'; 'The philosophical school of mechanistic materialism of the 1920s took Pavlov as its figurehead'; see also *The Cinema of Eisenstein,* London 1993, pp. 116–119
35 Léon Moussinac, *Le Cinéma soviétique* , Paris 1927, p. 49; Winifred Ellerman (Bryher), *Film Problems of Soviet Russia* , Territet 1929, pp. 46–47
36 Leyda, pp. 205–206; *Experiment in the Film*, ed. Roger Manvell, London 1949, p. 271:'Amongst documentary films, the remarkable *Mechanics of the*

Brain ... is certainly worthy of special mention'; also Marchand & Weinstein:, *Le Cinéma*, Paris 1927, p. 145

37 Thorold Dickinson and Catherine de la Roche, *Soviet Cinema*, London 1948, p. 65; Peter Dart, *Pudovkin s Films and Film Theory*, New York 1974, p. 10

38 A. Mariamov, *Pudowkin: Kampf und Vollendung*, [1951] Berlin 1954, p. 85; compare Nikolai Iezuitov, *Pudovkin*, Moscow 1937, pp. 44–54

39 Paul Rotha, *The Film Till Now*, London 1951, p. 233

40 Jean and Luda Schnitzer, *Cinema in Revolution*, tr. D. Robinson, London 1973, p. 136

41 Anatolii Golovnia, 'S"emki kartiny "Povedenie cheloveka"', *Sovetskii ekran* no. 40 1926, p. 4; Golovnia's anecdote about a particularly amorous hippopotamus is endorsed by Voskresenskii!

42 Pudovkin, 'Kak delaetsia kul'turfil'ma "Povedenie Cheloveka"', p. 5

43 with regard to the banning of *The Mother* and deletions from *The End of St. Petersburg*, see IMC/BFI/Special Materials Item 67; for bans on Pudovkin's films in Britain, the Empire and elsewhere see also J.C. Robertson, *The Hidden Cinema*, Londn 1993 p. 34 and Tom Dewe Mathews, *Censored*, London 1994 pp. 43 & 86: 'After examining *The Mother*, which he inexplicably viewed within the privacy of his flat, T. P. O'Connor astonishingly misread Pudovkin's unsubtle plot to the extent that he thought *The Mother* contributed towards better understanding of Russian conditions. The Baldwin government brought power to bear on the BBFC to veto the film'; IMC/BFI/SM Item 11, correspondence with the Home Office concerning the licensing of educational films.

44 Royal Society of Medicine, Neurology Section (minutes of meetings 1907–1936) pp. 394 & 398. Montagu says that in 1930 University College London bought the film and this is corroborated by Iezuitov, *Pudovkin*, Moscow 1937

45 see Ellerman (Bryher), *Film Problems of Soviet Russia*, p. 48; also in *Close-Up* 3/4; *Kino i kul'tura* 1, 1929, p. 95 refers to articles by Bryher advocating the use of film in education: *Times Educational Supplement* 606, 616, 617 (1927)

46 see Ivor Montagu, *The Political Censorship of Films*, London 1929, p. 31: 'Social: ... Scenes connected with childbirth ... which are considered too intimate for public exhibition'; see also IMC/BFI/SM Item 67, letter 23 December 1929 to BBFC

47 IMC/BFI/SM Item 15, letter 20 June 1930 to Sidney Bernstein: 'Mr. Dickinson has just drawn my attention to the fact that the London Workers' Society have announced "Mechanism of the Brain" for its next performance. He feels that this might lead to difficulties for us – the film was rejected by the BBFC ... it should only be shown by special permission of the LCC.... we applied to the LCC but just at the time of the troubles re Sunday performances. Under the circumstances it was decided to show the film after quite a good deal was cut out of it ... If London Workers show it without making such careful cuts as we made it may well

lead to trouble. There was no doubt that a number of our members disliked the film very much ...'

48 Babkin, *Pavlov: A Biography,* London 1951; Hilaire Cuny, *Pavlov and his School*, London 1962; J. Gray, *Pavlov,* Brighton 1979

49 I. P. Pavlov, *Selected Works*, Moscow n.d., p. 377

50 Jean and Luda Schnitzer, *Poudovkine,* Paris 1966, p. 20

51 Jay Leyda, *Kino,* London 1960, p. 174; C.A. Lejeune, *Cinema*, London 1931, p. 134; see also Lee Atwell, *G. W. Pabst*, Boston 1977, pp. 37–42

52 Mariamov p.74; *Sovetskoe kino* 1 (1926) p. 10; Iezuitov, p. 44

53 Iezuitov, p. 53

54 Pavlov, *Lectures on Conditioned Reflexes,* tr. Gantt, London 1928, p. 42

55 Pudovkin, *Kino*, 26 April 1927

56 see for instance Tolstoy's description of Count Oblonsky at the beginning of *Anna Karenina*, tr. Rosemary Edmonds, Harmondsworth 1978, p. 14, or Dostoevskii's staged 'show' trial of Raskolnikov in *Crime and Punishment*, tr. David Magarshack, Harmondsworth 1951, pp. 272 and 544; on the intervention of Tsarist authorities in the availability of foreign popular science materials see Todes, 'From Radicalism to Scientific Convention', p. 79; see also Jeffrey Brooks, *When Russia Learned to Read*, Princeton 1985, pp. 247 & 268: '... no luboki were genuine works of popular science-writers did not communicate much about scientific method nor impart an understanding of how science differs from magic – but in the limited task of combatting superstition popular writers made important contributions to promoting a modern outlook among common readers ... At the lower level of popular literature occasional attempts to demonstrate the marvels of technology or to enthrone ... science in place of familiar popular beliefs may have meant no more than the replacement of one vague and mysterious explanation or phenomenon with another'.

57 V. M. Bekhterev, *General Principles of Human Reflexology* [1923], tr. Murphy, London 1933, p. 141; Boris Babkin, *Pavlov: A Biography*, London 1951, p. 87

58 I. P. Pavlov, *Conditioned Reflexes*, tr. Anrep, Oxford 1927, p. xi

59 Babkin, p. 109

60 I. P. Pavlov, *Lectures on Conditioned Reflexes,* tr. Gantt, London 1928, p. 42

61 I. P. Pavlov, *Lectures on Conditioned Reflexes,* tr. Gantt, p. 144

62 'Organizatsiia "sluchainogo" materiala', *Kinorezhisser i kinomaterial*, *SS* I, pp. 108–109; also Jay Leyda, *Kino,* London 1960, p. 206

63 Voskresenskii, 'O nauchnykh', p. 12

64 I. P. Pavlov, *Conditioned Reflexes*, tr. Anrep, p. 169

65 Mikhail Bulgakov, *The Heart of a Dog* [1925], tr. Glenny, London 1968

66 Y. P. Frolov, *Pavlov and His School* [1938], London 1970, pp. 238 & 261

67 Alexander Vucinich, *Science in Russian Culture*, Stanford 1970, p. 308

68 I. P. Pavlov, *Twenty Years of Objective Study of the Higher Nervous Activity in Animals*, London 1928, preface

69 Bekhterev, p. 141

70 Joravsky, *Soviet Marxism*, p. 241, re Pavlov boycotting congresses as a mark of disapproval of the regime

71 Bekhterev, pp. 41, 55, 61, 64
72 Pavlov, *Lectures on Human Refexology,* tr. Gantt, p. 40
73 Pavlov, *Selected Works*, Moscow n.d., p. 624
74 Pavlov, *Selected Works*, pp. 578–595
75 Karl Popper, *The Logic of Scientific Discovery,* London 1972, p. 30
76 William James, *Psychology,* London 1892, p. 467
77 Meyerhold wrote to Pavlov on the occasion of his 80th. birthday: 'We congratulate you as the man who has at last dispensed with such a disreputable thing as the soul' and was duly informed 'As far as the soul is concerned, we must wait a little while'. B. Picon-Vallin, *Vsevolod Meyerhold* III, Paris 1990, p. 146, qu. *Sovetskoe iskusstvo* 20 December 1933.
78 David Joravsky, *Soviet Marxism*, p. 93 re Enchenism and Mininism
79 Pudovkin, *Kino-zhurnal ARK* 9, 1925, p. 10
80 Lisa Cartwright, *Screening the Body,* Minneapolis 1995, p. 1
81 see Aaron Scharf, *Art and Photography,* Harmondsworth 1974, p. 204; Charles Darwin, *The Expression of the Emotions in Man and Animals* [1872], Chicago 1965, pp. 5 & 25; Eisenstein too was familiar with Duchenne's experiments
82 *Sovetskoe kino* 1, 1925, p. 5
83 Pudovkin, *Kino-zhurnal ARK* 9, 1925, p. 10
84 Hilaire Cuny, *Ivan Pavlov,* London 1964, p. 72
85 Charles Darwin, *The Expression of the Emotions in Man and Animals,* Chicago 1965, p. 75
86 Boris Pavlov, 'L'animation', in Valérie Posener, ed. *Le studio Mejrabpom,* Paris 1996, p. 95; the animation studio was set up in 1925
87 Pudovkin, *Kino-zhurnal ARK* 9, 1925, p. 10
88 Pudovkin, *Kino-zhurnal ARK* 9, 1925, p. 10
89 Pudovkin, *Kino-zhurnal ARK* 9, 1925, p. 10
90 Babkin, p. 310
91 *Pravdà*, 14 December 1926, qu. Zapasnik and Petrovich
92 Pudovkin, *Kinogazeta*, 28 July 1925

3. *The Mother* and the return of the actor

A concern with the specificity of media

Film theory in Soviet Russia, as elsewhere, heralded its subject as a new phenomenon, celebrated it for its prerogative as the most contemporary of all the arts. Ippolit Sokolov, in *Kino-Fot* 1 (1922), celebrates film as the new philosophy, the new science and the new art, a new form of education and propaganda, entirely suited to the new needs of the century. In his 1927 'The Nature of Cinema', the Formalist theoretician Boris Kazansky endorses the earlier enthusiasms of Elliot and Münsterberg:

> Cinema arose within our own memory and literally developed before our eyes. Thus its study presents possibilities and promises results which cannot be obtained for the other arts, whose origins extend far back into the darkness of time, hidden from sober investigation by the fog of legend and the dogma of tradition.[1]

Theory strove to identify cinema's peculiar characteristics and to establish terms by which film could be evaluated as an art. Paradoxically, to this end it often resorted to the authority of a cultural heritage, discovering in it portents of cinematic practice.

> Thus we can see that the *principle of cinema* is not something which dropped upon mankind from the heavens, but is something that has grown out of the very depths of human culture. It seems to us that this cinematic *principle* is growing and developing within the cinema

> itself; and that since all forms of cinema are determined by the nature of the society which creates them, it is in the highest form of social organisation – ours – that we are moving towards the fullest understanding of the aesthetics of this art form.[2]

Furthermore, in the course of establishing its own aesthetic (even an aesthetic which was sometimes fiercely anti-art), writing on cinema partakes in a discussion of more general cultural issues: the purpose of art, the means whereby the art work affects its audience and the relationship of the artist to that audience. Film is acknowledged as something distinct but simultaneously as an amalgam which espouses a number of other arts, which inherits its content and form from other arts and which is most often received by the audience for whom it is intended as part of a syncretic experience, aided and abetted by its musical accompaniment.

In *The Film Director and Film Material*, Pudovkin narrates the history of film as a progression away from theatre. In its first phase, film was no more than living photography and did no more than record the art of the actor. In its second phase, he says, film managed to accomplish distinct transitions of space and time of which the traditional theatre was incapable: between acts such concentrations and leaps had been made but not within the duration of a single scene.[3] 'The film director ... can concentrate in time not only separate incidents but even the movements of a single person. This process, that has often been termed a "film trick", is, in fact, nothing other than the characteristic method of filmic representation'.[4]

However, it should be noted that Pudovkin uses a conventional example of theatrical practice to underscore the line of progression which he wishes to trace. Not only had various cinematic strategies been indicated in avant-garde theatre but the two areas of practice were becoming mutually informing, exchanging personnel and procedures and sharing a range of theoretical concerns. Pudovkin praises Meyerhold for discovering and representing a contemporary theme in his staging of the classics.[5] Regarding the disciplines broadly, it is significant that Meyerhold had used a form of close-up in the over-scaling of his props for his production of *Masquerade* (1917) and in the isolation of essential set dressings for the artist's studio in *Krampton* (1905).[6] Close-ups of objects were already familiar in films of the teens and Meyerhold himself commented in 1914 upon a difference in procedure which he then perceived:

> ...in cinema an object appears on screen for utilitarian reasons; in the studio (in a pantomime) an object appears so as to afford the actor the chance to make use of it in order to make the spectator happy or sad ... The cinema's principal aim is to grip the spectator by means of the plot. In pantomime, the spectator is gripped not by the plot but by the manner in which the actor's free inspiration manifests itself through his sole desire to dominate the stage.[7]

Meyerhold had attempted to stage flashbacks and in 1907, in *Spring Awakening*, had lit action in different parts of the stage space to present them to the spectator in quick succession, juxtaposing the isolated pieces in a putative montage.[8] Eisenstein carried the programme of disparate elements of his stage spectacles (which had included such stunts as a boxing match and the short film *Glumov s Diary* inserted into *Enough Simplicity for Every Wise Man*) into the collage of grotesques in *The Strike* [Stachka, 1925]. In a narrower aspect, it is significant that Meyerhold's collective, including Eisenstein, shared a building with Kuleshov's workshop in the early 1920s, enabling their actors to train together.[9] Meyerhold's elemental exercise in biomechanics, the intention, realisation and refusal of action, have much in common with Kuleshov's reduction of basic tasks into separate attitudes, à la Delsarte. Whereas, in rehearsal, the complete action was differentiated into its separate units by the deliberate and adept control of the actor over the body, with Kuleshov the units could be separately shot then assembled.

Pudovkin says that his own awareness of the potential for film as an art came with a fortuitous meeting with Kuleshov. He has little to say in *The Film Scenario* and *The Film Director and Film Material* of his previous apprenticeship with Gardin, certainly he does not choose to credit him as a formative influence.[10] (see chapter one, above) Pudovkin, like Balázs, says that the Americans were the first to seize the peculiar possibilities of film as other than a photographic record and is dismissive of film practice before Griffith.[11] Pudovkin reiterates Kuleshov's thesis that film needs must discover its own proper materials and usage, is required to reveal its 'core' in order to be recognised as an art alongside its ancient predecessors:

> It appears to me that every art has its own specific quality which is what makes it an art. Painting cannot exist without colours;

> sculpture without plastic material. The cinema consists of fragments and the assembly of those fragments, elements which in reality are distinct ... All this ... convinced me of the necessity to consider montage as the basic means of cinema art, the specific fundamental quality of the medium.[12]

Montage, and more especially Kuleshov's use thereof, is proclaimed by Pudovkin as the conspicuous founding moment of film as art, dismissing any debt to the efforts of 'primitive' film-makers. Meanwhile, Kuleshov is keen to draw a parallel between his art and exemplary style elsewhere: he says that Tolstoy refers to the equivalent of montage as 'connection' and Kuleshov and Eisenstein refer to Pushkin: 'You can take any poem by Pushkin and number the shots...';[13] Eisenstein refers to the pertinence of imagery to theme in Zola: '...his pages read like complete cue sheets', and recommends him in retrospect to Pudovkin: 'I criticised Pudovkin because he did not read *Money* before filming the stock exchange for *The End of St. Petersburg*. It would have turned out even better if he had'.[14]

The over-emphasis in the 1920s on montage, later to be censured, was surely prompted in no small part by this compunction to affirm artistic status for film. However, even in the 1920s Pudovkin seems to deal in the theoretical currency without being consistently tied to it in practice. Whereas Kuleshov can tend towards the apprehension of fragmentation as the end product in the spectator, Pudovkin is often more intent upon accomplishing summation and synthesis.(see chapter one, above) Pudovkin likewise is aware of Meyerhold's sequence from preparation to completed action and that the impression of the action is enhanced in the representation of the sequence. However, rather than cutting between successive segments Pudovkin employs a strategy which is less visually disruptive and which better retains an image of unity: in *Storm over Asia*, the withdrawal of the Mongol, the gathering of his strength before he strikes the white man, is fast-cranked and decelerated for the viewer, the blow itself appears accelerated in force within the context of the sequence.(see chapter six, below) The movement is performed whole, partially intensified. 'Slow-motion in editing', says Pudovkin, 'is not a distortion of an actual [deistvitel'nogo] process. It is a portrayal more profound and precise, a conscious guidance [coznatel'no rukovodia] of the attention of the spectator. This is the eternal characteristic of cinematography'.[15]

Pudovkin declines additive montage in favour of more pressing concerns.

A respect for the integrity of a particular performance sometimes urges Pudovkin to opt for a locked-off, frontal mid-shot of a scene, purposefully using conventional dramatic chiaroscuro lighting to direct the spectator's attention and emotion. Golovnia refers also to the influence of painters, Rembrandt especially, on Kozlovsky's spartan sets and his own stark lighting.[16] Pudovkin asserts:

> There is one more element characteristic for the work of the director with the actor- that is light, that light without which neither object nor human being nor anything else has existence on the film ... An actor unlit is nothing. An actor lit only so as to be visible is a simple, undifferentiated, indefinite object. This same light can be altered and constructed in such a way as to make it enter as an organic component into the actor's work. The composition of the light can eliminate much, emphasise much, and bring out with such strength the expressive work of the actor, that it becomes apparent that light is not simply a condition for the fixation of expressive work by the actor, but in itself represents a part of this expressive work. Remember the face of the priest in *The Battleship Potemkin*, lit from underneath.[17]

In *The Mother*, Mikhail Vlasov's body is laid out centre frame, foreshortened. As the scene opens, two figures, shrouded in black, sit with their backs to the spectator, camera left. The mother sits immobile to the right of the body, her face white against the dark background. The two figures turn and are seen to be wailing babushki. They move away and the mother continues to sit, motionless eyes fixed blankly. Although Pudovkin here uses a tonal and volumetric construction resembling a form of 'internal montage' in Eisenstein I suggest that its employment is the consequence less of a reluctance to detract from the dull resignation conveyed in the duration of Baranovskaias's performance. Here again, the scene defers to Pudovkin's general pronouncement that 'arousing emotion in the spectator is the true end of all art' and that it is the film-maker's task to find the means whereby this can best be achieved on screen.[18]

Pudovkin prefaces the German edition of *The Film Director and Film Material* with an analogy between film practice and literature. It is a common-sense statement directed at persuading his readers of what is to follow:

> To the poet or writer separate words are as raw material. They have the widest and most variable meanings which only begin to become precise through their position in the sentence ... To the film director each shot of the finished film subserves the same purpose as the word to the poet.[19]

The Film Scenario and *The Film Director and Film Material* were both published in 1926. Boris Eikhenbaum published *The Poetics of Cinema* [Poetika kino] in 1927, including Viktor Shklovsky's 'Poetry and Prose' (in which he discusses *The Mother*).[20] His article 'Semantika kino' appeared in *Kino-zhurnal* in 1925.[21] However, Pudovkin does not enter into a theoretical debate with these contemporaries much exercised by the possible psychological or semantic foundations of his analogy (see chapter eight, below). Amidst the wranglings of the Formalists and the contentions of Eisenstein and Vertov towards a suitably Realist theory, Pudovkin is wont to express vague and vaguely idealistic sentiments. Montage is for Pudovkin '...a selection conditioned in advance [zaranee opredelialcia] by that filmic image ... which exists in the head of the director long before its actual appearance on the screen'.[22] Beyond paying his required obeisance to montage, Pudovkin seems untroubled in the early writings by any pressure to appear intellectually or culturally *au courant*. Pudovkin does not refer to contemporary avant-garde practice in literature or criticism in an attempt to locate his own work favourably alongside it. In contrast, Eisenstein not only cites major literary figures at home and abroad but also subjects their work to specifically cinematic scrutiny:

> ...Fedorchenko is a more accessible and less expensive 'edition' of James Joyce.
>
> *Ulysses* is of course the most interesting phenomenon for cinema in the West.
>
> I don't know about the literary aspect but I think the same applies there.
>
> At any rate, however odd it may seem, I am familiar with Joyce's writings.
>
> I don't have to read him at night in a hurry, like I did Dreiser the

> night before my official meeting with him.
> Fedorchenko and Joyce are very close to contemporary cinema. Certainly more than half way to what lay ahead.
> They use the same 'de-anecdotalisation' and the direct emergence of the theme through powerfully effective raw material.
> This may be completely tangential to the plot that only figures in the work because the author is conscientious.
> The same 'psychologism' of detail.
> In close-up.
> In a purely intellectual effect, an abstract conclusion from their physiological methods.
> Cinema again.
> There is, of course, significantly more in Joyce. To meet the demands of the denunciatory, polemical and other multiple tasks that *Ulysses* or *The Portrait of the Artist as a Young Man* set themselves. Fedorchenko is more like a fixing agent but her construction is the same.[23]

When Pudovkin refers to Mayakovsky or Meyerhold it comes more by way of a personal anecdote. Even when referring (rarely) to classical authors, Pudovkin is predominently concerned with his personal preferences and their potential as sources of cinematic impulses, of 'plastic raw material', or, as for Eisenstein, of the deliberacy with which details are selected, rather than with finding in them precedents for a definite structure. Of his adaptation of *The Mother*, Pudovkin says: '*The Mother* began for me with the image of the mother crushed, firstly in a general perception of the atmosphere of Gorky's novel and secondly in the final emotional shock: the mother under the horses' hooves'.[24]

A film adaptation

Soon after the Revolution, major works of Russian literature, including those of Pushkin, Tolstoy, Turgenev, Gogol and Gorky, were declared the property of the state. There was, says Jeffrey Brooks, 'a widely shared belief that Russian literature could serve as a bridge between classes';

> There was a perception on the part of many educated Russians that they had a moral obligation to influence and contribute to cultural

> development ... a shared common belief that 'proper' literature was a necessary beacon to guide the Russian peasant...
> Efforts to mould the literary taste of the common reader were also an expression of a more fundamental desire to bring common people into a consensus of values shared by educated Russians or to create a new consensus incorporating the values of the common people ... Success in this endeavour would both discharge the intelligentsia's debt to the people and close the gap between the common people and the rest of society.[25]

These efforts took the form of disseminating cheaper editions of the approved texts and, in recognition of the high rate of illiteracy (3 out of 5 Russians in the 1920s could not read) cinema was enlisted as a suitable means of acquainting a broad public with its cultural heritage.[26] Indeed, literary adaptations, as period costume pieces, had been a staple of the pre-revolutionary 'Film d'Art' movement (including Gardin's 1914 *Anna Karenina*, Protazanov's 1915 *War and Peace*, Persky's 1911 and Sabinsky's 1917 *The Living Corpse*) and in 1918, a competition was launched for a scenario based on a work by Turgenev, to mark his centenary.[27] More specifically, cinema was to be exploited as a medium capable of popularising an officially approved canon of masterworks in which the lineage of the revolution was affirmed. 'Once a work was officially recognised as a classic its ideological soundness was taken for granted', observes Anna Lawton.[28] *The Mother* was held in especially high regard for the favour which it found with Lenin and for its reputedly having been written with his consultation;[29] Richard Stites dubs him 'the semi-official bard of Bolshevism'.[30] Furthermore, Gorky as an individual was esteemed as something of a hero, a son of the soil sharing 'the values of the common people', and a political descendant of Chernyshevsky, having suffered censorship and exile under the ancien-régime[31] (see chapter two, above).

Gorky had based his novel on events at the Krasnoe Sormovo plant in Nizhny Novgorod and the character of Pavel Vlasov on the leader of a May Day demonstration, Pavel Zalomov. In court, the demonstrators conducted their own defence before being sentenced to prison.[32] Natan Zarkhi, Pudovkin's scenarist, drew additionally on reports in *Pravda* of cavalry troops being sent in against strikers in Tver (Pudovkin's chosen location) in 1905;[33] Eisenstein similarly based *The Strike* on events in Rostov-on-Don. Fault had been found by Lunacharsky with Razumny's 1919 film adaptation for being merely episodic. Mariamov, Pudovkin's biographer, says that the earlier version was found wanting in precisely those capacities which critical opinion was to find exemplified in its successor:

> The film was no more than a period piece, accounting for a single episode in social history. The sense of Pavel as a type representative of his class and his time was thereby lost, but also the film lost the connection between Pavel and his comrades with the generation of the October Revolution, binding the theme with the general public seated in the auditorium. The film did not treat its subject matter correctly ... a return to the broader ideological and artistic foundation of Gorky's work was called for.[34]

Razumny names Pavel's comrades individually and occupies himself with a quantity of background information; the mother similarly nurses her husband in spite of his dissolute past and his cruelty towards her; her religiousness is more clearly marked (paintings on the wall, icons on a corner shelf) as is her later contribution to the comrades' conversations and her reading of 'Proletarians of all Countries'. As in the Gorky original (but unlike the Pudovkin version) seditious pamphlets are shown as sufficient cause for Pavel's arrest. The 1926 adaptation took liberties with the original in order to emphasise a political theme. 'The idea of content does not refer to subject matter, in the ordinary sense of the term, but to social purpose', said Trotsky.[35] Strategic revisions were similarly made by Shklovsky in his scenario from Pushkin's *A Captain s Daughter* and in various interpretations of Tolstoy's *The Living Corpse*. Otsep's version [Zhivoi trup, 1929], in which Pudovkin took the part of Fedia, deviates from the original in that obstruction to a divorce between a loveless couple is seen to emanate from the Orthodox Church rather than (as Tolstoy would have it) from a rigid state bureaucracy. In *The Mother*, the necessary summation is pointed by the particularity of location at the end of the film; at the beginning, Pudovkin's film shares with the novel a general sense of the location being abstracted to any place, the protagonists to unnamed characters, any of a number of anonymous industrial suburbs and their inhabitants to which such incidents occurred.

In addition to Gorky, Pudovkin acknowledges Tolstoy (his favourite author) as a source. In the trial scene in *Resurrection*, the judge is distracted by thoughts of his mistress, in *The Mother* a conversation about 'a fine-looking filly' is revealed to concern a horse, which the judge then draws on his blotter as the trial proceeds. *The Death of Ivan Ilyich* volunteers itself as a secondary source for the cynicism of the legal functionaries towards the practice of the law.[36] In his 1928 article 'How I Work with Tolstoy', Pudovkin indicates that he found in Tolstoy a species of pertinent detail which Eisenstein prefers to identify in Joyce:

> He works with enormous persistence upon every detail. He denies himself any simple rules of elegant compositional style and doesn't shy away from using one and the same word repeatedly in a single passage in order to confer upon it the greatest persuasive power. Tolstoy leaves the reader no room to see something other than as he shows it. Everything that he writes accords perfectly with a real object ... The form of his language is so fundamental to the idea that any relativity is ultimately lost.[37]

The Mother deviates from Gorky's novel significantly in the role of the father. In the latter, he is merely referred to in passing:

> Living a life like that for some fifty years, a workman died. Thus also lived Michael Vlasov, a gloomy sullen man, with little eyes which looked at everybody from under his thick eyebrows suspiciously, with a mistrustful evil smile. He was the best locksmith in the factory, and the strongest man in the village. But he was insolent and disrespectful towards the foreman and the superintendant and therefore earned very little; every holiday he beat somebody, and everyone disliked and feared him.[38]

In the film, the role is expanded to serve a number of purposes, both dramatic and ideological, and material which in the novel might be deemed to compromise or confuse the clarity of the theme is deliberately discarded. For instance, in the novel the son behaves badly towards the mother immediately after the death of Vlasov senior (indeed, 'he knew no better') whereas in the film the older generation is consistently identified with reprehensible behaviour, or with ideas which are shown to be held falsely in contrast with the younger generation's enlightenment (Gorky's 'Children of the Sun'). It is significant that the story tells of the political awakening of a woman of peasant stock: such as she were regarded by the state as generally conservative and resistant to change.[39] The babushki wailing at the side of the corpse warn the mother against her son, it is he, they say, who has brought this trouble upon her. The character of Vlasov is used to endorse the official campaign against alcoholism (prominently voiced by Trotsky) and to promote the idea of a new Soviet citizenry who would reject alcoholic excess (see chapter two, above): 'Drunkenness is a violation of our class, proletarian communist morality. Vodka poisons and destroys the organism, it bears us out of the world of reality into a world of illusion, it deprives us of judgement'.[40] In order to buy vodka the father attempts to take the flat iron which serves as a weight to the clock, then to take the clock itself. This is the only adornment of the bare interior and the mother intervenes to prevent him. Vlasov's vast shadow overwhelms the cringing mother and the father succeeds by brute force to take the iron. Vlasov then presents it at the tavern, drawing it out from a torn and dishevelled pocket. His fecklessness is contrasted with the mother's thrift and fortitude: meanwhile, she sets to, endeavouring to piece together the broken clock, evidently much repaired previously. Alcohol is the root of further evil: unaware that he is an object of public mockery (an accordion player in the tavern winks connivingly at the film's audience) the refusal of the bar tender of the iron is seized upon by the members of the Black Hundred conspiring in the corner as an opportunity to manipulate him to their ends (Vlasov's addiction renders him, a working man, susceptible to bribes to betray his class). Here again, the naming of the group contributes particular resonance. In the 1905 revolution the Black Hundred were agents provocateurs, acting against Jewish groups and strikers.[41] Thus Zarkhi crucially brings together father and son on either side of the factory owners and the workers. The manager flicks cigar ash from a gloved hand (he will not sully his hands himself); a paid lackey from the tavern draws out a knuckle-dustered clenched fist. Vlasov is shot in the ensuing fight, but the cronies who were so keen to enlist him into their gang on the previous night now slink away and desert him.

The mother is converted to the cause of the young, she turns from the established order and towards the promise of the new. At first unquestioningly she responds to the police officer's word that Pavel will be treated better if he surrenders his arms; she bows and fawns to his authority and pleads with Pavel to act to save himself. The simple obedience of a peasant woman ('it's good to be simple', Gorky has her say) is a sign of political naiveté. In the novel, her folk roots are repeatedly signalled in the language in which her point of view is described: the mother is central to the novel in her becoming an heroic protagonist but also in that the text is suffused with Orthodox and folkloric images. The lawyers at the trial are 'four large blackbirds', uttering 'hailstorms of unintelligible long words'.[42] One is reminded of the old woman in *The Twelve* [Dvenadtsat'], 'like a hen', wondering how many pairs of footcloths for the children could be made from a red flannel banner . . . yet they all go barefoot.[43] Pudovkin takes the Gorky original as his 'object of imitation' and also adopts its 'manner and style'. However, political enlightenment is effected in the film not by the series of long conversations with Pavel's comrades by which she is persuaded in the novel (and in the Razumny version), but by growing dissaffection with the old regime. Surrounding characters are employed to demonstrate her emotional state in their reaction or appearance to her. For instance, in the arrest, although she defers to the officer's authority, it is her growing distrust of him which is shown in the camera's look askance and in the obscuring of his eyes with the wire frame of his spectacles (whereas the comrades look directly to camera, eyes clear and bright, looking forwards like the comrades in *The End of St. Petersburg*. While the mother approaches her son's trial with trepidation (anxiously arriving long before anyone else), fearful of what darkness in his soul may be uncovered by the probing of the court, she then comes to realise that the pomp and gravity of the judges is no more than superficial and sham, their participation no more than routine (one functionary is intoxicated, it is observed): grandiose histrionic oratory leaves the guards unmoved (it is tediously usual and familiar) and a dowager onlooker, viewing the scene through a lorgnette, applauds the fine-ness of the show. It is the mother's sense of injustice which is conveyed at Pavel's trial, at the failure of the established order to command authority any longer (the trial, clearly figured by the double-headed eagle as a Tsarist performance, is reduced to an entertainment staged for a bourgeois audience): 'Here was nothing to frighten her by its power or majesty'.[44]

Pudovkin and Zarkhi consistently argue for the primacy of theme (the 'supra artistic concept' [poniatie vnekhudozhestvennoe]) conveyed in a written scenario as the 'hard skeleton' governing the clear organisation of a film, but reiterate the difficulties involved in transfering a literary work to the screen:

> The theme is almost the most that one can take from a literary work in changing it into a scenario. The development and treatment of the plot of a literary work (especially in the hands of a great master) are the result of purely literary methods. Their translation to the screen is quite impossible.[45]

The scenario must be written in visual and active terms. Pudovkin disparages the literary scenario and the use of long explanatory intertitles. Pudovkin and Zarkhi were far from alone in addressing the problems of effecting such a transition, M. Smelianov's 'The Literature of Cinema' in *Kino-zhurnal ARK* and V. Dekabrsky's 'Literature and Cinematography' in *Art-ekran* voice similar concerns.[46] Numerous scenarios are rejected, says Pudovkin, because they are written in terms which are not susceptible to plastic expression: 'often' is not a cinematic term, he says, discussing the example of the life of the family Nikonov.[47] Indeed, the several year span of Gorky's novel is contracted in the film to a number of significant events. In the book, the characters who take care of the mother while Pavel is in prison are individually identified by name and origin; the comrades serve to demonstrate the solidarity of proletariat (Pavel), peasant (Andrei) and intelligentsia (Riabin and Sonia) during the revolution against capitalist exploitation. This solidarity is hard won: there is much discussion of the relative merits of revolutionary methods and programme. The comrades' interim disputations are unsuitable for direct translation to film and there is less differentiation between them. When they point to one another in turn as 'Pavel Vlasov', it is I would suggest, not merely a mocking gesture, a manoeuvre to impede the course of the arrest: any one of these comrades could become the character Pavel and take his part in what is to come. Selflessly, Pavel foregoes the fond longings of the woman revolutionary who delivers the guns, for the sake of a higher cause. In the book, the characters who take care of the mother are enumerated; in the film it is sufficient to render that she is comforted: the action is abstracted to its typical expression in the stroking of hands, in feet taking someone to the hob to prepare a meal for her. The gesture is repeated sufficiently for it to be understood that this was done over a period of time.

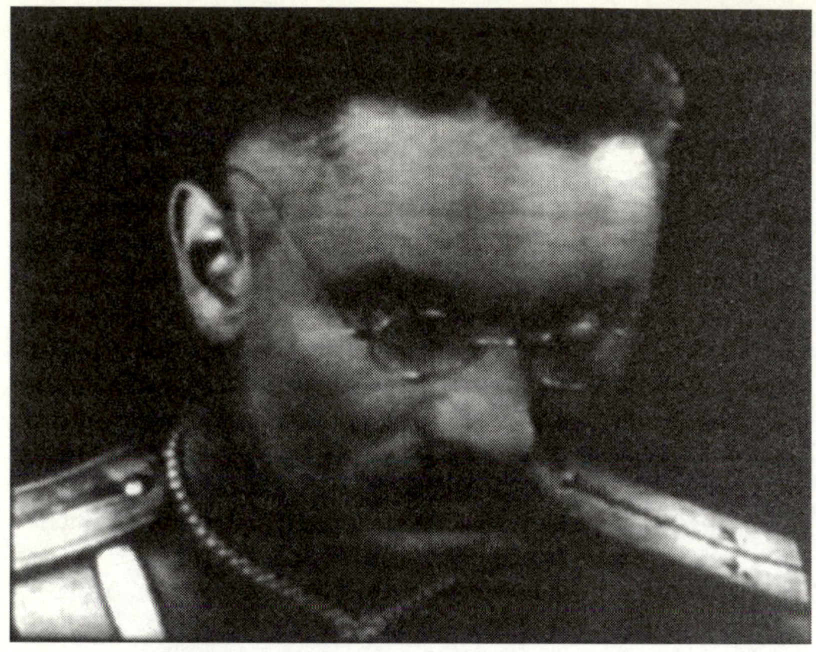

Pudovkin as a police officer

The film uses individual figures to point a general understanding of theme. Intertitles and single shots are used not only as formal 'keystones' (in Pudovkin's terminology), conceived 'in plastic (externally expressive) images' which structure the shape of the work but also as keys whereby the meaning of the theme is to be extrapolated. THE MOTHER is introduced to the viewer in her defining territory, 'penned-in' in her 'narrow cage', between the washing line and the hob. To THE FATHER is attributed his characteristic realm: the tavern.[48] The juxtaposition of words with images becomes a means of rendering emphatically apparent a connotation lost or submerged in common usage. The intertitle PILLARS OF THE ESTABLISHMENT is framed by a shot of the colonnaded portico of the Palace of Justice and a low close-up shot of the sturdy, booted, akimbo legs of a soldier guarding the palace. Montage does not merely materially connect shots but effects 'a differential exchange' of content; the intertitle WORD WENT ROUND is coupled with a frontal shot of a metal grille denoting the cellular structure of the revolution: the shot is simultaneously feasible within the spatial continuity of the sequence locating the film action in the factory *and* opportunistically effecting as an arrested, emphatic affirmation of theme. The intervention of the inter-title, as a visual phenomenon, the punch of white on black, is employed to stimulate the viewer's imagination into activity. It initiates the operation of the viewer's imagination, where the very requirement of participatory imagination is construed as a method of registering and fixing in the audience an intended meaning. Pudovkin presupposes  a mapping of the viewer's experience on to his directorial intention, affirming a shared social purpose: 'The director and scenarist lead despotically along with them the attention of the spectator ... the smallest error in clearness of vividness of construction will be apprehended as an unpleasant confusion or as a simply unimpressive void'.[49]

In the novel, the mother for a long while remains unnamed and unidentified, until the Ukrainian asks her to introduce herself; Pudovkin transfers this passivity to a performance which conspicuously lacks voice: Baranovskaia plays the role with her mouth clenched shut, as though dulled into submission. She is not so much silent as forcibly muted. The slowly dripping tap by the body of her husband marks time and the heavy thud of tears, although her face, unlike those of the wailing babushki, registers Vlasov's death as a blank. Her increased animation, expressiveness and radiance accompanies her growing participation in the new cause and draws from the novel her heightened and accelerated sense of the passage of time: the '...bygone days in which her past dragged along, a thin, black thread' as against 'the days glided by one after the other, like the beads of a rosary' and 'the pendulum which always beat with an energy that seemed to say: "I must get to the goal; I must get to the goal"'.[50] At the trial, Gorky says, it seems to the mother that the judges are slavering after Pavel's blood, preying upon the health and vitality of his body; in the film the commanding officer, old and gaunt, is shown with his hound at his feet and the cavalry horses sweat and chew at their bits in anticipation of the imminent charge.[51] The mother's optimism for a new age, 'The life is for our children; the earth is for them', is introduced in her encounter with a young mother suckling her own child, a baby boy as was once her own.[52] The mother's growing love for Pavel's friends, beginning with her adoption of Andrei ('unthinkingly she called him Andriusha') shows the expansion of an individual, selfish love ('we love that which we need') to a generous fellow-feeling for an entire generation, for the Children of the Sun who will lead the world to a better future. Her political awakening is staged as a religious conversion, to which she herself gives testimony:

> Why, this is like a new god that's born to us, the people. Everything for all; all for everything; the whole of life in one, and the whole of life for everyone and everyone for the whole of life! This I understand all of you; it is for this that you are on this earth I see. You are in truth comrades all, kinsmen all, for you are all children of one mother, of truth.[53]

For Pudovkin's mother, taking hold of the red banner at the head of the demonstration is staged with as grand a gesture as the signing of the cross in mourning.

In spite of all these translations from novel to screen, Gorky himself is said to have disapproved of the Pudovkin version, accusing it of political tendentiousness at the expense of maternal motivation and was mollified only when Zarkhi and Pudovkin appealed to him in person.[54] Subsequently, examining the film in the light of the new regime's pronouncements towards the political recognition of women, Judith Mayne has judged *The Mother* wanting and regressive in the centrality of the son to her awareness and social enfranchisement: 'Ultimately, then, *The Mother* is not the mother's film; it is Pavel's'.[55] The martyrdom of the son is not only Christ-like but also reminiscent (as is Bair in *Storm over Asia*) of the self denial of saintly princes in Russian folklore[56] (see chapter five, below). It is as though, in seeking to legitimise and endorse the revolution by finding for it a social equivalent of its Christian pre-cursor, to build a new God, the old mythology cannot withstand demolition. Gorky's mother herself faces this dilemma; what will she have left if her God is taken from her?[57]

The significant keystones of the scenario, the clear articulation of character to serve the theme, refers Pudovkin's *The Mother* to the celebratory spectacles orchestrated by the Commissariat of the Enlightenment in imitation of popular ritualistic forms, even though the conventions are here effectively humanised by Baranovskaia's performance and such details as the prison porridge and the boy having his ear clipped by his bourgeois father as he cheers on the joyful demonstrators. Contemporary commentators were wont to herald film as the vehicle of a new urban folklore, peculiarly adept at addressing a new and migrant proletariat dispossessed of its rural traditions.[58] Both novel and film owe much to a received form in folklore, a conventionalised, national form which Propp identifies in its Soviet succession: 'Epic poetry shows whom people consider a hero and for what deeds . . . the content of epic poetry is struggle and victory . . . waged not for narrow, petty goals, not for personal interests, not for the well-being of the individual hero but for the people's highest ideals'.[59] In the novel, the mother's politicisation and gradual involvement in the struggle is registered partly in the move from a passive to an active role in the events described. She forms her opinion as a witness to the conversations of Pavel and his comrades, she struggles with her own confusions which are then resolved in crucial events: the arrest; the trial; Pavel's death. It is less important that the viewer derives a sense of the real time elapsed over events represented than that a sensation of a continuous sequence of episodes be appreciated in the theme's coming to fruition. It is characteristic of pictures that they live only in the present and that the spiritual dynamic of the film is sensed as a present continuous.

To this purpose, it is significant that Pudovkin draws upon Griffith as more than a source of images (the breaking ice floes of *The Mother* owe much to *Way Down East*, where Bartlett jumps across the ice to save Anna Moore). Piotrovsky analyses the construction of *The Mother* in comparison to the Griffith schema of catastrophe-chase-rescue, preceded by the briefest introduction of characters and limited delineation of preparatory circumstances. The crucial events of the film, 'representing treachery, judgement, flight', are each 'constructed according to the schema "preparedness for catastrophe-catastrophe"'.[60] Furthermore, Piotrovsky observes: 'The emotional tension of the whole is enormous and it, as distinct from the melodrama of Griffith, is spread in equal measure'. As an analysis of the narrative content alone of the scenario this conclusion may be satisfactory, but for Pudovkin the scenario plans for a film as a physical event. It seems to me that the end of *The Mother* produces a markedly heightened tension which is physically effected and effecting: shots of the marching demonstrators' shadows cast over the flakes of ice flowing downstream; shots of demonstrators marching regularly horizontally across frame (eventually abstracted to a flickering staccato punctuation of light and shade), shots of the flag being passed in action to the head of the march (the flag ascending from bottom to top of the frame, culminating in its appearance atop the Kremlin) create an urgent, forceful rhythm which is appreciably retarded, tautly wound-back and strained by parallel interjected shots of the prisoners slowly walking counter clockwise in the prison yard. The explosive sense of physical release which is experienced at the end of the film serves to sublimate the moment of the mother's death. Piotrovsky is of the opinion that the theatrical basis of 'a tragic dénouement' is 'seriously obstructed in cinema' because in film the person of the performer is wholly identified with the mask of the character. Piotrovsky volunteers this incapacity as an explanation for the prevalence of 'happy endings'.[61] *The Mother* is seemingly epic cinema; it accomplishes a specifically cinematic catharsis.

Lunacharsky was lavish in his praise of Pudovkin's film, proclaiming it an astonishing success for a young director, remarkably accomplished with the maturity of a master, 'a genuine masterpiece of Russian cinematography'.[62] Lunacharsky commended *The Mother*, firstly, for its truthfulness of imagery and performance, in which a staged theatricality was never present, in which Batalov and Baranovskaia completely fused themselves with the typical characters presented. Secondly, he finds that Pudovkin employs images in a manner constituting a distinct film language, where images are the stuff of the film and not merely ancillary and decorative. Thirdly, he appreciates *The Mother* for its lyricism, achieved by the emotional associations between connected images. For Lunacharsky it is by these means that Pudovkin renders the reality, pathos and glory of the first workers' revolution. And Lunacharsky, too, honours Pudovkin by comparing his style with the beautiful manner of Tolstoy.[63] Eisenstein, in 'Our "October"' and Shklovsky, in 'Poetry and Prose', criticised disparities in the film:

> When we examine Pudovkin's *The Mother*, in which the director has taken great pains to create a rhythmic construction, we observe a gradual displacement of everyday situations by purely formal elements. The parallelism of the nature scenes at the beginning prepares us for the acceleration of movements, the montage and the departure from everyday life that intensifies towards the end. The ambiguity of the poetic image and its characteristically indistinct aura, together with the capacity for simultaneous generation of meaning by different methods, are achieved by a rapid change of frames that never manage to become real. The very device that resolves the film – the double exposure angled shot of the Kremlin walls moving – exploits the formal rather than the semantic

> features: it is a poetic device ... *The Mother* is a unique centaur, an altogether strange beast. The film starts out as prose, using emphatic intertitles which fit the frame very badly and ends up as purely formal poetry. Recurring frames and images and the transformation of images into symbols support my conviction that this film is poetic by nature.[64]

Rudolf Arnheim subsequently adds to Shklovsky's observations by complaining that the 'Joy' sequence inadequately prefaces its figurative intention: 'Each shot is substantive ... Film's affinity for physical reality compels each shot to maintain its literal significance':

> It is very questionable whether the symbolic connection of smile, brook, sunbeams, 'happy prisoner' and 'joyous child' can add up to visual unity. It has been done thousands of times in poetry; but disconnected themes can easily be joined in language because the mental images attached to words are much vaguer, more abstract and will therefore more readily cohere. Putting actual pictures in juxtaposition, especially in an otherwise realistic film, often appears forced. The unity of the scene, the story of the prisoner who is rejoicing, is suddenly interrupted by something totally different. Comparisons and associations like the brook and the sunbeams are not lightly touched upon in the abstract but are introduced as concrete pieces of nature – and hence are distracting.[65]

Arnheim admits that, however unsuccessful he finds this particular instance, the possibility of the kind of montage which it represents nevertheless exists. He does not qualify his criticism by reference to the reception of the film by the audience for which it was intended, nor to any familiar conventional cinematic cues on which the sequence may be relying. But in pre-revolutionary cinema and Soviet film, the close-up of a face staring full forwards was often used as an announcement of introspection. Razumny's *Brigade Commander Ivanov* [Kombrig Ivanov, 1923], for instance, uses such a shot as a lead into a revelation of the commander's thoughts. Furthermore, in the 'Joy sequence', Pavel's vision of laughing children playing in the open is matched with the other prisoners' 'Dreams of Freedom': back on the farm, working the land. The 'Joy sequence' is also worked into the diegesis in parenthesis (to employ a grammatical analogy from the preface to the German edition of *The Film Director and Film Material*), with the mother returning from the prison through the field and past the duck pond at which the children play; the ice floes break as Pavel is attempting to escape across the river, heightening the urgency of the drama, as much as signalling the cataclysmic revolution which is to follow. The title 'And outside it is spring' simultaneously conveys narrative information, necessary to the plot, and functions metaphorically, conveying the subject of the parable contemplated by Pavel on hearing of the escape.

The Mother and the Moscow Art Theatre

In spite of his 1929 London address, 'Types instead of Actors', Pudovkin later dates his move away from Kuleshov's 'naturshchik' (see chapter one, above) to his work on *The Mother.* Certainly, as Ivor Montagu was quick to point out, by 1929 Pudovkin's own practice (his performance as Fedia in Otsep's *The Living Corpse*) did not appear to correspond to this theoretical position. Although *The Living Corpse* was received well in Germany (Otsep and Anna Sten opting to remain after completing the production there) in Russia, too, it was accused of pandering to bourgeois tastes. Montagu wrote to Pudovkin:

> As you will see, *The Living Corpse* has been well received and highly praised. Personally I did not like it or indeed your acting which seemed to me in some places to illustrate the defects which you have taught us are inseparable from professional actors! However I look forward to discussing it.[66]

On *The Mother,* Pudovkin worked for the first time with professional actors from the Moscow Art Theatre (MKhAT). Although Stanislavsky himself was not himself enthusiastic about cinema, directors and actors from the Theatre were frequently enlisted. In the planning stage of *The Mother,* it was even intended that Nikolai Batalov and Vera Baranovskaia should be joined by Ivan Moskvin, in the role of the father.[67] This was subsequently taken by Chistiakov, who also worked with Pudovkin on *The End of St. Petersburg*, *The Deserter* and *A Simple Case,* and who had known Pudovkin since their apprenticeship with Kuleshov. Pudovkin says that his own training left him feeling ill-equipped initially to create the necessary rapport with artists themselves trained with Stanislavsky. He later claims that he discovered the System as an effective means of establishing trust between themselves:

> On what could one base this confidence? ... I still looked at actors from a formalist point of view, entirely externally ... How could I reach the intelligence and the heart of those whom I had to direct, whom I had to guide in the creation of characters which still existed only in my imagination. How to find a common language?[68]

Vera Baranovskaia, a principal from MKhAT, remembers for *Sovetskoe kino* how she too approached her work on *The Mother* with some trepidation, unaccustomed as she was to the procedures of its director. The 'naturshchik' in avant-garde cinema, she relates, served as no more than a model unquestioningly carrying out the director's instructions ('Again from the beginning! To the right! To the left') and less as a model for an artist's painting, drawn from life. She identifies the difficulty in film-acting of overcoming its practical exigencies, shooting a role in separate pieces and out of sequence, and says that the craft of the professional actor is that which enables him or her to master 'mosaic work'.[69] Pudovkin in 1934 repeats her formulation:

> In the cinema, exactly as in the theatre, we immediately come right up against the problem posed by the discontinuity of the actor's work being in direct contradiction with his need for a continuous creative 'living-into' [vzhivaniia] and embodiment of the image played.[70]

Baranovskaia, like Valeri Inkizhinov, claims that Pudovkin was a director who respected the contribution of actors (see chapter six, below). However, although Pudovkin, his scenarist Zarkhi and assistant Doller (himself an erstwhile actor and director for the stage) worked in alternation or collaboratively, there is little sign that impromptu interventions were welcomed from elsewhere: once determined, the scenario, 'the hard skeleton', absolutely governed its realisation by the group as a whole. Baranovskaia says that discoveries made in rehearsals could be accommodated, but the instances she cites do not extend beyond details of performance. Pudovkin quotes for *The Mother* the precedents of the court scene in Tolstoy's *Resurrection* and the hands of Mae Marsh in *Intolerance*:[71] 'the actress was probably crying when she pinched the skin of her hands; she lived a full and real experience and was completely in the grip of the necessary emotion as a whole'.[72] However, when it came to filming Baranovskaia in her role he sometimes found mannerisms performed by the actress, almost unselfconsciously, without deliberation, most suitable to his intentions:

> First I removed all that seemed to me superfluous and exaggerated and then I decided ... to suggest that she should act this scene without making a single gesture or movement ... then ... I allowed the actress to make a single gesture which I had noticed among the many she had made in the beginning. It was a movement of the hand as of someone naively fending off some terrible threat.[73]

With the official rehabilitation of Stanislavsky, Pudovkin advances a claim on his behalf as a visionary precursor for a naturalistic trend in cinema, presuming for cinema a more adequate realisation and validation of Stanislavsky's theatrical project. But although life-like credibility was claimed by the younger medium as its particular preserve (sometimes as a virtue, sometimes as an impediment), constraints were imposed on the style of performance in order that its rendition on screen prove acceptable. Large gestures in front of the camera were functionally enlarged when screened and looked simply ridiculous when accompanying speech could not be heard (Pudovkin cites the example of Moskvin in *The Postmaster*).[74] Stage make-up was to be discouraged (Vera Baranovskaia was induced to play the Mother without make-up, and *Sovetskoe kino* emphatically offers an illustration of her decked out in powder, pearls and feathers as a 'Film d'Art' diva). Hence, in part, Lunacharsky's commendation of the truthfulness of Pudovkin's material. Discussing *The Battleship Potemkin* at the time of its release in 1925, Pudovkin had observed: 'As far as the performances in the different roles are concerned, everything is bad, apart from the almost static moments of people who are not acting. This is partly the fault of the director, who has not mastered his human material'.[75] Critical reaction to *The Mother* suggested that in 1926 Pudovkin had already achieved his own distinct and avowed aims:

> The film *The Mother* can be compared with *Potemkin*. The battleship,

the first film of general significance produced by Soviet cinema, is a creative triumph for the director and cameraman. In this picture Eisenstein was able to demonstrate astonishing mastery in directing the mass and the magnificent art of montage. In *The Mother*, in addition to these achievements, the triumph of the actors deserves just as much attention: they have been employed by their director to the full extent of their creative ability.[76]

Notes

1 Boris Kazanskii, 'The Nature of Cinema', tr. Herbert Eagle, *Russian Formalist Film Theory*, Michigan 1981, p. 101; see also Eric Elliott, *Anatomy of Motion Picture Art*, Territet 1928 and Hugo Münsterberg, *The Psychology of the Photoplay* [1916], New York 1970
2 Eisenstein, *Selected Works* II, ed. Richard Taylor, London 1991, p. 117
3 Pudovkin, 'Metod kino', *Kinorezhisser i kinomaterial*, *SS* I, p. 97
4 Pudovkin, 'Metod kino', *Kinorezhisser i kinomaterial*, *SS* I, p. 97
5 Pudovkin, 'Teatr i kino', *Akter v fil me*, *SS* I, p. 188
6 Edward Braun, *Meyerhold on Theatre*, London 1969, pp. 43 and 79
7 Braun, *Meyerhold on Theatre*, p. 147
8 see 'Chaplin and Chaplinism' [1936], Braun, *Meyerhold on Theatre*
9 Mel Gordon, 'Meyerhold's Biomechanics', *Drama Review* 18.3, 1974, p. 78 and *Kuleshov on Film*, tr Ronald Levaco, Berkeley 1974, p. 112
10 Luda and Jean Schnitzer, *Poudovkine,* Paris 1966, p. 12: '...above all, Pudovkin owed to him his respect for the actor, for his own thoughts and feelings'; Peter Dart, *Pudovkin s Films and Film Theory*, New York 1974, gives a full filmography
11 Pudovkin, 'Metod kino', *Kinorezhisser i kinomaterial*, *SS* I, p. 96
12 Pudovkin, 'Naturshchik vmesto aktera', *SS* I, p. 181
13 Kuleshov interviewed in Schnitzer, *Cinema in Revolution*, tr David Robinson, London 1973, p. 71
14 Eisenstein, *Selected Works* I, p. 95
15 Pudovkin, 'Vremia krupnym planom', *Proletarskoe kino* 1, 1932, p. 32
16 Anatolii Golovnia, *Svet v iskusstve operatora*, Moscow 1945, pp. 114–115; see also M. Bliumbert, 'Osveshchenie kino atel'e', *Kino zhurnal ARK* 11–12, p. 18 for the effects of directional lighting on perceived expression
17 Pudovkin, 'Akter i svet', *Kinorezhisser i kinomaterial*, *SS* I, p. 123; on the limitations of depth of focus see 'Operator i apparat'
18 Pudovkin, 'Diktsiia, grim, zhest', *Akter v fil me*, *SS* I, p. 220
19 Pudovkin, *Film Technique*, New York 1949, p. xiii
20 Boris Eikhenbaum, ed. *Poetika Kino*, Moscow [1927], ed. Richard Taylor, *The Poetics of Cinema*, Oxford 1982
21 *Kino-zhurnal* ARK 8, 1925, p. 5

22 Pudovkin, 'Analiz', *Kinorezhisser i kinomaterial*, *SS* I, p. 102
23 Eisenstein, *Selected Works* I, p. 96
24 Jean and Luda Schnitzer, *Poudovkine*, p. 128
25 Jeffrey Brooks, *When Russia learned to Read*, Princeton 1984, pp. 317 and 319, also in Stites, Kenez, Gleason, eds. *Bolshevik Culture*, Bloomington 1985, re the difficulties of book distribution; Richard Stites suggests that the insistence on 'correct' reading material led to a fall in literacy after 1917
26 Richard Stites, *Russian Popular Culture*, Cambridge 1992, p. 42 and Peter Kenez, *Cinema and Soviet Society*, Cambridge 1992, p. 30
27 for pre-revoutionary adaptations from Pushkin, Tolstoi et al see Yuri Tsivian, ed. *Silent Witnesses*, London 1989 and B. S. Likhachev, *Istoriia kino v Rossii 1896-1913*, Leningrad 1927, pp. 176–201
28 Anna Lawton, *The Red Screen*, London 1992, p. 7
29 A. Mariamov, *Pudowkin,* Berlin 1958, p. 93 re Lenin on the exceptional 'timeliness' of the novel; Katerina Clark, *The Soviet Novel*, London 1985, p. 52
30 Richard Stites, *Revolutionary Dreams*, Oxford 1989, p. 33
31 Maxim Gorkii, *The Mother*, tr Isidore Schneider, Secaucus 1977, p. 403
32 Katerina Clark, *The Soviet Novel*, London 1985, p. 52, says that Zalomov complained to Gorky about the supposed mis-representation of his mother
33 report by comrade D. Smirnov, '1905 god', *Pravda* 10 January 1926, p. 3
34 Mariamov, *Pudowkin*, p. 98
35 Leon Trotskii, *Literature and Revolution* [1924], Ann Arbor 1960, p. 232
36 Leo Tolstoi, *Resurrection,* tr Rosemary Edmonds, Harmondsworth 1979, chapter 34 ; *The Death of Ivan Ilyich*, tr Rosemary Edmonds, Harmondsworth 1960, pp. 99–101
37 Pudovkin, 'Kak ia rabotaiu s Tolstym', *SS* II, p. 58
38 Maxim Gorkii, *The Mother*, tr. Isadore Schneider, Secaucus 1977, p. 6
39 Barbara Evans Clements, 'The Birth of the New Soviet Woman' in Stites, Kenez, Gleason, *Bolshevik Culture*, Bloomington 1985, p. 221: '[The Bolsheviks] believed that the woman of the masses was both a conservative who could be the enemy of the revolution and the long-suffering victim of oppression who must be liberated by the revolution'
40 Richard Stites, *Revolutionary Dreams*, p. 117 quoting Komsomol authors in 1927; see also Trotskii, 'Vodka, the Church and the Cinema' [1923] *Problems of Everyday Life*, New York 1973, pp. 31–35
41 Orlando Figes, *A People s Tragedy: the Russian Revolution 1891-1924*, London 1997, pp. 196–197
42 Gorkii, pp. 132 and 352; for a structured comparison of the novel with the scenario, see Doris Lemmermier, *Literaturverfilmung in sowjetischen stummfilm*, Vienna 1989
43 Aleksandr Blok, *The Twelve* [1918], ed. Avril Pyman, Durham 1989, I
44 Gorkii, p. 356
45 Pudovkin, 'Mat'', *Sovetskii ekran* 35, 1926 in *SS* II, p. 49; see also Zarkhi's

undated, incomplete book manuscript, 'Kinematurgiia (teoria kino-stsenariia)' RGALI 2003/1/92 and his scenario for *Mat*, RGALI 2003/1/37; Iezuitov suggests that the films and 'school' of Pudovkin should more properly be recognised as the combined effort of Pudovkin-Zarkhi: Nikolai Iezuitov, *Pudovkin*, Moscow, 1937, pp. 203–204

46 M. Smelianov, 'Literatura kino', *Kino-zhurnal ARK* 1 (1925), pp. 59–64; V. Dekabr'sky, 'Literatura i kinematograf', *Art-ekran* 5 (1923), p. 12

47 Pudovkin: 'Siuzhetnoe oformlenie temy', *Kinostsenarii, SS* I, p. 59

48 Gorkii, p. 195; the mother remains unnamed for much of the novel and only gradually Pavel's comrades come to address her as comrade; Griffith was not unique in introducing protagonists similarly in *Hearts of the World* etc., but Pudovkin says nothing of this

49 Pudovkin, 'Konstruktsiia stsenariia', *Kinostsenarii, SS* I, p. 55

50 Gorkii, p. 197

51 Gorkii, p. 364

52 Gorkii, p. 188

53 Gorkii, p. 392

54 Jay Leyda, *Kino*, London 1960, p. 206; see also A. Karaganov: *Vsevolod Pudovkin* , Moscow 1973, pp. 50–53 and Nina Glagoleva, *Mat*, Moscow 1975

55 Judith Mayne, *Kino and the Woman Question*, Columbus 1989, p. 108

56 Clark, *The Soviet Novel*, p. 49

57 Gorkii, *The Mother*, p. 60: The novel abounds in religious imagery, which is less conspicuous in the film; on Gorkii as a God Builder see Lunacharskii, *Religion and Socialism* and Stites, *Revolutionary Dreams*

58 Taylor, *The Poetics of Cinema*, p. 8

59 Vladimir Propp, *Theory and History of Folklore* [The Morphology of the Folktale, 1928], Manchester 1984, p. 149

60 Taylor, *The Poetics of Cinema*, p. 104; for Pudovkin's own enthusiastic observations on *Way Down East* see ' Liudi v srede', *Kinorezhisser i kinomaterial*, *SS* I, p. 115

61 Taylor, *The Poetics of Cinema*, p. 93; the 'kheppi' ending was the subject of much critical comment, but tragic endings were common in Russian melodrama and were expected by film audiences: see Tsivian, *Early Cinema in Russia and its Cultural Reception* and Kenez, *Film and Soviet Society*, Cambridge 1992, p. 20: 'Most Russian films did not conclude happily ... in order to penetrate Western markets on occasion Russian directors prepared two endings for a film, a tragic one for domestic audiences and a happy ending for export'

62 Anatolii Lunacharskii, *Kino na zapade i u nas*, Moscow 1928, pp. 17–20; but Lunacharskii, like Shklovskii writing in the same year, notes that the film fared disappointingly outside the cities and sometimes even ran at a loss

63 Pudovkin archive, RGALI 2060/1/246

64 Eisenstein, *Selected Works* I, p. 102; Viktor Shklovskii, 'Poetry and Prose', *The Poetics of Cinema*, p. 88; Pudovkin, ever sensitive to criticism, was

sufficiently personally piqued to reply: 'If this film was a success, it seems to me that this is because I really showed everything that I felt and experienced in a very simple manner. I like this film more than any other of my works. There is a unity in it. Shklovskii calls me a centaur. Personally I think that I was a young puppy, with one paw shorter than the others. I do not want to be a mythological beast – it has no future. But I know that a puppy becomes a grown up and lively dog – and it's this dog that I want to become': Jean and Luda Schnitzer, *Poudovkine*, Paris 1966, p. 129

65 Rudolf Arnheim, *Film as Art*, London 1958, p. 81; also Ernest Lindgren, *The Art of the Film*, London 1950, pp. 81–85

66 IM/BFI/SM item 89, letter to Pudovkin 23 July 1929, sent together with a review of the film; by 1934 Pudovkin was reluctant to use the misleading term 'type' and Montagu, in his translation of *Akter v fil me*, duly remarked upon the change of stance: see Pudovkin, *Film Technique and Film Acting*, New York 1949, p. 118 and 'Rabota s "neakterom"', *Akter v fil me*, *SS* I, p. 226

67 on Zarkhi's original scenario, then intended for direction by Zheliabuzhskii, and in which an even larger role for the father was destined for Moskvin, see N. Iezuitov's introduction to N. Zarkhi, 'Otets', *Iskusstvo kino* 3, 1936, p. 52 and Leyda, *Kino*, p. 206

68 Pudovkin, 'Rabota aktera v kino i "sistema" Stanislavskogo' [1952], *Izbrannye stat'i*, Moscow 1955, p. 217

69 Vera Baranovskaia, 'Akter dramy v kino', *Sovetskoe Kino* 38, (21 September 1926) p. 4

70 Pudovkin, 'Preryvnost' akterskoi raboty v kino', *Akter v fil me*, *SS* I, p. 193

71 Mae Marsh, *Screen Acting*, Los Angeles 1921, p. 117, corroborates Pudovkin's suspicion: 'Mr. Griffith is quick to appreciate the involuntary action of one of his actresses while a scene is being played or rehearsed. As, for instance, in the court room scene ... (the mother and the law) when I began unconsciously to wring my handkerchief and press it to my face'.

72 Pudovkin, 'Akter i ekrannoe izobrazhenie', *Kinorezhisser i kinomaterial*, *SS* I, p. 122

73 Baranovskaia, 'Akter dramy v kino', *Sovetskoe kino* 38, gives the same example as Pudovkin in 'Rabota aktera v kino i "sistema" stanislavskogo' [1952], *Izbrannye stat i*, Moscow 1955, p. 207

74 Pudovkin, 'Vyrazitel'noe dvizhenie', *Kinorezhisser i kinomaterial*, *SS* I, p. 120

75 Richard Taylor, *Film Propaganda,* p. 90 and A. Karaganov, *Vsevolod Pudovkin*, Moscow 1973, p. 61, both citing *Kino* 2 February 1926; however, this did not prevent Pudovkin from otherwise praising this film

76 *Kino,* 11 October, 1926; see also Khrisanf Khersonskii, 'Mat', *Pravda* 21 October 1926, p. 6 and in Tatiana Zapasnik and Adi Petrovich, eds. *Pudovkin v vospominaniiakh sovremennikov,* Moscow 1989, p. 158

4. *The End of St. Petersburg*

Mechanism, Vitalism and physiological psychology

The attachment of Soviet Marxism to Pavlov lay largely in his usefulness in accounting for change, through time and across space. (see chapter two, above) For Soviet Marxism, Pavlov's work was of material concern in the understanding it afforded of the integration of the individual in the dynamics of society, of history, of evolution in time and with the natural environment (see chapter five, below). 'Along with strength, equilibrium and mobility', wrote Pavlov in 1935, 'another very important property of the nervous system incessantly manifests itself – its high plasticity. Consequently, since this is a question of the innate type of nervous system, we must take into account all the influences to which the organism has been exposed from the day of its birth to the present moment'.[1] Bekhterev similarly, in 1923, claimed for his 'reflexology' that:

> ... it investigates all manifestations of so-called psychic activity or the spiritual sphere from an objective standpoint and confines itself to the external peculiarities of the activity of man; his facial expression, his gestures, voice and speech as a coherent integration of signs in correlation with exciting external influences – physical, biological and social – but also with internal influences, regardless of whether either of these two types of influence is referable to the present or the past, even the very remote past.[2]

Lenin took his rendition of Nature from Engels, who in turn inherited it from Hegel: 'There is no matter without movement any more than there is movement without matter ... The study of the different forms of movement is therefore the essential object of the science of nature'. In *On the Question of Dialectics* (1921), Lenin wrote:

> Dialectics is the science of general laws of motion, both of the external world and of human thought ... as a doctrine of development concerning itself with forces and tendencies acting on a given body, phenomenon or society; the interdependence and close indissoluble connection between all aspects of any phenomenon; universal process of motion..that follows definite laws.[3]

Marxism viewed science as a function of human activity derived from society as a whole and, in turn, insisted that Marxism was rooted in Nature. Soviet Marxism was not alone in stressing that movement was an essential function of Nature, but Lenin was especially concerned to render a Nature in which matter retained its objective reality and in which the continuum was clearly articulated around decisive moments. For Lenin, the reflex is decisive as a reaction between an internal organism and an external stimulus; the reflex marks the boundary between physical and psychical activity in the individual. But Lenin's Natural Philosophy has a political imperative: *Materialism and Empirio-Criticism* (1909) was written in direct response to the new physics' denial of the primacy of matter, and more specifically, to the Machians' claims to have constructed a more correct world view on the basis of this discovery of how the world is and has come to be. In 'The Relations of Mechanics to Physiology', Mach declares:

> The majority of natural inquirers ascribe to the intellect the implements of physics, to the concepts mass, force, atom etc., whose sole office is to revive economically arranged experiences, a reality beyond and independent of thought. Not only so, but it has even been held that these forces and masses are the real objects of inquiry and if once they were fully explored, all the rest would follow from the equilibrium and motion of these masses ... we should beware lest the intellectual machinery employed in the representation of the world on the stage of thought be regarded as the basis of the real world.[4]

Mach advocates tolerance of an incomplete conception of the world and disputes the notion of cause and effect in nature; he opposes the primacy which Lenin accords to matter: 'Space and time are ordered systems of sets and sensations'. Lenin, as the successor of Engels, opposes Mach for his alignment with Dühring.[5] Lenin criticises Mach for being wrong in principle and inconsistent in application:

> In Mach, the first sensations are declared to be 'real elements of the world' ... then the very opposite view is smuggled in, viz that sensations are connected with definite processes in the organism. Are not these 'processes' connected with the exchange of matter between the organism and the external world? Could this exchange of matter take place if sensations of particular organisms did not give them an objectively correct idea of this external world...? ... Natural Science instinctively adheres to the materialist theory of knowledge ... Materialism, in full agreement with natural science, takes matter as primary and regards consciousness, thought, sensation as secondary, because in its well-defined form sensation is associated only with the higher forms of matter (organised matter) while 'in the foundation of the structure of matter' one can only surmise the existence of a faculty akin to sensation ... Machism holds to the opposite idealist point of view and at once lands into an absurdity: since in the first place, sensation is taken as primary in spite of the fact that it is associated only with definite processes in matter organised in a definite way; in the second place, the basic premise that bodies are complexes of sensations is violated by the assumption of existence of other living beings and in general of other 'complexes' beside the given great *I*.[6]

Marxists were not alone in requiring an attachment of knowledge of reality to scientific discovery, but early Soviet Marxism required a doctrine which described mechanically the process and structure whereby objects were set in motion rather than assuming movement as a transcendant vitalising force, nor was it sufficient to assume that logical order reflected natural order. The reflex was a decisive moment for philosophy in that it located the origins of consciousness, both in the process of evolution of the individual being from birth to maturity and in the process of evolution of life forms. 'The view of subjective psychology does not harmonise with the law of evolution, if it cannot tell at what level of development in the animal kingdom the phenomenon called consciousness begins'.[7] Thus Bekhterev criticises James and Bergson (published in Russia in 1908 and 1914 respectively) for idealism in their adherence to the vague notion of a 'cosmic consciousness', subsuming all nature, animate and inanimate, organic and inorganic. 'Haeckel, le Dantec, Petri and de la Grasserie and others regard the psychic and consequently consciousness as resident in every cell and every molecule and atom ... a "psychology of minerals".'[8] But Bekhterev, ever equitable, cannot entertain a rigidly mechanistic position either:

> The view holds undisputed sway among modern psychologists that, in investigating the behaviour of man, it is not possible to exclude the psychic altogether because every reality and every process is first of all a psychic reality, for our knowledge of nature is second hand, through the medium of the psychic world, which the mechanists deny ... if we turn to the objective investigation of the external person and regard that individual's logical process and his behaviour as reactions to stimulii from the external world, we shall have direct evidence that development of these reactions is inevitable, if we take into account the individual's bio-socio development under the influence of his experience and consider the utilisation of external influences for his own presentation and that of the community.[9]

Conversely, the vitalist Bergson repudiates Spencer for a misplaced attachment to the reflex and an inadequate evolutionism which falsely emphasises isolated states over the process of becoming. Bergson calls for 'A PHILOSOPHY WHICH SEES IN DURATION THE VERY STUFF OF REALITY. Matter or mind, reality has appeared to us as a perpetual becoming. It makes itself or it unmakes itself, but it is never something made'.[10]

Dynamism, plasticity and organic unity

Moreover, science was not the only area of knowledge to enter the mechanist/vitalist debate and to pursue new relationships of space and time and a new fascination with movement. 'Plastic art discloses what science has discovered', says Mondrian, aspiring to found art on an objective basis. 'Neo-Plasticism should not be considered a personal conception. It is the logical development of all art, ancient and modern; its way lies open to everyone as a principle to be applied'.[11] Here, too, Bergson makes a notable contribution:

> Pure change, real duration, is something spiritual, impregnated with spirituality. Intuition is the quality which reaches the spirit, duration, pure change ... There is, however, a fundamental meaning: intuitive thinking is thinking in duration. Intelligence arises ordinarily from the immobile and constructs the quality of movement as well as it may from juxtaposed immobilities. Intuition arises from movement, posits it or rather notices it as reality itself and sees nothing in immobility but an abstract, instantaneous moment which our mind has singled out of mobility. Usually it is of things – that is to say of the stable – that intelligence is given and change becomes an accident that is supplied afterwards. For the intuition, change is the essential.[12]

Throughout the arts, there was an enthusiasm for dynamism, movement per se, and for plasticity, both as the description of form in space and its representation in movement through time. The term 'plasticity' is prominent in the manifestos of the artistic avant-garde in Europe. For the artists of de Stijl the 'new plastic' was defined as 'a new organisation of the surface';[13] the Italian Futurists presented their 1912 credo under the title 'Pittura, Scultura, Futurista (dinamismo plastico)'[14] Lászlo Mohóly-Nagy urged that 'the significance of the plastic features of a face, of shells, flowers and a thousand other matters ... be rediscovered again',[15] and Léger, on behalf of Purism, concluded that 'plastic beauty is totally independent of sentimental, descriptive and imitative values'.[16] Lunacharsky noted the rise of 'rhythmic' and 'plastic' studios of dance, following the example of Isadora Duncan.[17] The meaning ascribed to 'plasticity' by those who employed it was various, but, broadly, 'plastic' denotes the organisation and articulation of material in movement. Even stillness, says Mondrian, is in plastic terms no more than the poising in equilibrium of potentially generative forces: 'In plastic art, reality can be expressed only through the equilibrium of dynamic movement of form and colour ... dynamic equilibrium, the unification of forms or elements of forms through continual opposition ... destroys static balance'.[18] In the manifestos, 'plasticity' indicates an enthusiasm for movement as a proper theme for the modern work of art (as distinct from any previous subsidiary concern with the expression of the plastic attributes of such and such a subject), with movement (natural or mechanical) as the generator of forms and with the means by which dynamism and flux (as opposed to stasis) are to be conveyed in an art work truly representative of a modern perception of the world.

In the theatre, Appia, Tairov and Meyerhold similarly celebrate plasticity, but their exploration of its dramatic potential extends beyond a formalist enthusiasm for abstract sculptural settings of mass and light. Meyerhold discusses the plastic as a means of involving the audience as the fourth creator in a ritualistic performance:

> . . . the spectator is compelled to employ his imagination creatively in order to fill-in those details suggested by the stage action . . . stylisation employs statuesque plasticity to strengthen the impression made by certain groupings on the spectator's memory . . . the stylised theatre wants to abolish scenery which is located on the same plane as the actor and the stage properties, to remove the footlights, to subordinate acting to the rhythm of dialogue and plastic movement; it anticipates the revival of the dance and seeks to induce the active participation of the spectator in the performance . . .[19]

Film, as the art of the moving image, was accorded a peculiarly privileged position. Film was welcomed by avant-garde artists as a medium which responded to, could even materially fulfil, these various aspirations. In 1934, Panofsky recognised in film unique possibilities for the 'dynamisation of space' and 'the spatialisation of time'.[20] In 1923, Elie Faure observed: 'The cinema is plastic first; it represents a sort of moving architecture which is in constant accord – in a state of equilibrium dynamically pursued'.[21] The duration and disclosing of a film referred it qualitatively, for some critics, to older and exotic precedents, for instance, Egyptian reliefs and Chinese roll paintings.[22] More often, film commended itself as a symptom of modernity and a celebration of a modern aesthetic: 'cinema fits naturally into the rhythm of the world', said Léger.[23] The plastic arts increasingly adopted terms descriptive of the performing arts to express their aesthetic ideals. Film not only juxtaposed performing and plastic art but presented a unity in which the traditional distinction could be overcome. Faure continues:

> Let us not misunderstand the meaning of the word 'plastic'. Too often it evokes the motionless, colourless forms called sculptural – which lead all too quickly to the academic canon, to helmeted heroism, to allegories in sugar, zinc, papier-mache or lard. Plastics is the art of expressing form in repose or in movement by all the means that man commands: full-round, bas-relief, engraving ... drawing in any medium, painting, fresco, the dance; and it seems to me in no wise overbold to affirm that the rhythmic movements of a group of gymnasts or of a processional or military column touch the spirit of plastic art far more nearly than do the pictures of the school of David. Like painting, moreover, and more completely than painting, since a living rhythm and its repetition in time are what characterise cineplastics – the later art tends and will tend more every day to approach music and the dance as well. The interpenetration, the crossing and the association of movements and cadences already give us the impression that even the most mediocre films unroll in musical space.[24]

St. Petersburg ... Petrograd ... Leningrad

It seems to me worth setting film against this broad swathe of intellectual enquiry into dynamism, plasticity and organicity, before investigating the various interpretations evinced in Pudovkin's films and in his writings. Pudovkin does not stand conveniently on one side or the other of the mechanist/vitalist debate, he is concerned with film both as a conspicuously additive construction and as duration, as the absorption of time fluidly passing: in the same breath he uses an analogy from architecture (bricks, keystones) alongside an analogy from music (crescendo, diminuendo).[25] A film, for Pudovkin, has objective identity and existence, it stands as a deliberate abstraction from the indifferent natural visual and rhythmic continuum, but simultaneously plays and functions in real time. Unlike his contemporaries in the pure film movement in the rest of Europe (Richter, Eggeling, Lye, Léger), Pudovkin does not make abstract qualities of line, volume, tone and movement the subject of his work, but rather requires of an aesthetic that it serve a particular social and political imperative.[26]

Pudovkin uses 'plastic' in a narrow sense to denote the selection of subject matter to be photographed. The camera directs the attention of the viewer towards a particular object, an ability akin to that identified by Kuleshov in Pushkin and by Eisenstein in Zola to locate pertinent details in a given scene (see chapter eight, below). Golovnia recounts that he and Pudovkin would often spend hours searching out a particular tree or river at a particular time of day and then insert the shot in a sequence of material entirely unrelated in actuality. Sometimes they would encounter their ideal entirely by chance. In *The Mother*, morning is shown by mists over still water and the cockerel crowing; waves and the stirring of the wind appear after the death of Vlasov; the elemental imagery culminates in the ice floes breaking as Pavel escapes and the demonstrating mass advances[27] (see chapter three, above).

The choice of shot entails exploiting or contriving lighting which reveals the object in its ideal aspect: in *The End of St. Petersburg* [Konets Sankt-Peterburga, 1927], Golovnia attempted to capture the idiosyncratic quality of the twilight and the White Nights, 'when contours become uncertain, the space nebulous, when the image loses its naturalistic quality'.[28] But the 'plastic' denoted more than the search for a natural object which can be photographed more effectively than another example: it means more than unusually photogenic, it means commitment to the centrality of theme, for instance in Zarkhi's working title *St. Petersburg ... Petrograd ... Leningrad*. Equally, for Pudovkin, 'plastic' equates with more than the Impressionists' 'photogénie', that which Delluc defined mysteriously as the capacity of the camera to transform pictorially the natural aspect of an object, to reveal appearances beyond the usual: for Delluc, Photogénie is *the* law of cinema, it is 'the poetic truth of moving photography'.[29] Delluc was known in Russia for his contributions to the international magazine *Veshch'-Gegenstand-Objet* and for his 1920 publication, *Photogénie*.[30] In his *Kino-zhurnal ARK* article 'Fotogeniia', responding to the 1924 Russian translation, Pudovkin says that for Delluc the term comprises 'the photographic representability of such and such an object, with the "genius" of film' but says that he seems to 'have considered the question of the film material itself of scarcely any importance'. One thinks here of Eisenstein's later response to Balázs, 'Béla Forgets the Scissors'.[31] Pudovkin continues:

> So it is that something appears on the film strip. Now, if we go on to study the completed picture on the screen, every moment one piece of the strip is replaced by another (a kind of leap) and certainly it will have a distinct impression (on the spectator), in its

> being perceived and apprehended, as a kind of visual shock – an accent, as I choose to call it, even if the change is registered only mildly.
> These accents (points of change) are to be distributed throughout the film, or, rather, in that time which it takes to show the entire film. They are planted in some pattern, grounding the relative pieces and their combination ... The accented moments, the organisation in time by the division of the division of the various intervals, is this not – precisely – a form of temporal rhythm?[32]

Eisenstein answers Delluc with a useful definition which corresponds to 'typage' (see chapter six, below): 'An idea expressed in its completeness is photogenic; that is, an object is photogenic when it corresponds most closely to the idea that it embodies'.[33] For Pudovkin, the 'plastic' incorporates a similar notion, meaning the appreciation at the outset of an element in sequence and the selection of visual material appropriate to the expression of a particular theme, 'a supra-artistic concept' [poniatie vnekhudozhestvennoe] commanding the film as a whole:

> The scenario-writer must bear always in mind the fact that every sentence he writes will have to appear plastically upon the screen in some visible form. Consequently, it is not the words he writes that are important, but the externally expressed plastic images that he describes in these words ... The scenarist must know how to find and to use plastic (visually expressive) material: that is to say. he must know how to discover and how to select, from the limitless mass of material provided by life and its observation, those forms and movements that shall most clearly and vividly express in images the *whole content* of his idea.[34]

Pudovkin intends by 'clear and expressive' that which readily and economically conveys a definite idea or feeling, an intention on the part of the director to avoid confusion or misunderstanding between the making and the viewing of the film. In *The End of St. Petersburg*, the garlanded statue of Alexander III, 'the peace-maker', weeps as Europe goes to war. The series of shots of landmarks of St. Petersburg includes the distinctive silhouette of St. Isaac's Cathedral and the tympanum of the cathedral portico bearing its dedication to its patron on the entablature; the equestrian statues of Peter the Great, Alexander III and

Nicholas I precede the officer on the bridge, similarly mounted; a close-up of the cross on the flank of Tsar Nicholas' steed becomes a figure for the union of the city with the lineage of the tsars and of the tsars with the church, repeated later during the war sequence the single silhouette of St. Isaac's dome is used to locate parallel action in St. Petersburg alongside the trenches. Pudovkin wills a particular interpretation of an image by its position in a sequence: images may be introduced in an apparently narrative sequence which grounds them in the diegesis, then are subsequently interspersed as individual frames in later montage sequences in which they figure metaphorically, as a momentary tendentious reminder of a larger synthesis. A shot of a factory worker, collapsed from exhaustion, is established early in *The End of St. Petersburg* and then recurs; a soldier dying agonisingly slowly in the mud in the trenches is cut successively into the stock market sequence, the frenetic activity as prices rise ('both sides are satisfied'). With the opening shots of the film, Pudovkin and Golovnia sought to convey Russia in general and not just the particular landscape of the Volga region:

> The first shots ... show hilly countryside with sheaves of rye, ploughed fields which reach as far the horizon to merge with the

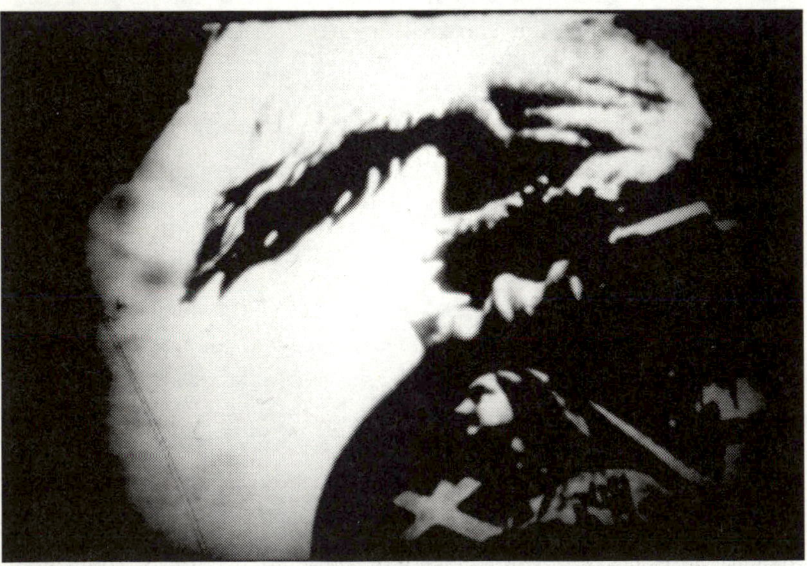

The church and autocracy (the statue of Nicholas II)

> sky ... In these pictures a sense of space was achieved by the well considered succession of graded tones, of the yellow rye and blue sky with white clouds. The troughs and furrows conveyed the feeling of an infinite distance and the cutting from landscape to landscape determined the extension of vision.[35]

'It is well known', says Pudovkin, 'to the specialist and to the general public alike, that some shots turn out well on screen and some badly'.[36] The selection of individual elements, ultimately the choice of shot and camera angle, is always to be subordinated to the general theme and the will of the director. Although Pudovkin quotes Kuleshov's analogy of film as a putting together of bricks (or of 'pieces of clay'), these separate individual pieces are not free to find or to generate their own form of combination.[37] 'Plasticity' is implied by Pudovkin more loosely in the internal feel, fundamentally intuitive, for a film as a whole, as material clearly organised within very definite boundaries. 'Cinematography is, before anything else, limited by the definite length of a film. A film more than 2,200 metres long already creates an unnecessary exhaustion'.[38] A director must 'feel' the division of the film into its reels and shape his material accordingly. 'A reel must not exceed a certain length ... a reel runs through in under fifteen minutes and the whole film in about one-and-a-half hours. If one tries to visualise each separate scene as a component of a reel, as it appears upon the screen and consider the time each will take up, one can reckon the quantity required as content of the whole scenario'.[39] In this respect, Pudovkin speaks of the appearance of movement of the screened image, the fact of its movement and the time accorded to it, as that which specifically distinguishes film from photography. Here the director's activity is somewhat akin to orchestration: 'A film is only really significant when every one of its elements is firmly welded to a whole ... When one calculates that in a film of about 1,200 metres there are about 500 pieces, then one perceives that there are 500 separate but interlocked groups of problems to be solved ... by the director'.[40] I suggest that for Pudovkin there is an additional sense in which the 'raw material of film' acquires a substantial plastic meaning apart from its appearance on screen. Pudovkin says that many technicians have become proficient directors by first learning to handle material shot by others, to feel the balance between different lengths and tones (elements, unlike bricks, dissimilar in kind);[41]

Pudovkin advocates that cutting is the basic skill of the director, not only in relation to the spectator's apprehension of the screened image but also as a craft underpinning the film-making process. Iezuitov and the Schnitzers have published excerpts from the lists held by VGIK, giving the exact lengths of Pudovkin's individual shots (and consequently their relative proportions) of sequences in *The Mother* and *The End of St. Petersburg* (Eisenstein's example of 'perfect metric montage').[42]

As a distinct element, titles are for Pudovkin a case in point. Titles may have plastic content, by means of an expressive type face or by size of font: German films were known to use gothic black letter to indicate officialdom; Gardin, amongst a number of expressionist devices, uses fancy lettering in the style of a calling card to introduce the Baron in *Locksmith and Chancellor* [Slesar' i kantsler, 1923]. In *Hunger ... Hunger ... Hunger* [Golod ... golod ... golod, 1922], notes Pudovkin, the title 'Comrades' appeared normal size, followed by the larger title 'Brothers' and thereafter 'Help' filling the whole screen. Dovzhenko's *The Arsenal* [Arsenal, 1928], Kuleshov's *The Female Journalist* [Vasha znakomaia, 1927] and Pudovkin's own *The End of St. Petersburg* use a similar effect. But Pudovkin notes further that 'more important than the plastic aspect of a title is its rhythmic significance ... it must be borne in mind that with the length of a title must be considered the speed of the action in which it appears. Rapid action demands short, abrupt titles; long drawn out action can be linked only with slow ones'.[43] In *The End of St. Petersburg*, the staggered single caption 'from Penza, from Novgorod, from Tver' recurs as a graphic leit-motif through the film. Pudovkin is wary of the disruption of the fluid movement of a sequence by an unwieldy, halting title and, again, is eager to facilitate the address of the film to the audience in an aesthetic unity of word with image:

> The main consideration affecting spoken titles is: good literary treatment and, certainly, as much compression as possible. One must consider that, on the average, every line of title (two to three words) requires one metre of film. Consequently a title twelve words long stays on the screen from twelve to eighteen seconds, and can, by a temporal interruption of this kind, destroy the rhythm, and with it the sequence and impression, of the current shots.
>
> Clarity is as important for the spoken as for the continuity title.

> Superfluous words that may enhance the literary beauty of the sentence but will complicate its rapid comprehension are not permissible ... It must be added that in construction of the scenario one must be careful of the distribution of titles. A continual, even interruption of the action by titles is not desirable. It is better to try to distribute them ... so that the remainder is left free for development of the action. Thus work the Americans, giving all the necessary explanations in the early reels, strengthening the middle by use of more spoken titles, and at the end, in quicker tempo, carrying through the bare action to the finish without titles.[44]

The organisation of literary material is hereby structured in accordance with a general ideal schema, as exemplified for Pudovkin by Griffith. Pudovkin observes that *Intolerance* (released in Russia in 1916) combines 'the inner dramatic content of the action and a masterly employment of external effort (dynamic tension)' and seemingly follows his own advice to directors to take Griffith's films in general 'as models of correctly contrasted intensification':

> At the very last moment, when the noose is being laid around the neck of the hero, comes the pardon, attained by the wife at the price of her last energy and effort. The quick changes of scene, the contrasting alternation of the tearing machines with the methodical preparations for the execution of an innocent man, the ever increasing concern of the spectator ... all these compel an intensification of excitement that, being placed at the end, successfully concludes the picture ... A working out of the action of the scenario in which all the lines of behaviour of the various characters are clearly expressed, in which all the major events in which ... the tension of the action is correctly considered and constructed in such a way that its gradual intensification rises to a climactic end – this ... is a treatment already of considerable value and useful to the director in representation.[45]

In *The End of St. Petersburg*, images are accorded an appropriate length of time, indeed are inseparably matched to screen time, for the comprehension of their content, in their own right and in sequential context. The quivering reflections of the palaces on the banks of the Neva remain on screen for long enough to allow contemplation

St. Petersburg's shaking foundations

of the unstable foundations of this fated city, '...the most abstract and intentional city in the whole round world', observed Dostoevsky[46]; there was, some said, a constant need 'to puzzle out the enigmatic existence of a city founded on all contraries and contradictions, physical and moral' a striving to understand 'this contradictory chaos of mutually devouring forces';[47] said Pushkin, of this city 'clothed in granite':

> Almost a century – and the city young
> Beauty of the Northern world, amazing,
> From gloomy forest and muddy swamp upsprung,
> Proudly risen in splendour blazing.[48]

These shots announce the guiding theme for Pudovkin and Golovnia, 'St. Petersburg ... Petrograd ... Leningrad', in this their contribution to the tenth anniversary of the October Revolution. In *The End of St. Petersburg*, sequences are balanced like separate movements in a single shot or like separate elements in a single composition; dynamic movement is balanced against stillness and an appropriate speed and direction is determined for each sequence. The film opens with a calm, stratified picture of a sunrise; the day breaks and the blades of a windmill slice vertically, chopping regularly through the sky; winds blow left to right across the plains and the tide passes over the estuary. 'It was not a single windmill', says Golovnia, 'destined to be looked at and studied, but a detail of the countryside considered as an uninterrupted shot, consisting of a whole series of elements rhythmically unified ... by montage into a single picture'.[49] The younger man waits motionless while the older breaks bread; neither is perturbed by the child (rushing into foreground from top of frame to bottom) reporting the screams of the mother: the men, worldly wise, know all too well that these pangs herald birth and not death and they continue their toil regardless. There is resignation: 'one more mouth to feed; one more proletarian must leave to find work'. The slow monotonous pace of the sequence sets the ensuing action of the film against the immutable course of the day and the seasons. As a train speeds the peasants away, windmills are seen on the horizon, turning ever turning. The spectator is suddenly jolted to attention by the rushing, lilting carriage transporting the minister through the city of St. Petersburg: a sense of urgency is afoot. A slow-cranked shot of clouds passing over the statue of Peter the Great enhances the feeling of unnatural acceleration. Belching factory chimneys and close-ups of fast-moving wheels and pistons continue the sense of urban dynamism, of men working to the rhythm of machines: when the strike is called the same wheel will be shown in close-up, stationary.

Raw material is selected to situate the narrative but simultaneously is employed to establish visually the momentum of the action: the factory smoke mirrors the clouds. Before the storming of the Winter Palace a bridge is shown closing, but as the camera seemingly passes under, the screen becomes a stark composition in black and white: night falls like the slow closing of an eye. The raising and lowering of the ship's guns over the Neva is a recurring motif: its recurrence lends shape and visual structure to the film and dynamically punctuates the narrative; the guns denote the ominous power of the state over the workers, but it is their labour, feverishly polishing shells, which keeps the guns primed; the guns are garlanded for war; the guns of the Aurora salute the fall of the Winter Palace. The effect of a passing train in Chaplin's 1923 *Woman of Paris* (well known and much discussed in Russia) could have provided a source for Pudovkin's shots of the lift. When the manager is offered promotion by the industrialist Lebedev, the alternating black/white cast flashingly by the grille-work of the elevator cage on his face serves to mark the speed of his ascent to dizzying heights: Panofsky's 'spatialisation of time' is applied to metaphorical purpose. Pudovkin equally employs dramatic content and external effort reciprocally. To effect a diegetically accommodated transition from one scene to another without disrupting the flow of the sequence, Lebedev advances upon the camera; his bulk consumes the screen in an encroaching blackness. The artful convention of a fade is effected apparently artlessly and effortlessly.

Yuri Tsivian says that early viewers frequently remarked jolts and shakes which rendered the act of projection all too appreciable.[50] Münsterberg observed (as did Arnheim thereafter) that the momentum of projection functions quasi transparently.[51] Certainly the mechanical progress of the film through the projector is not normally consciously perceived, one is not normally aware of the vehicle of movement itself moving. I contend that, in Pudovkin, an appreciation of filmic momentum, through the rigorous manipulation of movement in and between frames, verges on the palpable:

> Always there exist two rhythms, the rhythmic course of the objective world and the tempo and rhythm with which man observes this world. The world is a whole rhythm while man receives only partial impressions of this world through his ears and skin. The tempo of his impressions varies with the rousing and calming of his emotions while the rhythm of the objective world he perceives continues in unchanged tempo.[52]

Echoing Meyerhold's understanding of plasticity as a participatory relationship between performance and audience, in his notes on rhythmic montage, Pudovkin lavishes praise on Ruttmann's *Berlin* (Germany 1927): 'In his film Ruttmann never merely places something in front of the spectator, always he works with the montage of the material and the spectator together, as one'.[53] Certainly the city scenes in *A Simple Case* and in *The Deserter* owe something to Ruttmann (see chapter six, below). At the end of *The Mother*, the tension of the dramatic action (anticipation of the son's impending escape) is visually wound-up by the intermittent succession of shots of the prisoners walking round and round in a circle, counter-clockwise, in the prison yard. In *The End of St. Petersburg*, the spectator is emotionally engaged via a sensational assault. Images are often assembled to produce a sequence with the capacity to arouse a particular response, irrespective of their subject matter. In context, their source is often difficult to ascertain and is of no consequence. In the introduction to the German edition of *Film Direction and Film Material*, Pudovkin recalls:

> At the beginning of that part of the action that represents war I wished to show a terrific explosion. In order to render the effect of this explosion with absolute faithfulness I caused a great mass of dynamite to be buried in the earth, had it blasted, and shot it. The explosion was veritably colossal – but filmically it was nothing. On the screen it was merely a slow, lifeless movement. Later, after much trial and experiment I managed to edit the explosion with all the effect I required – moreover, without using a single piece of the scene I had just taken. I took a flame thrower that belched forth clouds of smoke. In order to give the effect of the crash I cut in short flashes of a magnesium flare, in rhythmic alternation of light and dark. Thus gradually arose before me the visual effect I required. The bomb explosion was at last upon the screen, but, in reality, its elements comprised everything imaginable except a real explosion.[54]

With fast cutting bombarding the eye, it seems that the sensational impulse is transferred from one shot to the next rather than the attention being held to allow for an identification of content. It would seem that this impulse operates independently of any residual image on the retina.[55] Even the howling baby in *The End of St. Petersburg* seems to be employed for purely physiognomic effect rather than to convey dramatic action. 'Single features ... appear in space; but the significance of their relation to one another is not a phenomenon pertaining to space, no more than are the emotions, thoughts and ideas which are manifested in the facial expressions we see. They are picture-like and yet they seem outside space; such is the psychological effect of facial expression', says Béla Balázs.[56] The cutting of shots during the central section of the film (the war years) is so rapid that the eye cannot catch all the images clearly, the combination of speed and brightness agitates, even aggravates the eye in the manner of op. art. Knowingly or by experiment, Pudovkin applies the phi effect, whereby two graphic forms projected alternately produce an illusion of transformation or simultaneity or movement.[57] Vertov uses a similar effect in *The Man with a Movie Camera* [Chelovek s kinoapparatom,1929], staging the trick with virtuosic aplomb.[58] In *The End of St. Petersburg*, the symbol of the 'Aurora' is transformed into the symbol of the Bolshevik leader with his arm outstretched, previously located in the action. The silhouette of the battleship (60 frames) is replaced by the negative of the same image (7 frames), proceeded by the blast, white on black (3 frames) superseded by the Bolshevik (20 frames). Petrograd becomes Leningrad.

> On the sailors' hat bands were 'Avrora' and 'Zaria Svobody'- names of leading Bolshevik cruisers of the Baltic Fleet. One of them said, 'Kronstadt is coming!' ... it was as if, in 1792, on the streets of Paris, someone had said, 'the Marseillais are coming!' For at Kronstadt were 25,000 sailors, convinced Bolsheviks and not afraid to die.[59]

Ivor Montagu later commented to Pudovkin that the 'historical classic' film succeeds in 'creating a reality so vivid that it even replaces history itself in the imagination of the beholder'.[60]

Selection of individual shots

Theoretically, the closest approach Pudovkin makes to Pavlov's reflex is in his isolation of the shot or camera angle as the most reductive element. Pudovkin suggests that the making of a film can be likened to the process of differentiation and integration in mathematics. Ivor Montagu notes that the analogy with calculus extended to (or was derived from) Pudovkin's understanding of perception as a computation of stimulii in the brain; Vance Kepley traces it to Pudovkin's early training as a chemist[61] (see chapter two, above). Shots, of moving and static objects, are to be selected by virtue of their ability to express in concrete form the theme of a particular scenario. In *The End of St. Petersburg*, Pudovkin shows the monotony of the trenches by the painstaking grinding of a blade; the time while the Bolshevik's wife waits is shown by the waning wisp of steam from a glass of tea, akin to the famous ashtray in *The Leather Pushers* [USA, 1923], perhaps.

Pudovkin acknowledges that the director is predisposed, obliged, to photograph the external world in a particular, purposeful way. The selection of a particular camera position can in itself render ordinary reality extraordinary, can lend an analytical interpretation to the usual or familiar. 'To show something as everyone sees it is to have accomplished *nothing*', says Pudovkin.[62] For instance, in *The End of St. Petersburg*, shots frequently deviate from an orthogonal stance: the camera is placed to re-orientate decisively the perspective (literally and metaphorically) of the viewing subject. Contrary to Dart's complaint that Pudovkin's orientation is destructive of audience identification in the film, I suggest that Pudovkin constructs a particular position in which the viewing subject is of necessity placed.[63] The shot of the two peasants walking across the pale open courtyard is more emphatically contrasted in scale by having the equestrian figure of Alexander III heavy and black in foreground; or, again, in the steep distorting angle of a shot of the isolated peasants overshadowed by the statue of an apostle of St. Isaac's cathedral, seeming even more insignificant and insect-like;[64] the housing-block on the Petrograd side to which they go to find lodging is first shown to the spectator as a distant object, looking, with its regular grid of bare black rectangular openings, more like a pigeon coop than apartments.[65] The low shots of the ministers who declare war on behalf of the nation are framed to show their legs in relation to the cabriole legs of chairs (these are stout bandy-legged old men, unlikely themselves to be despatched to war), to show their

the Petrograd side housing blocks

richly embroidered costumes emblazoned with the regalia of state (these are not medals attained in battle), to exclude recognition of accountable individuals (these are mere faceless functionaries). One is reminded of Bely's description of Nikolai Appollonovich, 'with his cap clutched in a white gloved hand, he would ascend the stairs behind the dignitaries, the old men in gold braid and white trousers'.[66] An old man and a young woman lean out to wave to the troops departing for war: all the young men are leaving; photographed from below, the flowers cascading down on them are omens of the grenades to come. As Balázs observes generally, sometimes a picture can make a point strikingly which would in words be no more than a cliché.[67]

Unlike Vertov, who in theory likened the camera lens to a window, a fixed flat plane parallel to the action which streamed past (at one stage even suggesting the burying of a camera in a wall to record whatever happened to pass before it), Pudovkin (like Kuleshov) lays stress on the choreographing of the pro-filmic event, on the organisation of the mise-en-scène within the boundaries of the frame and within an appropriate depth of field; that which is enclosed by the frame is not an accidental portion of a temporal and spatial continuum but is deliberately assembled. The absolute boundary of the picture frame concentrates the director's attention on the subject matter enclosed, it establishes a particular relation of subject with frame. This corresponds to the eventual focus of the spectator on the projected image in relation to the boundary of the screen: in the projected image the picture frame retains a directed and substantive presence (see chapter one, above). Lebedev is generally shot in *The End of St. Petersburg* such that he exceeds the limits of the frame; standing front to camera (his head swivels above his stiffly starched collar).

Pudovkin acknowledges that the limitations of the recording apparatus (the camera angle of vision, the focal length of the lens) impose constraints upon that which can be photographed effectively and that such a photogenic evaluation of potential raw material refutes the film's claim to be a direct representation of the natural world. But in this transposition also resides the camera's extraordinary potency. Extreme close-ups, as a means of de-familiarising the original subject matter had been used previously in *Le Ballet mécanique* (France,1924). However, with Léger these magnifications remained little more than a startling novelty, an entertaining party trick. Pudovkin photographs a shell axially foreshortened and a ship's gun hole, and alternates these with the cropped shot of the face of the howling baby. The similarity of the shots as abstract compositions combine to register graphically the idea that making war brings pain and suffering to those at home and at the front. Pudovkin never becomes entirely formalist: recognition of an actual object in the image is always an active element.

Kuleshov seemed in general to favour the positioning of the camera to correspond to the eye of a spectator viewing a scene played in the same horizontal ground plane. The picture stands perpendicular to the ground plane. Kuleshov regarded as affectation the practice of Expressionist and Constructivist photographers 'to seize things from above and below', and certainly Kuleshov was not alone in doubting that unusual camera angles rendered Rodchenko's photographs any more politically correct.[68] Kuleshov entertained the notion of a spatial web embracing the entire mise-en-scène, a three-dimensional grid radiating from the lens, akin to the cone of vision employed by a standard perspectival presentation of natural optics, with a single sight line similarly drawn parallel to the ground plane. Kuleshov, endorsed by Eisenstein, advocates this conceptual pyramid as a tool assisting the clear and distinct arrangement of elements within the shot frame.[69]

Pudovkin generally endorses Kuleshov's mise-en-scène, and, indeed, frequently reiterates tenets of his mentor's theories, but there is no mention of the web. Furthermore, the camera is often set *not* in the limiting vertical plane of the space in which the dramatic action is performed but rather is placed in a continuous space such that action is deemed to extend behind the camera: entrances are made from camera left, exits are made past camera right. Pudovkin uses the height, angle and tilt of the camera not only as devices which effect a particular interpretative expression in the screened picture; sometimes the picture is a means of rendering more forcibly a sense of the camera being somewhere, of situating the camera point of view as an authentic eye witness: in *The End of St. Petersburg*, a view from the war trenches is shot as a thin horizontal slit of white at the top of the frame above a black base; a view from the roof of the Winter Palace reverses the proportion. Kuleshov says that his *Dura lex* [Po zakonu, 1926] similarly deviated from the normal division of the frame by thirds and cites this as an extension of cinema's expressive potential.[70] In theory, Kuleshov is seemingly more proscriptive and the web indicates consistent spectator placement. The screened image is for Pudovkin a thing in its own right in and to which the spectator can re-orientate his or her point of view at the director's will. Pudovkin assumes that such re-orientations are customarily and habitually incurred in film-viewing.[71] Indeed, inter-titles could not be accommodated without it. However, Pudovkin's advice that these be limited and judiciously distributed (explanatory titles towards the beginning, dialogue titles in the middle, with as few as possible towards the end) suggests that titles obstruct subject incorporation, which is abetted by the unimpeded progress of the action.

Rather than using the film camera to obtain an image which conveyed the illusion of three dimensional depth, Pudovkin frequently seems to have deliberately flattened his image. Pre-Revolutionary directors, notably Bauer, had used props, and a succession of vertical planes and contrasted tones to enhance the apparent depth of field, to counter the loss of focus in depth, and employed this spatial articulation theatrically.[72] By the same token, Kuleshov noted that uncluttered carefully positioned sets and the selection of colours and textures which produced flat, dark tones on film, could seemingly bring the action towards the picture plane[73] (see chapter one, above). Perspectival distortion can also be productive of a flattened image: the tilted shots in *The End of St. Petersburg* of the peasants crossing the courtyard have a quality, I would suggest, reminiscent of Léger paintings of trapeze acts (significantly enough also painted from photographs). Pudovkin seems to use flat backgrounds to intensify the graphic, surface quality of some gestures and some images. Like Kuleshov, he is concerned for their ability to communicate efficiently, for their ready apprehension. These serve, like posters, to arrest the spectator's attention within the duration of the film, just as do the over-sized titles: FREEDOM!, BROTHERS!. These shots are not the constitutive fragments of a conceptual, single united pro-filmic space in which actions have been simultaneously or consecutively performed. These shots are often uniquely declamatory rather than mutually conversational. Consequently I think that Peter Dart misses Pudovkin's intention when he complains of lapses in continuity (continuity in a normative sense is not here at issue):

> Several times in *The Mother* and in *The End of St. Petersburg* especially people who are supposed to be confronting each other are shot in close-up, each looking toward the same edge of the screen.

> Thus, they do not appear to be looking at each other but rather they appear to be looking at some third thing while they speak.[74]

Dart criticises Pudovkin under the presumption that identity of space and causality of image is inherently necessary or natural to filmic coherence and comprehension; but such a presumption is I think, generally insubstantiated and here, specifically, misplaced. Sometimes the same arresting image is repeated several times in a sequence (for instance, the strike leader and the peasant boy in absolute profile, earnestly gazing out of frame left) or the silhouetted shot of the strike leader, arm outstretched as he addresses the workers. When the Bolshevik's wife is shown as the officer holds a bayonet to her throat, her chin uplifted, one is being presented with a gesture of defiance rendered in its most archetypal and photogenic form. Indeed, the shot appears to be specifically lit to this purpose: hitherto the face has been shown with the eyes sunk in shadow, the cheeks hollow (the low level of a basement): now the eyes open and the face is fully illuminated.[75]

When the peasant boy demands that Lebedev release his comrade, his determined features are starkly lit from below, exaggerating the set of the brow (there does not appear to be any explanation 'natural' to the mise-en-scène for this effect). Indeed, Barry Salt dubs such a shot 'a cliché of the Soviet avant-garde'.[76] The snapshot of the single gesture is itself, commented Rodchenko, a phenomenon not ordinarily available to the spectator; Rodchenko prefers a series of reductive snapshots to the synthetic portrait.[77] Noël Burch suggests that Eisenstein uses separate shots intending a synthesis, towards the plastic construction of an object in space;[78] by contrast I suggest that these poster shots of Pudovkin retain their singularity and thereby derive their impact. Where Pudovkin does take the same object from a succession of clearly differentiated angles or positions, (for instance, of himself as the police officer in *The Mother*), this characterises the figure (his evasion of the direct gaze, his want of literal 'glasnost'), it is again subjectively expressive rather than sculpturally exploratory. Sometimes Pudovkin's snapshots imitate agitational posters more directly: hands raised in support of the Bolshevik leader recall posters of the revolution showing workers and the Red Army saluting the flag. (See, for instance, Moor's 1918 'The glorious promise' or Klucis' 1930 'A practical plan for good work').[79]

Pudovkin cites various distinguishing filmic devices which have become conventional and to which audiences have become accustomed. The portrayal on film of simultaneous events in different locations and flashes backwards and forwards, are spatial and temporal transpositions of naturally available experience. The screen close-up signifies a similarly altered perception, a similar cue. Theoretically, Pudovkin found no reason why 'close-ups in time' could not be applied to concentrate and intensify attention and experimented with these in *A Simple Case* and in *The Deserter* (see chapter six, below).

> When the director shoots a scene, he changes the position of the camera, now approaching it to the actor, now taking it farther away from him, according to the subject of his concentration of the spectator's attention ... This is the way he controls the spatial construction of the scene. Why should he not do precisely the same with the temporal? Why should not a given detail be momentarily emphasised by retarding it on the screen, and rendering it by this means particularly outstanding and exceptionally clear.[80]

Indeed, contrivances of performance speed were called for customarily. Pudovkin notes that Ivan Moskvin's rhythmic, emphatic movements in *The Postmaster* [Stantsionnyi smotritel', 1925], made to accompany stage delivery of speech, did not achieve on film the desired effect:

> During the shooting, when the words were audible, the scene was effective ... but on the screen it resulted as a painful and often ridiculous shuffling about on one spot ... Gesture – movement accompanying speech, is unthinkable on the film. Losing its correspondence with the sounds that the spectator does not hear, it degenerates to a senseless muttering. The director in work with an actor must so construct the performance ... that the significant point shall lie always in the movement, and the word accompany it only when required.[81]

In *The End of St. Petersburg*, the Bolshevik's wife frenetically rocks her baby, which the spectator perceives as expressive of her extreme anxiety. Similarly, the bourgeois' applause of Kerensky contributes to the rabid pace of the war. Pudovkin observes that fast cranking had been used by Epstein in creating a dream-like aura around his adaptation of *The Fall of the House of Usher* [La Chute de la maison Usher, France, 1928], but censured the use of the device in this instance as too general.[82] *Entr'acte*, also cited by Pudovkin, includes a slow-motion sequence of a cortege and Murnau's *Nosferatu* [Germany, 1922] features slow-cranking. Slow-motion was familiar in educational and scientific films, slow-cranking had hitherto been used humorously and fast-cranking had been used to emphasise the balletic qualities of the stunts of such as Fairbanks, to further enhance what Shklovsky and Delluc coined 'his grace and natural poetry'.[83] In *Storm over Asia*, Pudovkin uses slow motion to heighten tension, as the troops turn against the Mongolians (see chapter five, below).

Ivor Montagu, in his notes to *Film Technique*, claims that the Russians, 'as naturalists' were inclined to disfavour tracking shots as drawing attention to the camera.[84] The appellation and the explanation seem hard to credit (Bazin was later to praise Renoir for employing tracks and dollies as a naturalised, self-effaced technique) and odd given the conspicuous manoeuvring of spectator placement in different rapidly juxtaposed camera angles.[85] Furthermore, Montagu claims (more plausibly), tracking shots were resisted as inordinately expensive. Eisenstein argued that such shots proved unwieldy in cutting.[86] Certainly tracks had been used before the Revolution, for instance by Bauer in *A Child of the Big City* [Ditia bol'shogo goroda, 1914], where the spectator's attention is drawn to the dancer on stage in the background of a restaurant scene; or in *Day Dreams* where a track identifies a character's stream of attention as it is caught by a passing woman who reminds him of his dead wife.[87] Pudovkin similarly uses a moving camera subjectively. In the *End of St. Petersburg*, the slow track and pan as the Bolshevik's wife walks through the Winter Palace conveys the grandeur of the building, its monumental symmetry, her awe in attempting to encompass it in her gaze (and possibly also her trepidation). Intercut shots of her battered metal potato kettle remind one of the incongruity, of her not being well acquainted with such finery. Given tracking as an acceptable option, when Pudovkin chooses not to use a track, I would contend, there is also significance in the selection of an alternative, in his favouring the use of a more effective means of 'dynamisation of space'.

When the peasants arrive in St. Petersburg there is a close-up, full-square shot of the base of a marble column; the shot lends appreciable scale to the subsequent shot of the colonnaded portico, thereafter dissolved into subsequent similar shots. The dissolve and the fade, states Pudovkin, are commonly used to carry film action from one location to another, denoting a transition in time compressed and across space unseen.[88] Where the colonnade shots overlap and mix into one another, one moving sideways behind another in the opposite direction, there is a subjective impression of repetition, of the same thing being seen time and time again, of multiplicity and perplexity on the part of the peasants in this vast city of Italianate palaces and monuments, 'which appear in the usual accounts of letters and poems', says Golovnia.[89] The shots of rising share prices are overlaid top to bottom in the war sequence to suggest that they are no sooner chalked up, than they are erased and superseded. The intervening title, 'Forward, Forward!', matches the profiteering of the manufacturers' share-holders to the engagement and re-engagement of troops in battle. Fervour on the floor of the stock exchange is rendered subjectively, the camera shoots in the face of the frenzied, slavering speculators, it keels as the crowd jostles:

> While taking the first shots of the stock exchange we observed that wide shots of the action in the background, on the staircase, turned out badly, the scene became static. We wanted to achieve a dynamic mass, because these shots of the agitation in the exchange were to be edited in parallel with the action at the front. To render the concept clearly, this composition was constructed to forward the action: a marked diagonal movement in the shots of the attack and a chaotic linearity in the shots of the exchange. In this way the conceptual difference of the two actions was emphasised plastically. The exchange is frenetic confusion, speculation, febrile movement, disorganised. The front is tension, decisiveness, strength.[90]

'Rhythm is a modern catchword', says Pudovkin, 'rhythm guided by the will of the director can and must be a powerful and secure instrument of effect'.[91] For Panofsky, movement in a literal sense is of the essence of cinema, both in its founding and in the experience of it by an audience. The question remains whether cinema was experienced as a really new phenomenon or whether its particular aesthetic properties, the 'dynamisation of space' and the 'spatialisation of time' allowed for a new apprehension of the world. Certainly the mechanists found in the discovery of cinema a powerful means of asserting a theoretically consolidated world view; Bergson complains that absolute duration is wanting from their reality.

Notes

1 ed Jeffrey Gray, *Pavlov s Typology*, Oxford 1964, p. 37

2 Vladimir Bekhterev, *General Principles of Reflexology* [1923], tr Murphy, London 1933, p. 33

3 Vladimir Lenin, *On the Question of Dialectics* [1921], Moscow 1980, p. 8

4 Ernst Mach, *The Science of Mechanics*, London 1919, p. 505

5 Mach, p. xi: ' [because I had already published] Dühring . . . did not particularly influence me – nevertheless there are many points of agreement with Dühring and Avenarius and the criticisms here expressed'

6 Vladimir Lenin, *Materialism and Empirio-Criticism* [1909], London 1952, p. 37; for Lenin's shortcomings as a philosopher in this work, see Richard T. de George, *Patterns of Soviet Thought*, Michigan 1966, pp. 146–160; for faults in Lenin's understanding of science, see David Joravsky, *Russian Psychology*, Oxford 1989, p. 193

7 Bekhterev, p. 74

8 Bekhterev, p. 61

9 Bekhterev, p. 43

10 Henri Bergson, *Creative Evolution* [1907] tr Mitchell, London 1911, pp. 287 and 386: Bergson is replying to Herbert Spencer, *The Principles of Psychology*, London 1855, note p. 534: 'The reflex action being the lowest form of psychical life, is, by implication, that which is most nearly related to the physical life – that in which we see the incipient differentiation of the psychical from the physical life'.

11 Piet Mondrian, 'Toward the True Vision of Reality', *Plastic Art and Pure Plastic Art*, New York 1945, p. 14

12 Bergson, *Pensée et mouvement* [1935] qu. Frank Popper, *Origins and Development of Kinetic Art*, London 1968, p. 224

13 Popper, p. 57

14 qu. Lászlo Mohóly-Nagy, *Vision in Motion*, Chicago 1956, p. 237

15 Mohóly-Nagy, p. 218

16 Fernand Léger, 'The Machine Aesthetic' [1925], *Functions of Painting*, ed. E.F. Fry, London 1973, p. 63

17 Ilya Ilyich Schneider, *Isadora Duncan*: *The Russian Years*, tr. David Magarshack, London 1968, pp.23 and 63.: 'Duncan abhorred the "rhythmic" and "plastic" studios for they adopted only her 'bare feet' and tunics, and forgot the chief thing – the naturalness of movement, its simplicity and expressiveness'.

18 Piet Mondrian, p. 27

20 Erwin Panofsky, 'Style and Medium in the Motion Pictures', ed. D. Talbot, *Film: An Anthology*, Berkeley 1967, p. 18

21 Elie Faure. 'The Art of Cineplastics', ed. D. Talbot: *Film: An Anthology*, p. 5

22 Rudolf Arnheim, *Film as Art*, London 1958, p. 58; Roger Fry, 'An Essay in Aesthetics', [1909] *Vision and Design*, London 1990, p. 23; this 'unrolling' was similarly noted also by Eisenstein

23 Léger, 'Speaking of Cinema' [1933], *Functions of Painting*, p. 101
24 Faure, p. 6
25 Pudovkin, 'Siuzhetnoe oformlenie temy', *Kinostsenarii*, *SS* I, p. 58
26 see Grigori Roshal 'Soviet Film', *Experiment in the Film*, ed. Roger Manvell, London 1949
27 see selection of stills in VGIK archive
28 Anatolii Golovnia, *Svet v iskusstve operatora*, Moscow 1945, p. 124; see also Pudovkin, 'Petersburg ... Petrograd ... Leningrad', *Sovetskoe kino* 2, 1927, p. 6; see also 'Repertkom tov. Mordvinkinu', *Lunacharskii o kino*, Moscow 1963, p. 272
29 qu. Marcel Tariol, *Louis Delluc*, Paris 1965, p. 48; see also David Bordwell, 'The Nature of the Filmic Image', *French Impressionist Cinema*, New York 1980
30 Eisenstein, *Selected Works* I, ed. Richard Taylor, London 1988, p. 57; see also 'Literarura i kinematograf', *Veshch -Gegenstand-Objet* 1–2, Berlin 1922, p. 11, for an earlier reference to Delluc
31 see Eisenstein, 'O pozitsii Bela Balasha' [1926], *FF*, p. 145
32 Pudovkin, 'Fotogeniia', *Kino-zhurnal ARK* 4–5 (1925), pp. 9–10
33 Eisenstein, *Selected Works* I, ed. p. 56
34 Pudovkin, 'Plasticheskii material', *Kinostsenarii*, *SS* I, p. 64
35 Golovnia, p. 123; Pudovkin's sketches in the margins of his own shooting script show what care he and Golovnia took: for instance, as the small boy runs down the field to the father and son, the furrows are deliberately shown curved rather than straight: Pudovkin archive, Zarkhi scenario 'Peterburg ... Petrograd ... Leningrad', 2060/1/1, shots 58–64. For the particular part played by the Volga region in Revolution, see Orlando Figes, *Peasant Russia, Civil War*, Oxford 1989, p. 21
36 Pudovkin, 'Fotogeniia', p. 9
37 Ronald Levaco, ed. *Kuleshov on Film*, Berkeley 1974, p. 7
38 Pudovkin, 'Tema', *Kinostsenarii, SS* I, p. 56
39 Pudovkin, 'Siuzhetnoe oformlenie temy', *Kinostsenarii*, *SS* I, p. 61
40 Pudovkin, 'Tekhnika rezhisserskoi raboty', *Kinorezhisser i kinomaterial*, *SS* I, p. 111
41 Pudovkin, 'Priemy obrabotki materiala', *Kinostsenarii*, *SS* I, p. 69
42 VGIK Kabinet Kinovedenia, *Mat* ; see also Iezuitov: *Pudovkin*, Moscow 1937 and Jean and Luda Schnitzer: *Poudovkine*, Paris 1966
43 Pudovkin, 'Nadpis'', *Kinostsenarii, SS* I, p. 67
44 Pudovkin, 'Nadpis'', *Kinostsenarii, SS* I, p. 66
45 Pudovkin, 'Siuzhetnoe oformlenie temy', *Kinostsenarii*, *SS* I, p. 61; see also Vance Kepley Jr., 'Pudovkin and the Classical Hollywood Tradition', *Wide Angle* 7.3 (1985) and '"Intolerance" and the Soviets' *Wide Angle* 3.1 (1979)
46 Fedor Dostoevskii, *Notes from Underground* [1864], tr. David Magarshack, Harmondsworth 1972, p. 17
47 qu. Grigory Kaganov, *Images of Space: St. Petersburg in the Visual and Verbal Arts*, Stanford 1997, p. 103
48 Aleksandr Pushkin, *Mednyi vsadnik* [1833], London 1961

49 Golovnia, p. 123
50 Yuri Tsivian, *Early Film in Russia and its Cultural Reception*, London 1994, p. 52
51 Hugo Münsterberg, *Psychology of the Photoplay* [1916], New York, 1970; a contrary, non-neutral effect was produced when films were shown at incorrect projection speeds, for instance, the notorious case of the first London screening of *The Battleship Potemkin*, synchronised to Meisel's score, rendered the rising lions sequence ridiculous
52 Pudovkin, 'Asinkhronnost' kak printsip zvukovogo kino' [1934], *SS* I, p. 159; Andrey Tarkovsky suggested that succumbing to the temporal substance of a film was the primary phenomenal attraction of the experience; see *Sculpting in Time*, London 1986
53 Pudovkin, 'O montazhnom ritme', *SS* II, p. 270; for Vertov's disparaging view of the same film see 'Speech to the First All-Union Conference on Sound Cinema', (1930) *FF*, pp. 301–302
54 Pudovkin, *Film Technique*, tr. Montagu, New York 1949, p. xv; also 'Predislovie', *SS* I
55 see Joseph and Barbara Anderson, 'Motion Perception in Picture' in eds. de Lauretis and Heath, *The Cinematic Apparatus*, London 1980 also Joseph Anderson, *The Reality of Illusion*, Carbondale 1996
56 Béla Balázs, *Theory of the Film*, London 1952, p. 61
57 The phi phenomenon depends on critical intervals between images shown; see Richard Gregory, *Eye and Mind* and *Visual Perception*, also Ernst Gombrich, *Art and Illusion*, London 1977, p. 260
58 see Vlada Petrić, *Constructivism in Film*, Cambridge 1987, p. 139
59 John Reed, *Ten Days that Shook the World* [1926], Harmondsworth 1982, p. 82; the cruiser 'Aurora' is now open as a museum, telling the story of the ship on the night of 24/25 October 1917 and describing conditions on the ship for the officers and men; the tone of John Reed's account suggests well the mythical status enjoyed by the ship, although some historians doubt the authenticity of the current exhibit. The Museum of the Revolution in Moscow also has memorabilia from the ship, including sailors' hat bands!
60 RGALI, 2060/1/151, letter 28 February 1944
61 Vance Kepley Jr., 'Pudovkin and the Classical Hollywood Tradition', *Wide Angle* 7.3 (1985) p. 59
62 Pudovkin: 'Material kino', *Kinorezhisser i kinomaterial*, *SS* I, p. 100
63 Peter Dart, *Pudovkin s Films and Film Theory*, New York 1974, p. 103
64 a photograph in RGALI, 2060/1/46, shows the camera crew intrepidly perched on a platform atop the cathedral
65 for a discussion of Mitrokhin's *On the Petrograd Side* (1925) and much else, see Kaganov, p. 146
66 Andrei Belyi, *Petersburg* [1913], tr. Cournos, London 1960, p. 251
67 Balázs, p. 111
68 Brandon Taylor, *Art and Literature under the Bolsheviks* II, London 1992, p. 107: Kushner's 1928 challenge to Rodchenko; Kuleshov's disagreement

with Rodchenko did not prevent their working together successfully, on *The Female Journalist*, for instance.

69 Eisenstein, *Selected Works* I, p. 57

70 Levaco, p. 82

71 see, for a useful discussion, Linda Williams, ed. *Viewing Positions*, New Brunswick, 1995

72 sometimes foreground architecture was darkened and backgrounds lightened, in imitation of Danish practice; see Yuri Tsivian, 'Cutting and framing in Bauer's and Kuleshov's Films' *Kintop* 1 (1993) pp. 103–113 and his comparison of Bauer and Hofer in Thomas Elsaesser and Michael Wedel, eds. *A Second Life: German Cinema s First Decades*, Amsterdam 1996

73 Levaco, pp. 73–74, on the sets for *The Female Journalist* conceived as a 'shot sign'

74 Dart, p. 110

75 an interesting location photo of the lighting set-up for the final shot of the mother's face in the Winter Palace, on the Jericho staircase, confirms my suspicion that such close-ups were re-rigged: see RGALI 2060/1/48

76 Barry Salt, *Film Style and Technology*, London 1992, p. 192

77 'Against the Synthetic Portrait', in John E. Bowlt, ed. *Russian Art of the Avant-Garde*, London 1988

78 Noël Burch, *Theory of Film Practice*, London 1973, pp. 32–50

79 see *The Soviet Political Poster*, Lenin Library Collection, Moscow 1984

80 Pudovkin, 'Vremia krupnym planom', *Proletarskoe kino* 1, 1932, p. 30

81 Pudovkin, 'Vyrazitel'noe dvizhenie', *Kinorezhisser i kino material*, *SS* I, p. 120

82 Pudovkin, 'Vremia krupnym planom', *Proletarskoe kino* 1, 1932, p. 32

83 Louis Delluc, *Cinéma et cie*, [1919], Paris 1965, p. 103

84 Pudovkin, *Film Technique*, New York 1949, p. 182

85 André Bazin, *What is Cinema?* tr. Gray, Berkeley 1967, p. 29

86 'Architecture and Montage' in Eisenstein, *Selected Works* II, ed. Richard Taylor, London 1991

87 for a discussion of early tracking see Tsivian, *Early Cinema*, pp. 205–207 and Tsivian and Cherchi Usai, *Silent Witnesses*, London 1989

88 Pudovkin, 'Prosteishie spetsial'nye priemy s'emki', *Kinostsenarii*, *SS* I, p. 67

89 Golovnia, p. 124

90 Golovnia, p. 125

91 Pudovkin, 'Ustanovka ritma fil'my', *Kinorezhisser i kinomaterial*, *SS* I, p. 116

5. *Storm over Asia*

Typologies

An impetus towards the subdivision of the entire spread of society into discretely differentiated groupings was derived in large part from the taxonomy of nineteenth century natural history (see chapter two, above). However, even Darwin cautioned that the term 'species' was fundamentally 'arbitrarily given for the sake of convenience', and that his conceptual model was no more than provisional.[1] The ideological imperative to found a vision of society on a scientifically authorised model was made manifest in literature and the visual arts. The theme of 'Darwinism and Marxism' was present in all academic programmes of the Commissariat of Enlightenment: this 'gave the progressive secondary school teacher the chance to work on the formation of a materialist world-view in his pupils, to inculcate scientific-atheistic views of the world, and to make them active transformers of nature'.[2] In Soviet practice specifically it found equivalence in a determinedly politicised vision of history, embracing the past and the future. Plekhanov, as founding father of Russian Marxism and himself greatly influenced by Darwin, declared the general agenda in 1898:

> At the present time, human nature can no longer be regarded as the final and most general cause of historical progress: if it is a constant, then it cannot explain the extremely changeable course of history; if it is changeable, then obviously its changes are themselves determined by historical progress. At the present time we must regard the development of productive forces as the final and most general cause of historical progress of mankind and it is these productive forces that determine consecutive changes in the social

> relations of men ... history is made by the social man, who is its sole 'factor'.[3]

In Soviet film, the impetus is systematically doubled and bi-focal in orientation: firstly, it concentrates essential traits and attributes which tend to distinguish individual characters one from another; secondly, in the identification of particular interest groups in the audience such that characters can be constructed to agitational and didactic (and entertaining) effect.[4]

In *Storm over Asia* (*The Heir to Genghis Khan*) [Potomok Chingiskhana,1928], an old Mongolian lies dying. Prayers are offered by a lama. The son, Bair, is told to sell a rare and wonderful fox fur. This pelt, advises his father, will fetch enough money to keep them for the winter. The lama, catching sight of the fur, demands a higher price for his services, but Bair sees him off and in the tussle an amulet is dropped. Bair takes the amulet and goes to market. Bair is offered far less than the true price for the pelt but the merchant, Hughes, insists that he accept his price. Bair becomes angry and a fight breaks out in which a white man is injured. In retaliation for the shedding of one man's blood, troops are despatched to pillage the native encampments and punish the whole population. Bair is urged to flee for his safety. 'Go to the Russians, they are kind and strong'. An intertitle interjects to locate the action in 1920, on the Eastern front between the partisans and the White Russians (supported by American and European battalions and services). Bair then encounters a partisan and a soldier fighting on a cliff edge. The soldier falls, but Bair holds the partisan fast. He is thanked as a friend. Other troops are heard advancing and Bair and the Russian needs must escape. Another partisan arrives, at the gallop. 'What are you waiting for?', cries this partisan and Bair leaps behind the saddle. Bair is then invited into the partisans' camp. There are old and young men, of various origins in the new Soviet Empire. A fellow Mongolian translates for Bair. Bair's eyes widen as he looks across at the partisan who saved him: in the depths of an engrossing fur coat, a child is being suckled. Bair had not realised that Daria, his saviour, was a woman. Another woman, with plaited braids, also with a young child, is shown sharing in the group's amusement at Bair's surprise. The Russian is now brought in on his death bier. He, the commander of the group, calmly and stoically utters his final words. 'Listen to Moscow', translates the Mongolian, 'that's where

Lenin lives', he explains. 'Moscow ... Lenin' are to become Bair's talisman in place of the monk's amulet which he carries. The sequence ends with a held shot of a primed gun mounted silhouetted against sky and a distant longshot of the Kremlin against a setting sun.

Although they are all applied to a common purpose, there are a number of typological strategies at work in this sequence and in *Storm over Asia* as a whole. Typification is used as a means of registering a wide sweep of individuals and activities. Broadly speaking, inclusivity of range is a defining function of realism in art, as is extensivity in its historical context: realism is defined in the perceived extension of preceding conventional limits. In Soviet films of the 1920s, the representation of characters is often adopted from (or at least shared with) reputable and approved novels, from Gogol or Gorky for instance. *My Universities* gives a description which befits Bair: 'His head was shaven Tartar fashion and he seemed to be tightly sewn up in his grey Cossack jacket which was hooked right up to his chin'.[5] Pudovkin's *The Mother* inherits from the Gorky original a range of typical individuals amongst the activists: intellectuals, well-bred young women (with portfolio), peasants of Good Soul[6] (see chapter three, above). The typological model was authorised not only for representation to the native audience, it had also been the chosen form of address of the nascent Soviet republic when represented abroad. In 1918, the delegation sent to peace talks in Brest-Litovsk contained several Russians, an Armenian, two Jews, a woman revolutionary, an old soldier and a rough-hewn worker. 'To complete the sociological mosaic of the worker-peasant state, they picked up on their way to the station in Petrograd a peasant from the streets and pressed him into service as the embodiment of the People'.[7] Political posters of the 1920s and early 1930s similarly show a range of types.

Judith Mayne has rightly observed the importance of 'the Woman Question' to the Soviets as an aspect of social egalitarianism and draws attention to the new equality instituted in state benefits, rights in marriage and education. She construes the representation of women in Soviet films as 'problematical'.[8] The social enfranchising of women is in some sense shown to have been earned by their active part in the revolutionary struggle, as is demonstrated in such figures as the shop-girl in *The New Babylon* [Novyi Vavilon, 1929], Daria in *Storm over Asia*, the Red partisan in Protazanov's *The Forty-First* [Sorok pervyi, 1927] and, later, the girl gunner and later nurse, Mashenka, in

Pudovkin's *A Simple Case* [Prostoi sluchai, 1932] and in the Vasilievs' *Chapaev* [1934]. This acknowledgement in film was predated by the appearance of 'the new Soviet woman' in periodicals, in the guise of 'nurse, political leader in the army, even as combat soldier':

> She was modest, firm, dedicated, sympathetic, courageous, bold, hard-working, energetic and often young, gave no thought to her personal welfare and could leave her children, although with regret, if she was needed at the front; she could put up with physical hardship, face combat and torture if captured and even endure death, believing that her sacrifice had contributed to the building of a better world.[9]

These films and periodicals also engage with campaigns for the further politicisation of women, but as women fighting for society rather than on issues exclusively of interest to women. Figures such as Daria were in some measure drawn from life, but more significantly were intended as an inspirational ideal for proletarian women, whom the Party leaders believed to be inherently conservative.

> The Party leaders insisted that agitation among women must do nothing to rouse 'feminist' attitudes, which meant that such agitation must emphasise women's responsibilities to the 'general revolutionary cause' ... women were to be persuaded to work for the good of all and to pursue their own special interests only to advance the revolution.[10]

The model is aspirational and utopian. True, these figures can be deemed to represent more of an idealised archetype than a statistical mean or abstract average, but I think that Mayne's complaint that none of these women are 'real flesh and blood' fails to acknowledge the stylistic conventions which govern the representation of all the individual types in these films. I think also that she posits a notion of spectatorship which consists in matching a particular individual character against the vagaries of personal experience: mis-match finds the characters defaulting. Such a notion is itself not unproblematical. The mass address of early Soviet films is formed inclusively in the accumulation of a number of distinct characters rather than in an attempt to construct an holistic amalgam concurring with and infallibly reproducing a full encounter with a living individual in everyday life, nor, as Eisenstein asserted, in an attempt to construct 'the objective co-ordination of sign and essence'. Nevertheless, such criticisms were equally levelled by contemporaneous Soviet audiences and the conventions shifted accordingly. The effect of the sign upon the audience is prioritised over its verisimilitude.

Conversely, *Storm over Asia* attaches itself firmly to the reality of everyday experience in its capacity as an anthropological and envirnmental document. Like *Little Red Devils* [Krasnye d''iavoliata, 1923], Vertov's earlier *One Sixth of the World* [Shestaia chast' mira, 1926] or later *Three Songs for Lenin* [Tre pesni o Lenine, 1934], *Storm* serves to demonstrate to its Soviet viewers the geographical extent of the Soviet empire and its ethnic inclusivity. It was not merely a matter of a correspondent submitting copy from 'the far flung outskirts' to the centre: films were carried by train, boat and camel into the regions in an attempt to reach as wide an audience as possible, 'acquainting people of various districts with each other's mode of life, habits and dress'.[11] The journals and contemporary commentators report the activities of regional studios and of Russian companies in the regions: Goskino and Mezhrabpom-Rus' both made films in the Caucasus, Proletkino in Turkestan; there were studios in the Ukraine, in Georgia, in Uzbekistan and Tatkino made films with Tartar subtitles;[12] *Kino-zhurnal ARK* discusses the activities of Bukhkino. *One Sixth* and Shub's *The Fall of the Romanovs* had shown Caucasians, Arabs, Negroes and Asiatics. The distribution of films throughout the Union was especially important given that, as late as 1927, more than 98 per cent of the peasantry was still living on small holdings, and amongst the peasantry especially, illiteracy was common.[13]

Part of the appeal of *Storm*'s scenario for Pudovkin and Golovnia was in the opportunity it presented to work away from the constraints of the studio, working with living material on location, recoding the exotic landscape and culture of the Buriat-Mongolian Republic.[14] Indeed, avant-garde and purist critics censured them for being entirely enthralled by their subject matter and indulgent towards its aesthetic and decorative (and commercial) possibilities:

> Pudovkin was definitely rejected and excommunicated by ... a group of theoreticians, partisans of montage cinema, 'grand' and 'pure'. *Storm over Asia* was considered as regressive, contrary to the

> general direction of cinema, submissive to its subject and to mere chances of fortune, and other reprehensible things ... there was a conspiracy of silence around this film.[15]

Reviewing the film for *Izvestiia*, Nikolai Osinsky complains that the 'symbolic' ending of the film (umpteen billy cans are rolled over the steppes by a tempest, followed by soldiers' caps, followed by soldiers themselves, unable to stand against the force of the storm, gusting and billowing a thousand leaves against them) was open to misinterpretation and that both ending and beginning of the film were too drawn out; he even suggests (horror of horrors) that the scene of Bair's release is slightly reminiscent of such scenes in mild comedies made before the revolution. Others, more sympathetic and tolerant, perhaps, have said that this film suited Pudovkin's temperament well.[16] Certainly, the original 1928 copy of the film includes considerably more peripheral, establishing travelogue footage of the Mongolians at market than survives in the later version, showing sword dancers and acrobats, different market stalls and Mongolians jostling with one another to see and hear a record player. Equally, the technical difficulties of filming in these conditions (like those of Flaherty's pioneering expeditions into the North) are logged in the manner of an explorer overcoming an obstacle to his path. Golovnia recalls:

> The feast of Tzai did not exist in the original scenario any more than the other scenes which resulted from our contacts with the actual life of the monasteries, which still existed there at that time and made a great impression upon us ... The feast of Tzai is always celebrated on a certain date. At Achirov's request the Bog Do Lama ... agreed to bring forward the date of the festival especially so that we could film it. But the performance of the ceremony could not be modified: the ritual had to be strictly followed, independent of the requirements of the filming. They paid absolutely no attention to us and of course there could be no retakes. I was just shown the plan of the ceremony in advance – what people would dance when, where etc ... Unhappily at this time there were no hand cameras. In order to shoot all this I had a harness which held the camera on my chest. It was an old Debrie; and the motor gave up the ghost at once so I had to operate it manually, turning the handle and all the time running right and left, 5,000 metres of film.[17]

Film expeditions to Central Asia produced good copy for the journals. In the year prior to Golovnia's expedition (covered by *Sovetskii ekran* over several weeks), *Sovetskoe kino* included the article 'With a cine-camera in the Buriat' and 'Some friendly advice about world travel', suitably illustrated with pictures of cameramen trekking for footage.

The recording of Mongolian culture was not a self-sufficient enterprise, in spite of appearances. It roots Bair in a particular environment and social organisation and serves to amplify a larger theme. Diversity and extensiveness are employed to demonstrate a transcendent humanism of body and spirit and to identify this with a specific ideology. 'All the emotions which we revolutionists, at the present time, feel apprehensive of naming', says Trotsky in 1924, 'such as disinterested friendship, love for ones neighbour, sympathy, will be the mighty ringing chords of socialist poetry'.[18] Fraternal love is similarly represented by Gorky and Lunacharsky, in quasi cultist terms as a putative substitute for religion: 'We will kindle a new sun ... a new life comes into being born of the children's love for the entire world'.[19] 'Take my hat, my mittens' say Bair's fellow trappers as he bids them farewell. Bair's help is offered to the partisan fighting the soldier on the basis of an enemy's enemy being a friend. Bair warms to the partisans because they likewise show him familiar kindness: this is a human transaction which transcends the barriers of language. In contrast, an inhumane exchange is demanded by the representatives of an oppositional ideology, the occupying forces. Want of humanity is indicated in the unequal exchange of blood – the shedding of one white man's blood demands an inordinate forfeit, a reparation of enormous suffering on the part of the native population (in seizing their cattle, a livelihood is denied them). In the sonorised version the theme is amplified further: blood is discriminately valued in the discussion between the white doctor and nurse: 'a white man's blood for him?', queries the nurse attending to Bair, the wounded Mongolian trapper; 'He has to live', replies the doctor, referring to Bair, the prince of ancient lineage.

In spite of the overlaying of different typological strategies in *Storm over Asia*, these remain clearly organised and correctly prioritised. Class type is favoured over national type in the identification of characters' interests. A distinction is made between the British foot-soldiers and their commanding officers. Decking out the mess-hall with with flags and tassels in readiness for the treaty-signing, Ronald complains: 'What's all the fuss about?'; 'It's for that prince they nearly shot', says his fellow rustic. Osip Brik, Pudovkin's scenarist, says that the episode of Bair's execution is drawn out as a matter of dramatic necessity (critics said that it was drawn out too long).[20] It is intercut with the parallel action of the deciphering of the amulet fragment, such that the discovery of Bair's supposed identity and the moment of his supposed execution occur together.[21] However, the suspense is not used gratuitously, merely to tantalise the audience. The episode is crucial to Pudovkin's thematic purpose. Grudgingly, Ronald goes out to perform the command to execute Bair. He procrastinates, slowly putting on his jacket, then his coat, then turning up the coat collar. Another soldier hides behind a penny magazine: he wants no part in this affair either. Ronald dithers over selecting a rifle, then decides to take a pistol too. On the way, he makes a detour around the edge of a large puddle, which Bair splashes through the middle of regardless. He then finds further ploys to postpone the shooting, filling a pipe for himself. Then he laboriously tears off a strip of paper and rolls a cigarette for Bair from his own pouch. He moves to untie Bair's hands, so that he can smoke it. But this is no routine enactment of a prisoner's 'one last request': Bair serenely, graciously, declines to smoke, he is already resigned to his fate. Ronald is angered I would suggest, less by the rejection of a gift kindly intended than by Bair's dispassionate disengagement from the situation; in refusing to save himself, even momentarily, Bair equally denies Ronald a momentary stay of execution from the task he dreads to perform. Bair is not complicit in the act of vengeance. The refusal of the comradely offer of the cigarette, albeit benignly intended, tacitly witholds from Ronald any easing of his own conscience.

A similar distinction is made between the Mongolian priests and the tribesmen who call upon their services. While the tribesmen may be held to be the innocent victims of superstition, their fears are deviously preyed upon by the priest at the old man's bedside: 'the gods demand a great sacrifice', he says. As he sways with the incantation of the prayers, his eyes flash open at the mention of the valuable fur, suggesting that his mind is really occupied with more worldly concerns and that his religion is sham. Hughes is similarly not to be trusted: the trappers bite the coins he throws to them to test and value their metal. Mercantile, ecclesiastic and military concerns are shown to be in cahoots with one another in their exploitation and oppression of the Mongolians, in 'THE INTERESTS OF CAPITAL', reads a title.

In 1922, a decree had been passed through the Commissariat for Enlightenment requiring the screening of 'films of specific propaganda content' alongside the entertainment pictures, intended for amusement and income. Films 'from the life of peoples of all countries' were to include, it was suggested, such material as the colonial policy of England in India. *Pravda* praises Pudovkin's film for its searing portrayal of the whites, the traders and the occupying forces intent upon the exploitation of the territory.[22] It is significant that in a film of 1928 the opposition is identified with imperialism (however insidious), feudalism and the intervention of foreign capital. No claim is made on behalf of the foreign army for support during the Civil War for the restoration of Tsarism.[23] Equally, it is historically significant that the focus of *Storm over Asia* should be symbolically centred on Moscow, indeed the death of the partisan leader and the held silhouetted shot of the Kremlin against a blaze of light is a structurally pivotal point in the film. Furthermore, in Brik's original scenario this was splendidly reiterated at the end of the film, with Bair escaping on horseback and galloping over the Mongolian steppe, through rivers and over mountains; at last a mirage is viewed in the distance and as Bair draws nearer it is seen to be a town ... the radiant city of Moscow.[24] Marx had indicated that communist revolution would occur worldwide. Informed by the Soviet experience, and the absence of revolution elsewhere, Lenin's revisions to this proposition in the early 1920s (thereafter adopted by Stalin) suggested that Communism was immediately possible or necessary within this single state. Under these circumstances, I would suggest, the appeal of *Storm over Asia* to foreign audiences is less an urge towards universal uprising and more a summons for support for the only state in which a revolution had been magnificently achieved. It is also an answer to fears on the part of individual nationalities of aggressive russification.[25] There is an open invitation to honour Bair's talisman, 'Lenin ... Moscow ... go to the Russians, they are good and strong'. In spite of the reach of the film to represent the periphery of the union ('far flung on the outskirts...') the partisans' attention is centralised.

Films of the earlier 1920s tended to use static types to represent character, these sometimes adopted from visual forms suited to a broad and general and immediate address, for instance posters, chap-books and street festivals. The depiction of Kerensky in *October* and *The End of St. Petersburg* as vain and foppish, the darling of the bourgeoisie

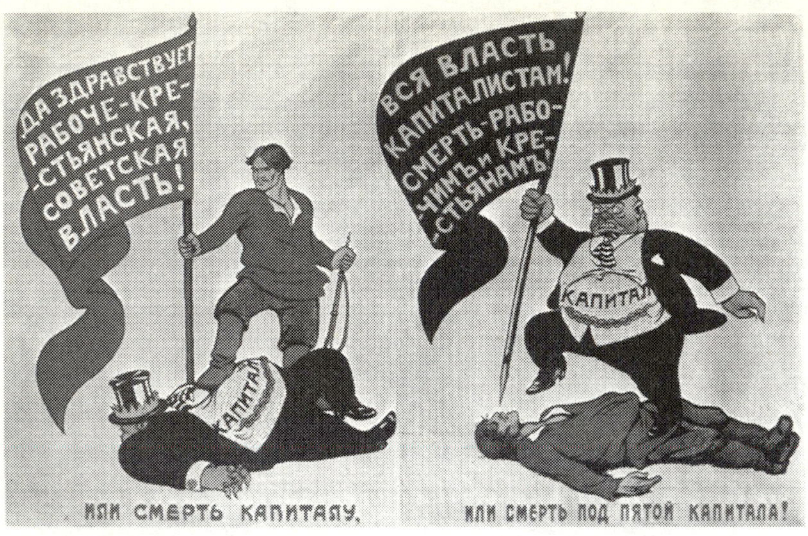

Deni poster, 1918

applauding him from the gallery, is predated by similar representations in Evreinov's *The Storming of the Winter Palace* [1920], the verses of Mayakovsky and elsewhere.[26] In November 1918, Meyerhold had staged Mayakovsky's spectatcular *Mystery Bouffe*, in which a world is divided into two camps, workers and non-workers. Mayakovsky did not depict more than a single interest in each camp, and the bourgeoisie was identified with tsarism. When the bourgeois opt for a republic it is of no effect for the workers: 'the republic is the same old tsar, just with a hundred mouths'.[27] Such types are specially clearly rendered in the puppet animations of Ptushko and Medvedkin and in Vertov's graphic animation *Soviet Toys* [Sovetskie igrushki 1924].[28] Trauberg identifies the hero, the ingénue, the coquette and the vamp as types identifiable in American cinema; *Sovetskii ekran* delineates a few standard comic types in Soviet film (including the alcoholic, the hooligan, the kulak, the bureaucrat and the female degenerate complete with powder puff).[29] In *The Mother* and *The End of St Petersburg* the lorgnette is a typical attribute of bourgeois women; in *The New Babylon* the capitalist is denoted by the typical attribute of a shiny top-hat. It adopts the atmosphere of a carnival by placing its principal figures close to the camera with a dancing, swirling throng as a backdrop. Trauberg and Kozintsev researched Daumier's caricatures for their presentation of the Paris commune and Pudovkin's portrayal in his film of a shop assistant seems to owe much to Zola's *Au bonheur des dames* (1883).[30]

However, while the oppositional types are flatly portrayed in poster fashion, meanwhile the character of the shop-girl at the centre of the story changes with the growing awareness of her responsibilities to her class. Once a timorous, set-upon creature, like Bair a political naif, she is later seen armed and mounting the barricade, like Daria, an active partisan. The bourgeois and aristocratic types serve merely as functionaries to the incidental articulation of this process. Indeed, their obligation to behave according to type, apparently oblivious and uncomprehending of the historic necessity which threatens to shatter their false security, is itself used as an object for satiric comment: they select a site for a fête-champêtre overlooking the city, affording a good prospect of the fire-works below; like the factory owner in *The Mother* and the gallery in *The End of St. Petersburg*, they are removed from the fray, decadently indulgent and blissfully ignorant of their impending extinction.

In *Storm over Asia* the opposition is similarly shown to be ignorant but here the commentary is, I would suggest, more subtle, more ironic than satiric and is effected within the enactment of the narrative rather than presumed in the audience's ready recognition of familiar types. The opposition, priestly and secular, is shown to be arrogant in its belief that it can manipulate Bair to its own ends. Although parallel cutting draws comparisons between the superficial gloss of both systems (the preening of the envoy and his consort; the dressing and polishing of the temple) the pomp and circumstance is equally undercut by the child-god, the medium of the protective deities (after all, really a child and less of a god) laughing at the expense of the British officer as he bows his shiny bald pate.[31] It is suggested that the proposed alliance of the priestly and secular interests is prompted by mutual self-interest rather than by understanding: the irony of a British officer pinning militaristic medals on the robes of pacifist Buddhist monks passes unacknowledged by either party. The society women are ignorant of the true majesty and power of the tribal inheritance borne by Bair (actual and imagined), insulting its dignity by passing comment on the ceremonial robes as though he were a figure merely affected to delight the eye. The sense of something at work more ponderous than broad satire is, I think, abetted by Bair's own sclerotic passivity. Whereas one feels encouraged to laugh spontaneously with

Bair at his ingenuous surprise in discovering Daria, one feels in the mounting tension that the later jokes are misplaced and at his expense.

Mythology and Ethnography

In the fuzzy mythology of the late twentieth century, Genghis Khan is surely a by-word in the West for absolute autocratic rule and ruthless barbarity. It seems worth indicating alternative representations which suggest that this is not an image universally nor historically consistently sustained. At different times and under different circumstances the image has been constructed otherwise. In the context of *Storm over Asia* how, one may ask, does the Tartar become yoked to a distinctively optimistic and celebratory Soviet view of the future? How did Bair the Mongolian figure for his audience in the new art described by Trotsky, 'incompatible with pessimism, with scepticism and with all other forms of spiritual collapse ... filled with a limitless creative faith ...'?[32]

In popular literature and song before the Revolution, says Jeffrey Brooks, the Tartars were unflatteringly presented as the most dangerous and terrible of peoples within the Empire, typically described in Suvorov's history of the Russian Empire: 'Out of the Asiatic steppe there surged into Russia the Tartars ... These people were terrible; they were ferocious in appearance and pitied no-one. Neither rivers nor mountains nor dark forests could stop them'.[33] The prevailing myth is attributed by Charles Halperin to the Westernising of Russia initiated by Peter the Great. This 'introduced European feelings of superiority into eighteenth century Russian historiography and racist and colonialist ideologies into nineteenth-century Rusian historical writings. Imperial Russian policy towards minorities at the turn of the twentieth century engendered rabid chauvinism'.[34] The suggestion that 'twas not ever thus and that a positive view of the Khans could be construed as the retrieval of a pre-Tsarist historiography is borne out by the account in Marco Polo's *The Travels*. This refers to the founder of the Mongolian Empire as the 'good Chingiz Khan', the first to hold lordship and to conquer half the world, 'a brave and prudent ruler', tolerant of all religions:

> Now it happened in the year of Christ's incarnation 1187 that the Tartars chose a king to reign over them whose name in their language was Chingiz Khan, a man of great ability and wisdom, a

> gifted orator and a brilliant soldier. After his election, all the Tartars in the world, dispersed as they were among various foreign countries, came to him and acknowledged his sovereignty. And he exercised it well and honourably, so that he was loved and honoured not as a lord but as a god ... The number of Tartars who rallied round him was past belief. When Chingiz Khan saw what a following he had, he equipped them with bows and their other customary weapons and embarked on a career of conquest. And I assure you that they conquered no less than eight provinces. And this was quite natural; for at that time the lands and provinces in these parts were either ruled by popular government or each had its own king and lord so that lacking mutual union they could not individually resist such a multitude. He did not harm the inhabitants or despoil them of their goods, but led them along with him to conquer other nations ... And those he had conquered, when they saw his good government and gracious bearing, asked nothing better than to join his following.[35]

Halperin suggests further that Mongolian rule exerted less impact on the Russian peasantry than on the aristocracy, pressed into slavery, he suggests that it was no worse than life under the warring princely factions who seized power after the disintegration of the empire. I should like to suggest that the film *Storm over Asia* engages with the revisionism of contemporaneous Eurasianist intellectuals, attempting to counter the prejudices of their Petrine precursors.[36] Dmitri and Vladimir Shlapentokh say that the advocates of Eurasianism praised Genghis Khan as the founder of the great Eurasian empire, which, in their view, preceded Imperial Russia and the USSR. The great Khan was extolled for his opposition to the West and his antipathy towards individualism and the idea of private property.[37]

In *Storm over Asia* (*The Heir to Genghis Khan*), the potency of the myth is acknowledged both in the behaviour of characters in the film and in its address: the British generals believe that they will be able to secure suzerainty and legitimise their power over the people through the authority of the Khan's lineage, in the individual agency of the strapped and bound puppet over whom they hold mastery. Bair, however, is not so much a false Khan as the true avenger of his people. Similar exemplary figures were adopted by Mardzhanov's *Law and Duty* [Zakon i dolg,1927], which, based on Stefan Zweig's *Amok*, tells of attempted British colonial expansion in the Caucasus, by Tarich's *The Revolt in Kazan* [Bulat Batyr, 1928], which celebrates the martyrdom of a Tartar leader who aided peasants in their revolt against the Empress Catherine II, and Mikhin's *Abrek Zaur* (discussed by *Sovetskii ekran*). The final heroic frames of *Storm*, not in the original Brik scenario but praised by Montagu as 'a pictorial resolution of a metaphor', show Bair multiplied many times over, a veritable Mongolian horde charging across the steppes. The increasing turbulence of the elements, throughout the film, culminate in the final frames. Bair as a type representative of his people is shown as a 'world historical individual' equivalent in his seizure of the force of the moment to the Great Khan himself. *Storm* uses popular mythology to promote an anti-popularist historical type, Plekhanov's type of 'social man ... who makes history'.

The translation of a raping and pillaging brigand into a positive figure of the revolution is not without precedent and parallel in Soviet popular culture. Stenka Razin was similarly a rebel chief famous in folk-lore and song and familiar in 'lubok' illustrations. He was the subject of one of the most successful pre-Revolutionary films, the first (made by Romashkov in 1908), appeared in a ballet by Alexander Gorsky, a Kashensky verse-play and numerous mass spectacles staged in the years following the revolution.[38] According to Jay Leyda a scenario about Stenka Razin was prepared by no less a luminary than Maxim Gorky, intended for direction by Protazanov in 1927, and in 1938 Olga Preobrazhenskaia responded to 'The Historical Theme in Cinema' with the same subject.[39] Jeffrey Brooks gives examples from Russian 'byliny' of other bandits, heroes 'whose adventures conformed both to the peasants' long struggle for freedom and to a traditional view on man's helplessness before the forces of whimsical nature'. Popular serials told the stories of the bandits Churkin, Anton Krechet and Buslaevich.[40]

Equally, one might find mythical sources for Bair in the dual cults of Russian Tsardom: firstly, passively, as a passion bearer imitating the holy suffering of Christ; secondly, actively, as a warrior prince (a portent of Eisenstein's *Alexander Nevsky*).[41] Here again, Brooks remarks upon other instances of such a paradoxical conjunction: 'Bandits were also identified in apocalyptic dreams with the myth of the redeemer tsar who would regain his rightful place on the throne and bring justice and freedom'.[42] The assimilation of such superficially antithetical myths into Soviet narratives served to lend popular credence and authority. Lunacharsky, Commissar for Enlightenment, seemingly sanctioned such opportunistc translations of Christian imagery in his *Religion and Socialism* (1908). Similarly, *The Mother*, both the Pudovkin film and the Gorky original, adopt Maryon myths from Russian folk belief (the mother who lays down her life), just as certainly as Christianity had borrowed from preceding pagan rituals and practices;[43] Vertov's *Soviet Toys* pictures the Red Army as a Madonna in Misericorda.

Both Valeri Inkizhinov (who plays Bair) and his father (who plays the father of Bair) have faces in which their ethnic origins are readily recognisable.[44] Indeed, Golovnia says that they were members of a tribe neighbouring the Buriat territory in which the filming took place: 'the land of his father and his father's fathers', reads a subtitle. Their features represent an appreciable mean value; they are cast for verisimilitude, but the plastic value of their distinguishing features (broad forehead, wide-set almond eyes, high cheekbones) are enhanced and emphasised with make-up and lighting. In later life, the younger Inkizhinov was cast indiscriminately in a range of Asiatic roles. There is a tendency in literature also towards the assiduous and detailed description of typical ethnic physiognomy. A Ukrainian is numbered amongst Pavel's comrades in *The Mother*:

Valeri Inkhizhinov as Bair, the Mongolian trapper

> The stranger leisurely removed his short fur jacket ... His head was perfectly round and close-cropped, his face shaven except for a thin moustache, the ends of which pointed downward ... his eyes large, grey, transparent, protuberant ... In the entire angular, stooping figure, with its thin legs, there was something comical, yet winning. He was dressed in a blue shirt and dark loose trousers thrust into his boots.[45]

Before the Revolution, there had been photographic catalogues compiled of various ethnic types in the Empire and their respective habitats, some overtly decorative in intent (for instance, Bukhar's *Album of Views and Types of the Orenburg Region*, 1872) others more strictly scientific (for instance, Kostenkov's *The Kalmuck Steppe and its Inhabitants*, 1860).[46] In the fine and applied arts, at the turn of the century, there was a fashion for the itemising of various regional differences in physiognomy and costume. The sculptor Konenkov made a series of ceramic portraits of the Russian people (now in the Tretiakov Gallery); Kamensky in 1907-8 modelled ceramic figures, amongst them a Buriat woman (now in the Moscow Museum of Decorative and Applied Art). However, this sort of appropriate casting according to ethnic type, as practicised by Pudovkin in *Storm over Asia*, should not be confused with the term 'typage' as used by Eisenstein, even though Eisenstein himself has contributed to the confusion by using the term variously on different occasions and has since been subjected to further re-interpretations. Eisenstein was aware of the distinction and duly commented on Pudovkin's idiosyncratic casting of Inkizhinov:

> Pudovkin works with actors: that is one point on which our views differ. He is doing something very interesting: he is looking for something between a professional actor and the people that I use in my films. He takes an actor like Inkizhinov and uses him once as if he were not an actor. He lets him play a role that corresponds to his temperament and his natural calling. He is thus at the same time an actor and a real person: but such coincidences are rare and that is why Pudovkin almost always uses each actor in only one film.[47]

The question of typage, variously understood, as that of the actor versus the non-actor, was commonly and vigorously debated in the film journals.[48] Jay Leyda's note to 'Form and Content: Practice' says that 'typage, as a term and as a method, might be defined as "type-casting" of non-actors'.[49] Such a practice had an ancient pedigree in the theatre for the casting of rustic or secondary characters according to facial physiognomy: in this tradition, Pudovkin and his assistant, Doller, cast non-professionals to play the prison guard and the 'babushki' mourning the death of Vlasov in *The Mother*. Such casting presumes upon a received notion of propriety, an abstracted average type to which a living human being is found to correspond naturally as closely as possible. This is casting for a socially amenable plausible representation of everyday life. Whilst Pudovkin held with this requirement for surface realism, he found that non-actors did not generally suit his working method: contrary to the citations in some editions of Pudovkin's writings, Inkhizhinov, like most of his performers, was a professional, previously for eight years a tutor in biomechanics in Meyerhold's workshop.[50] (see chapter one, above) In *Sovetskoe ekran*, Inkizhinov speaks of the rigorous training undertaken for the film, of the need to cast off the 'Russian pedestrian intellectual' and to rediscover his Mongolian self: stripped to the waist, he proudly displays his sportsman's physique, the result of much running, jumping and climbing and (under the instruction of a cavalry officer) riding confidently without stirrups, as if born 'in the saddle of the steppes'.[51]

Even the prison guard in *The Mother* presented problems. Pudovkin's account is reminiscent of the difficulties of working with children and animals for *The Mechanics of the Brain*. He also found that actors in conjunction with non-actors did not produce a satisfactory effect on film:

> ... as soon as I began to work with non-actors I immediately discovered that they are faced with a number of difficulties which threaten to destroy the precious truth of their behaviour. The unusual surroundings, the conventional demands made by the producer, the presence of the camera – all this puts off and creates a stiffness which they have to be helped to overcome. Here I discovered the decisive importance, in getting a man to behave unselfconsciously, of a simple physical task which completely absorbs his attention and thus frees him from stiffness. It is particularly important to make him believe in the reality of the task he is set ... I was taking a 'type' in the part of a soldier on guard at the cell where the meeting of

> mother and son takes place. Beside the soldier I set a plate with remains of food in which a black beetle was stuck. I had thought at first that the juxtaposition of the vacant face of the soldier, of Batalov behind the bars, and of the unfortunate black beetle hopelessly caught in the mess of porridge would give a certain symbolic emphasis to the general atmosphere of the scene. But the figure of the soldier taken simply as a symbol would not merge with the truth of the scene. In order to enliven the static figure of the sentry I suggested to the non-actor chosen for the part that he should push the black beetle into the porridge. He became extremely interested in this task and performed it very naturally. The result was most successful. Not only did the soldier come alive, but the very stupidity written on his face was transformed into action.[52]

Conversely, Baranovskaia says that the 'babushki' in *The Mother* were successful simply because they were required to do no more than be themselves, to sit 'vacant-faced'; the middling actresses from central casting whom Doller had auditioned initially tended to act too strenuously, wringing their hands and so forth, and quite stole the show.[53]

Eisenstein's method, in contrast, persuaded him that he could use non-actors in major roles, even to play the character of a real human being who had actually existed. He duly cast a non-actor who looked like Lenin to play the lead in *October* [1927]. Critical and popular opinion judged the performance a failure: 'I ... protest in every possible way', wrote Mayakovsky, 'against the portrayal of Lenin by various similar-looking Nikandrovs. It is disgusting to watch someone striking attitudes like Lenin's and making similar body movements when ... behind all this exterior, you can sense complete emptiness, a complete absence of thought ... Nikandrov is not like Lenin but like all the statues of him'.[54]

Eisenstein's notion of typage in 'Through Theatre to Cinema', 1934, also refers to a highly conventionalised theatrical tradition, but which equally employs audience expectations of a character instantly called forth by his or her appearance.[55] Such, for instance, were the seven stock types of Commedia dell'arte validated on stage by their reference to and interaction with one another. In the conventions of Commedia, the mask adopted by an actor at the outset pre-supposes and proscribes a particular range of actions.[56] In this these types are static. Eisenstein applies a similar set of conventional associations in the zoomorphic caricatures in *The Strike*: monkey, bulldog, fox, owl. Eisenstein makes no claim for a direct equivalence in the everyday. These figures are introduced 'to create first and foremost an impression, the subjective impression of an observer, not the objective co-ordination of sign and essence actually comprising character'.[57] Here, he casts for effect on his audience and not necessarily for empirical verisimilitude, he relies more on the immediate outward appearance than a process of performance and volunteers a distinction between type and character and personality.

Pudovkin observes that professional actors can function as stereotypical ciphers in their own right if they assume characters originating from elsewhere, not emerging 'organically' from the scenario:

> How is a 'star' made use of and made in the bourgeois world? If an actor has been accepted by the public in some film owing to his manner of acting, this latter being in most cases almost a trick, then the producing unit does all in its power to preserve, as carefully and rigidly as possible, all those properties in the actor that appealed to the public, and to adjust to them, by any makeshift, any material ... the 'star system' means no more than that the director presents the 'star' in his given discovered form, against some background dictated by his employers. An example of the kind is Adolphe Menjou, who acted brilliantly under Chaplin's direction. In a series of further, already desperately stupid films, mechanically preserving unchanged the appearance and general scheme of his behaviour, he has gradually become a less and less interesting empty doll.[58]

Being and becoming

Katerina Clark identifies the Marxist spontaneity/consciousness dichotomy as it is worked out in a number of Revolutionary novels.[59] Similarly, the apportioning of nature and nurture in the development of behaviour was a long-standing subject for debate in Russian science and literature. 'From the standpoint of reflexology', says Bekhterev, 'man is not only a living organism but a "bio-social being", acting in dependence not only on the natural but also on the social environment'.[60] Especially of concern was the determination of criminality in an individual's actions: Bekhterev continues:

> Let us remember . . . the unfortunate problem of absolute freedom of will, a doctrine which has led mankind into serious errors concerning the eradication of criminality . . . I have shown the complete dependency of the development of criminal actions on a totality of factors influencing the person at the moment of the crime as well as those which have influenced him earlier, even from birth, and lastly those which in their influence on the ancestors have determined the conditions of the conception of pre-natal life of that person.[61]

What could be attributed to malicious intent (which could be punished) and what to ignorance (which would benefit from instruction) and what to innate wickedness (for which one could but offer prayers)? Such, for instance, is the substance of Dostoevsky's *Crime and Punishment* and *Notes from the Underground*, also of Levin's dilemma in *Anna Karenina*. Dostoevsky stages such a 'set-piece' discussion between Porfiry, Raskolnikov and Razumikhin of the circumstances for culpability and describes the conclusions of the examining magistrate and the judges at Raskolnikov's subsequent trial.[62] In *Storm over Asia*, the temperament of Bair is I suggest, material to the course of events in the film. In *Sovetskii ekran*, soon after the release of *Storm*, Mikhail Devidov contributes to the then current debate about film heroes. He complains of heroes who are oppressed, suffering, humble about themselves and self-sacrificing: these may appeal, he says, to the high literary tastes of the intelligentsia. Devidov heralds the new heroism of Soviet cinema, conceived of revolutionary and creative optimism[63] (see chapter six, below).

Bair is the product of his tribal lineage and the natural environment which supports his tribe. The original silent version of *Storm* is considerably longer than the 1949 sonorised edition now commonly available in the West.[64] The opening sequences celebrate the shapes and atmosphere of the Baikal plains, the bare landscape, long, low horizons and rounded hills.[65] The trappers of the plains are shown laboriously trailing and stalking their prey, patiently waiting for the kill. All of this gives the film something of the quality of Flaherty's *Nanook*, released in Moscow in 1924. 'The mysterious barren lands – desolate, boulder-strewn, wind-swep, illimitable spaces which top the world', runs the film's first title. Of Nanook the Eskimo, Flaherty said:

> Here is a man who has less resources than any other man in the

> world. He lives in a desolation that no other . . . race could possibly survive. His life is a constant fight against starvation. Nothing grows; he must depend utterly on what he can kill; and all this against the most terrifying of tyrants . . . the bitter climate of the North, the bitterest climate in the world.[66]

Indeed, Nanook died on an unsuccessful expedition shortly after the film was made. Bair's peaceful resilience is a natural adaptive trait, borne of the material relationship of his people with their habitat. Tacitly an analogy is drawn between Bair as an historical type, like the boy in *St. Petersburg* and the Mother, shaped by significant events in which they participate actively, and Bair's character, as a product of temperamental disposition and experience. In Marxist terms, the conditions of production (Bair's life as a trapper) and contending productive forces (the sale of the fur, as the product of his labour) establish a basis for dramatic change.

There is propaganda value in this use of passive equilibrium and resignation. The character of Bair is constructed such that his type of temperament lends weight to the force effecting his awakening of conscience. In *The Deserter*, Pudovkin goes yet further, effecting a political conversion in the central typical figure[67] (see chapter six, below). On the one hand, in not resisting execution, Bair may be seen to be offering himself as a significant sacrifice. I tend to think that Bair's discounting of his individual self, his own self effacement, renders him less of an original hero in the popularist, Stenka Razin mould, and serves to make the later Bair all the more potent a figure. 'Men make history', says Plekhanov, arguing the case for the individual, 'and therefore the activities of individuals cannot help being important in history'.[68] Such a device is by no means peculiar to the ideological purposes of Soviet film in the 1920s, endeavouring to affirm and maintain the state through a founding mythology in the recent and distant past, but it does here carry particular political and historical force.

The evolution of the character of Bair is effected as much in reactions to him as in his own gradual arousal to rampant anger and indignation: Mr Hughes' floosie (the colonel's daughter) screams and quivers hysterically as Bair seizes the silver fox from her neck. Indeed, the spectators' sense of controlled rising tension renders the final explosive retaliation all the more forceful and emphatic. The camera is held on Bair, the anger intensifies as the condemned Mongolian calls to him: 'save me, my brother!'. An old man chews his lip in anticipation of an outburst when Hughes derisively throws down his pieces of silver for the fur: Bair looks down pensively, calmly, before decisively lashing out. Pudovkin is not, I contend, merely using the conspicuous expression in the reaction as an external sign juxtaposed with an inexpressive model (pace Kuleshov); Inkizhinov's taut reserve is significantly psychologised. The fish from the upset aquarium slither and squirm on the carpet around his bandaged head, as though the inner turmoil is forcibly restrained and bound. 'General historical circumstances are stronger than the strongest individuals', says Plekhanov. 'For a great man the general character of his epoch is "empirically given necessity" ':

> When the consciousness of my lack of free will presents itself to me only in the form of the complete subjective and objective impossibility of acting differently from the way I am acting and when ... my actions are to me most desirable of all other possible actions, then in my mind, necessity becomes identified with freedom and freedom with necessity; then I am unfree only in the sense that I cannot disturb this identity between freedom and necessity, I cannot oppose one to the other, cannot feel restrained of necessity – But such a lack of freedom is at the same time its fullest manifestation.[69]

'Concrete potentiality', says Lukács, 'is concerned with the dialectic between the individual's subjectivity and objective reality. The literary presentation of the latter thus implies a description of actual persons inhabiting a palpable, identifiable world. Only in the interaction of character and environment can the concrete potentiality of a particular individual be singled out from the 'bad infinity' of purely abstract potentialities and emerge as the determining potentiality of just this individual at just this phase of his development ... it is just the opposition between a man and his environment that determines the development of his personality'.[70] In *Storm over Asia*, not all the oppressed choose to seize the possibility for release; some of the Mongolians are shown serving the forces of reaction. Bair marks a particular coincidence of circumstance.

Storm over Asia's attachment to reality goes beyond its use of genuine locations, native actors and real events in the recent past, (the announcement in the intertitles of dates and known incidents). The source for Brik's screenplay in an actual anecdote is no more than fortuitous. Whereas Vertov finds it sufficient to screen real people from everyday experience, Eisenstein expediently uses the real features of these individuals as a fixed and given type. The evolving process of Bair's enlightenment during the course of the film imitates a concept of historical reality as process. *Storm* stands between the theory of the individual in Plekhanov and the development of the theme in Lukács. Bair is at once historic individual and dynamic stereotype. Bair marks a coincidence of concurrent scientific and historical reality, but is still made to embrace a truth at the core of a myth.

Notes

1 Charles Darwin, *The Origin of Species* [1865]; for a discussion of current thinking on taxonomy see Marc Ereshevsky, ed. *The Units of Evolution*, London 1992

2 Sheila Fitzpatrick, *Education and Social Mobility in the Soviet Union*, Cambridge 1979, p. 23; see also V. M. Bekhterev, *General Principles of Human Reflexology*, tr Murphy, London 1933, p. 206: 'In 1924 the Leningrad Congress of Psychoneurology passed a resolution to introduce instruction in the science of behaviour of animals and man, studied from an objective standpoint, and the fundamental content of this science must be the investigation of those internal (biological, physico-chemical) and external (physical and social) factors which determine the development of the human being and his behaviour'

3 G. V. Plekhanov, *The Role of the Individual in History* [1898], London 1940, pp. 58 and 60

4 for instance, the exhaustive study by Babitsky and Rimberg of heroes and villains in Soviet films arrives at an unremarkable conclusion: the majority of cinema goers (some with tickets subsidised by the Red Army) and the majority of screen heroes, are young and male: *The Soviet Film Industry*, New York 1955, pp. 230–233

5 Maxim Gorkii, *My Universities*, tr. R. Wilks, Harmondsworth 1979, p. 41

6 for a discussion of the new Bolshevik woman (leather belted coat and briefcase), as featured in Pudovkin's updated adaptation, and her male counterpart (leather jacket and Mauser) as seen at the end of *Mr West*, see Geoffrey Hosking, *A History of the Soviet Union*, London 1990, p. 86 and Richard Stites, *Russian Popular Culture*, Cambridge 1992

7 see Louis Fischer, *The Soviets in World Affairs* I, London 1930, p. 33 and Richard Stites, *Revolutionary Dreams*, Oxford 1989, p. 131; see also Hosking: *A History*, pp. 93–96, enumerating the variety of peoples in the empire

8 Judith Mayne, *Kino and the Woman Question*, Columbus 1989, p. 26; for her revised views of spectatorship, see Linda Williams, ed. *Viewing Positions*, New Brunswick 1995

9 Barbara Evans Clements, 'The Birth of the New Soviet Woman', Gleason, Kenez, Stites eds *Bolshevik Culture*, Bloomington 1985, p. 220: 'In 1920, 66,000 women were serving in the Red Army[2%]'; see also Beatrice Farnsworth's contribution to the same volume and Maya Turovskaya in Lynne Attwood, ed. *Red Women on the Silver Screen*, London 1993

10 Evans Clements: 'The Birth of the New Soviet Woman', p. 225

11 Jay Leyda, *Kino*, London 1960, p. 138, qu Huntley Carter

12 René Marchand and Pierre Weinstein, *Le Cinéma*, Paris 1927, pp. 64, 79 and 118

13 Brandon Taylor, *Art and Literature under the Bolsheviks* II, London 1992, p. 71

14 see *Sovetskii ekran* 31, 31 July 1928, p. 5: 'Kak rabotal Pudovkin s "akterami" buriatami i kitaitsami'

15 Sergei Iutkevich, interviewed by Luda and Jean Schnitzer, *Poudovkine*, Paris 1966, p. 159; see also Leonid Trauberg's criticisms of *Storm over Asia* in terms redolent of the 1928 Party Conference: 'Eksperiment, ponyatnyi millionam' from *Zhizn iskusstva* 1 January 1929, *FF*, p. 251; N. Osinskii, 'Potomok Chingis-khana', 14 November 1928: the review finishes by praising the film as a whole: 'On the release of *The End of St. Petersburg*, an American critic asked: what can be given to the Russian film industry, if at the outset it can produce such a film. Answer: it can already produce *The Heir to Genghis Khan* and is fully confident that it shall produce even better yet' ; *Buriato-Mongol skaia pravda,* 2 December 1928, repeats the *Izvestiia* review virtually verbatim

16 L. Rusanova, *Pudovkin*, Moscow 1939, p. 26; see also 'Opiat' krizis v kino', Nina Glagoleva ed., *Lunacharskii o kino*, Moscow 1963, p. 138

17 see Golovnia, *Svet v iskusstve operatora*, Moscow 1945 and Jean and Luda Schnitzer: *Cinema*, p. 146; for an appreciation of Golovnia's work see Fel'dman's review of the film in *Rabochaia Moskva*, 14 November 1928

18 Leon Trotskii, *Literature and Revolution* [1924], Michigan 1960, p. 230

19 Maxim Gorkii, *The Mother*, tr. Isadore Schneider, Secaucus 1977, p. 391

20 again, some of the stage business involving a puddle and puttees (Ronald after the supposed shooting) and boots and planks (officers crossing puddles) is cut from the 1948 version

21 Osip Brik, 'Theory and Practice of a Script Writer', *Screen* 15.3, 1974

22 Babitsky and Rimberg: *Soviet Film*, p. 272; S. Ermolinskii, 'Potomok Chingis-Khana', *Pravda*, 5 December 1928

23 the foreign powers were suspicious of and hostile to the Bolsheviks but did not care for Tsarism either; for a discussion of the various interests involved (and explanations as to why the depiction of British involvement caused political embarrassment on the home front) see Louis Fischer: *The Soviets*; Richard Luckett, *The White Generals*, London 1971, John Bradley, *Allied Intervention in Russia*, London 1968; John Swettenham, *Allied Inter-*

vention in Russia, London 1967; Arthur Ransome, *Six Weeks in Russia*, London 1919 and Richard H. Ullman, *Britain and the Russian Civil War*, Princeton 1968.

Screening of *Storm* was suppressed in Ontario and Australia, following a request from the Colonial Office: see Tom Dewe Mathews, *Censored*, London 1994, p. 85

Is the image of the British officer, silhouetted like a bronze statue against flames particularly tsarist, or rather a generalised symbol of imperialist autocracy before which Hughes, a mere merchant, is cowed?

I think the latter.

24 VGIK archive, nos. 695 and 1711 'Potomok Chingis-khana'; Viktor Shklovskii preferred Brik's scenario to the film as realised: see 'Beregites' muzyki', *Sovetskii ekran*, 1 January 1929, *FF* p. 252

25 the 1930s, of course, did see the extraordinary suppression of national culture and custom, not least in the Mongolian territories; foreign visitors such as the liberal Kurt London, commented on the standardisation, centralisation and russification of culture in these years: see *The Seven Soviet Arts*, London 1937

26 see Hosking, p. 43

27 James von Geldern, *Bolshevik Festivals*, London 1993, p. 67; see also Tolstoy, Bibikova, Cooke, *Street Art of the Revolution*, London 1984

28 Richard Taylor and Ian Christie, eds., *Inside the Film Factory*, London 1991, p. 166, an interview with Alexander Medvedkin: 'We used comedy, circus, lubok, farce ... We had all sorts of interesting scenes, like a lubok'; see also Jay Leyda, *Kino*, London 1960, p. 274

29 see Valentin Turkin, *Kino-akter*, Moscow 1929, p. 55; *Sovetskii ekran* 27, 3 July 1928, pp. 11–12

30 see Bernard Eisenschitz in *La Commune de Paris/Nouvelle Babylone*, Paris 1975, p. 124

31 see IM/BFI/SM item 4: notes to London Film Society 35th. season programme. 'The titling [in *Storm over Asia*] follows closely that of the Russian version; it is customary, in most title lists to identify the soldiers shown in British uniforms as Russian Whites (counter-revolutionary forces equipped with old uniforms); it is obvious, however, from the Russian titles in relation to the Colonel, referring to 'imperial necessity' etc. that the theme of the picture cannot credibly be interpreted in this sense'. Also see item 7a, reply to IM's query re films dealing with the Russian Revolution: minutes of exception issued by BBFC for *Storm*: 'We think that the conduct of the British troops wearing British uniforms is such as to make this film unsuitable for exhibition in this country'; 'this film was produced to satirise the exploitation of undeveloped peoples'

32 Leon Trotskii, *Literature and Revolution* [1924], Michigan 1960, p. 15

33 Suvorov, qu. Jeffrey Brooks, *When Russia Learned to Read*, Princeton 1985, p. 228

34 Charles J. Halperin, *Russia and the Golden Horde*, London 1987, p. vii

35 Marco Polo, *The Travels*, tr. Ronald Latham, Harmondsworth 1979, p. 93; see p. 97 for a description of the nomadic and pastoral life of the Mongols. Polo was in the service of Kubilai Khan in China and his account may not be impartial; he is also so hedged about with mythology himself that he may not be an entirely reliable source for quotation. The post-perestroika and glasnost revival of Genghis Khan is worth noting; for instance, the new monument in Delgerhann, Mongolia and the appeal of a millionaire Chess-champion to the ascendancy of the Khans as a means of promoting his political career; Genghis Khan is now officially regarded as a great strategist and unifying leader.

36 Halperin, pp. 104 and 107; see also his 'George Vernadsky, Eurasianism, the Mongols and Russia', *Slavic Review* 41.3 (1982)

37 Dmitri and Vladimir Shlapentokh, *Soviet Cinematography*, New York 1993, p. 93

38 see von Geldern, p. 77 and Richard Stites, *Russian Popular Culture*, pp. 31 and 57; also Alexander Dumas, *Adventures in Czarist Russia* [1858], London 1960, p. 174 and Phillip Longworth, 'The subversive legend of Sten'ka Razin' in Vittorio Strada, ed. *Russia*, Turin 1975, p. 22: 'The millenarian content of the legend is considerable. Razin is often represented as a messianic Christ-like figure, concerned for the people's welfare; and sometimes, like christ, he lives after death and is due to come again ... And legends speak repeatedly of his impending resurrection or immortality'.

39 Leyda, p. 349 and Ian Christie and Julian Graffy, *Protazanov*, London 1993, p. 77; for Pudovkin's verdict on the 1938 interpretation see 'Khoroshii fil'm, "Stepan Razin"', *SS* II, pp. 206–207

40 Brooks, p. 174

41 Michael Cherniavsky, *Tsar and People*, New York 1969, p. 18; for the reappearance of these figures in films of the '30s addressing Civil War themes, see Richard Taylor in *Inside the Film Factory*

42 Brooks, p. 177

43 Linda J. Ivanits, *Russian Folk Belief*, New York 1992, p. 21

44 Valeri Inkizhinov, 'Les Souvenirs d'Inkijinoff', *Cinéma* 167 (1972) p. 116, re his father being enormously helpful on location; for further comments on Inkizhinov as a 'pure-blooded' mongol, his background in bioMechanics, stunning physical prowess and so forth see N. Kaufman, 'Potomok Chingis khana', *Kino-gazeta* 9, 28 February 1928, p. 4

45 Gorkii, *The Mother*, pp. 21–22

46 Elena Barkhatova, 'Realism and Document', David Elliott, ed. *Photography in Russia*, London 1992; there were also cheaper versions of such pictures, more widely available: see Stites, *Russian Popular Culture*, p. 26: 'A postcard series called "Russian Types" offered images (often distorted) that helped people 'envision' social categories'. These would appear to provide the model for Kuleshov's wonderful 'Bolshevik Barbarities' in *Mr West*

47 Eisenstein, *Selected Works* I, ed. Richard Taylor, London 1988, p. 200

48 see, for instance, Konstantin Derzhavin's contribution 'Akter ili natursh-

chik' in *Art-ekran* (1923) 5, p. 4 and *Kino-front* 9 and 10 editorials written à la Punin

49 Sergei Eisenstein, *The Film Sense*, London 1968, p. 135

50 see, for instance, *Sight and Sound* XXII (1953), referring to 'Inkizhinov, who had never acted before, the trapper-king of "Storm over Asia"'

51 'Bair i ia', *Sovetskoe ekran* 33, 14 August 1928, pp. 8–9

52 Pudovkin, 'Stanislavsky's System in the Cinema', *Sight and Sound* XXII (1953), p. 118

53 Vera Baranovskaia, 'Akter dramy v kino', *Sovetskoe kino* 38, 21 September 1926, p. 4

54 Vladimir Maiakovskii, 'O kino', *FF*, p. 174; see also Esfir Shub, 'LEF i kino. Stenogramma soveshchaniia'

55 Sergei Eisenstein, *Film Form*, New York 1949, p. 8

56 see David George and Christopher Gossip, eds. *Studies in the Commedia dell arte*, Cardiff 1993

57 Eisenstein,'Film Form: New Problems', *Film Form*, p. 127

58 Pudovkin, 'Tvorcheskii kollektiv', *Akter v fil'me*, *SS* I, p. 235; in spite of the theoretical protestations of Pudovkin and others against the system, American stars enjoyed success with the avant-garde in the early '20s and with popular audiences (witness the 'mobbing' of Fairbanks and Pickford in 1924; thanks to Richard Taylor for drawing to my attention to Viktor Shklovskii's account of Pudovkin's meeting with the couple in *Eizenshtein*, Moscow 1973, pp. 134–135): journals frequently featured American personalities and were as interested in their lives both in and out of the studios (see, for instance, *Kino-zhurnal ARK*'s account of Pickford and Fairbanks, 4–5, 1925 and Asta Nielsen's account of her average day in *Sovetskii ekran* 17/18, 1926)

59 see Katerina Clark, *The Soviet Novel*, London 1985, p. 15

60 Vladimir Bekhterev, *General Principles of Reflexology* [1923], tr. E. and W. Murphy, London 1933, p. 33

61 Bekhterev, p. 63

62 Fedor Dostoevskii, *Crime and Punishment* [1866], tr. Magarshack, Harmondsworth 1951, pp. 272 and 544

63 Mikhail Devidov, 'Naschet geroev v kino i v literature', *Sovetskii ekran* 50, 11 December 1928, p. 7; Devidov is contributing to a debate which has been conducted over the previous few issues of the journal (see also *Sovetskii ekran* 47, Viktor Shklovskii, 'Sovetskaia shkola akterskoi igry'; 48 and 49)

64 Tatiana Zapasnik and Adi Petrovich, *Die Zeit in Grossaufnahme*, Berlin 1983, p. 624, give the 1928 version as 3092 metres, the 1949 as 2425 metres

65 Golovnia, 'Operatoraia rabota v nekotorykh fil'makh', *Svet v iskusstve operatora*

66 Arthur Calder-Marshall, *The Innocent Eye*, London 1963, p. 77; see also I. Erenburg, *Materializatsiia fantastiki*, Moscow 1927, p. 13

67 for a discussion of this as a standard device in political film-making see

Folke Isaksson and Leif Furhammar, *Politics and Film*, London 1971, and Jacques Ellul, *Propaganda*, New York, 1965

68 Plekhanov, p.23

69 Plekhanov, p. 16

70 Georg Lukács, *The Meaning of Contemporary Realism*, London 1962, p. 23

6. *A Simple Case* and *The Deserter*: the sound film and sound film acting

Sound in Pudovkin's Silent Films

Unlike Eisenstein, Pudovkin has little to say about the music which accompanied his own silent films, but the subject of appropriate scoring was frequently and variously discussed in the journals: Khristanf Khersonsky's 'Music in cinema' in *Kino-zhurnal ARK* 3 is concerned with the notion of melody, Sergei Budoslavsky's contribution to the same issue is highly technical; articles in *Kino* address the appropriate characterisation and suitable proportioning of music to film and a 1923 issue draws together the views of a number of professional commentators, including D. S. Blok and the conductor of the Goskino orchestra, M. Z. Basov. Evgeni Mandel's contribution to *Kino-zhurnal ARK* 9, 'Musical Illustration for Films', discusses the relative merits of written and improvised scores.[1] Blok, who became musical director at Goskino, composed a score in 1935 for *The Mother* and Shaporin's work on Pudovkin's first sound film, *The Deserter*, is mentioned in *The Actor in Film* and in 'Asynchronism as a Principle of Sound Film'. Sadly, in all of this, there is little precise information as to what exactly was played, nor does Pudovkin seem to have been sufficiently fussy or pedantic to specify a particular score for his own films. Marie Seton wrote to Ivor Montagu before the 1933 London screening of *A Simple Case*:

> I think Pudovkin has told you that he has no very definite ideas about it. The enclosed suggestions are his, they may give you some

ideas: middle of the second part from the first explosion in the civil war episode to the moment when the young soldier is dead, there must be *no* music; Pudovkin has not thought of any special music and he leaves the choice to [you]; first part (prologue): Bach; second part beginning and end must have an epic quality; third part: Beethoven.[2]

Golovnia is hardly forthcoming either:

...we always felt that films like *The Mother* and more particularly *The End of St. Petersburg* were perfectly understood by audiences, especially when they had a good musical accompaniment ... at that time special scores were written for important films and in the best cinemas they were always shown with their proper musical accompaniment ... for *The End of St. Petersburg* several musical phrases evoked immediate and very precise associations: in the scene of the patriotic demonstration the music played was a slightly distorted version of the national anthem: the two perceptions, visual and aural, were linked and mutually reinforcing.[3]

Golovnia suggests that the success of Pudovkin's films with audiences was due in part to the effective 'cuing' or 'signing' of the intended reaction by the music. Sovkino advocated that producers and composers work alongside one another 'while making the film and in particular for them to agree finally on the musical scenario when the picture is being put together'.[4] Shostakovich, an erstwhile cinema pianist himself, advocated that a composer should take no more than the theme from a film as an impetus to his own autonomous work. For *Sovetskii ekran*, Shostakovich comments upon other methods of working, such as using improvised scores which depend on the talents and inspiration of the musicians, scores which draw on familiar themes from Beethoven, Schubert and Schumann or, following the example of Tchaikovsky, interpret by means of such instrumental motifs as the trombone announcing royalty. He then describes how he set about composing the music for *The New Babylon* [1929]: 'Overall I was rarely guided by any principle obliging me to illustrate each picture. I proceeded from the essential form, from the main shot in one or other of a series of shots'. Kozintsev agreed: 'We had the same idea: not to illustrate shots but to give them new quality and scope; the music had to be composed against external events so as to show the inner sense of the action'.[5] As Kozintsev had turned to Zola and Daumier as a historical source for his starkly delineated caricatures of Paris in *The New Babylon*, Shostakovich turned to Offenbach's operettas and wrote a new orchestration of an old French song and of the Marseillaise. However, the orchestra and the audience proved resistant to their innovation. But Shostakovich's notion of producing a score as a counterpoint to the film was to become standard practice with sound films. 'Music must retain its own line', says Pudovkin, discussing the score for *The Deserter*. Sound can run counter to the content of a particular image and counter to the shape of the image track.

Eisenstein's 1928 'Statement on Sound' (to which Pudovkin and Alexandrov were signatories) was not opposed to the introduction to film of sound per se; rather it resisted the naturalistic constraints on the medium which the synchronisation of image with dialogue portended, 'the line of least resistance'.[6] Characteristically, Eisenstein argued the case by asserting that it was montage, the quintessence of cinema, that synchronisation placed under threat and that it was only in its potential for developing and advancing montage techniques that sound was to be welcomed:

> In the first place there will be commercial exploitations of the most saleable goods, i.e. of talking pictures: those in which the sound is recorded in a natural manner, synchronising exactly with the movement on the screen and creating a certain 'illusion' of people talking, objects making a noise, etc. The first period of sensations will not harm the development of the new art; the danger comes with the second period, accompanied by the loss of innocence and purity of the initial concept of cinema's new textural possibilities can only intensify its unimaginative use for 'dramas of high culture' and other photographed presentations of a theatrical order.
> Sound used in this way will destroy the culture of montage because every mere addition of sound to montage fragments increases their inertia as such and their independent significance; this is undoubtedly detrimental to montage which operates above all not with fragments but through the juxtaposition of fragments.
> Only the contrapuntal use of sound vis-à-vis the visual fragment of montage will open up new possibilities for the development and perfection of montage.[6]

Equally, Pudovkin had argued in *The Film Director and Film Material* that film acting applied its own peculiar selectivity towards 'indifferent nature', employing its own independent means, and that it was spurious to construe the absence of dialogue as a regrettable ommission. 'The idea that the film actor should express in gesture that which the ordinary man says in words is basically false. In creating the picture the director and actor use only those moments when the word is superfluous, when the substance of the action develops in silence, when the word may accompany the gesture, but does not give birth to it'.[7] For Pudovkin, acting for silent cinema is not a matter of restoring to a performance that of which it has of necessity been deprived, but rather of transposing the narrative from a constative to a performative plane, whereby the meaning of a gesture is its enactment. But, with the advent of sound, Pudovkin is characteristically less concerned with the preservation of artistic tenets inviolate, than with the capacity of sound to enhance an effect: 'The role which sound is to play in film is much more significant than a slavish imitation of naturalism; ... the first function of sound is to augment the potential expressiveness of the film's content'.[8] In practice, both Pudovkin and Eisenstein were to work productively in sound, although Romm (possibly as an apology for the formal and political 'line of least resistance' pursued in the late films) says that Pudovkin had difficulties adapting to dialogue.[9] For *A Simple Case* he attempted his first experiments in the manipulation of sound perspective; in *The Deserter* these were realised in such moments as the slow trickling then close-up crashing of a chain on the ship's deck and the distorted whining of a palm-court orchestra. My point is, that the early sound films can be regarded as a continuation and development of Pudovkin's theoretical position rather than as a complete break.

Of images which constructed in the spectator a sense of sound accompaniment, Pudovkin praises Eisenstein for the figure of the accordion player in *The Strike*, sustaining the impression as the characters move off into the far distance with an elongated fanning shadow from the bellows.[10] The accordion underwrites a satirical edge to the action (as do the tavern players in *The Mother* and the mechanical organ in *The Living Corpse*), and provides an emphatic pace (brutally interrupted by Vlasov's attack on the bartender). Pudovkin praises also the stone lion sequence in *Potemkin*, rising to the unheard sound of the ship's salvo in the bay. 'It is not just, as Pudovkin says, that this effect can be ''reproduced'' in words with difficulty' remarks della Volpe, 'it is impossible to reproduce it or translate it into words or verbal ''values'' without entirely losing its filmic-visual artistry'.[11] Indeed, the addition of a sound accompaniment to the sequence sometimes marred rather than assisted its reception: at the first London screening with the Meisel score, the film projection speed was slowed to match the tempo of the music and, to the amusement of the audience, the lions lumbered rather than sprang to attention.[12] The dripping tap in *The Mother* regulates a different tempo in the spectator's perception: its slow monotony effects the dull thud of her grief. 'There is a law in psychology', says Pudovkin, 'that lays it down that if an emotion gives rise to a certain movement, by imitation of this movement the corresponding emotion can be called forth'.[13] Asked by a foreign reporter in 1929, how he would convey the same scene in sound, Pudovkin answered:

> If this were possible I would do it thus: the mother is sitting near the body and the audience hears clearly the sound of the water dripping in the wash basin; then comes the shot of the silent head of the dead man with the burning candle; and here one hears a subdued weeping.
>
> That is how I imagine to myself a film that sounds, and I must point out that such a film will remain international. Words and sounds heard ... could be rendered in any language.[14]

A Simple Case (Life is Very Good)

After criticisms of *Storm over Asia* and the damning in Russia of Otsep's *The Living Corpse*, sometimes for its 'regression' to theatricality, elsewhere for its indulgence of bourgeois sensibilities, Pudovkin entered what Karaganov terms 'a difficult period'. More generally, the March 1928 Party Cinema Conference marked a shift in the terms in which films were evaluated and discussed. Henceforth, the official requirement that films contain the 'correct criteria of socio-political content' and be 'intelligible to the millions' [na formu poniatnuiu millionam] is routinely invoked against work which is judged and found formally and artistically wanting.[15]

Alexander Rzheshevsky's scenario for *Life is Very Good* [Ochen' khorosho zhivetsia], based on a short story by Mikhail Koltsov, was submitted for approval in September 1928 and in November 1928 *Sovetskii ekran* reports that work has begun.[16] For much of 1929 Pudovkin was abroad, partly in Germany for *The Living Corpse.* The filming of *Life is Very Good* was not completed until late 1930 and Pudovkin was required to account for the delay. He answers that the period of preparatory work on the written scenario was long and that the shooting schedule (103 days in total) was perforce interrupted by bad weather: in one whole month, he says, they could work for only four days.[17] In December 1930 the film was released, but to such a hostile reception that it was withdrawn after only two days. The official evaluation was scathing. The film, it was said, was poorly co-ordinated and assembled: 'With the exception of the prologue and the final manoeuvres of the Red Army, nothing much in particular seems to happen in this film. This misarrangement of the theme is fundamentally the fault of the scenario':

> The second failing, also arising from the cinematographic inadequacy of the scenario, is the abundance of literary, wearisome and boring dialogue delivered by the hero, who either sits in a room or roams aimlessly around the streets of Moscow.
>
> The third shortcoming of which we find the scenarist and the director culpable, is the patent deviation towards an already condemned psychologism, especially dismal and theatrical, verging on naturalism. In respect of silent cinema, this is undoubtedly a reactionary phenomenon.
>
> The fundamental and principal defect of the film consists in the absence of a topical subject, expressing actual life, to excite and appeal to today's mass audience ... To put it another way, basically the case in question appears unaware of the Party Conference directive towards 'a form intelligible to the millions'.

The character of the commander, Langovoi, is criticised for his preoccupation with his relationship with Mashenka. 'It is hard to imagine a more distressing result for the picture of a great master, such as Pudovkin'. But, deserving of a favourable mention, was the performance of the actress in the role of Mashenka (played by the VGIK student, Rogulina) the warm portrayal of comradeship and the splendid photography of locations and of numerous details. The report continues to accuse the film's authors of spending their budget on a

Mashenka

film for an extremely limited public, something which was to be considered entirely inadmissable. A number of harsh comments from working class viewers are then listed, such as 'I didn't understand a single thing'; 'The picture does not appeal to the working class viewer'.[18]

After these searing attacks, Pudovkin endeavoured to re-edit the film, supplementing it with out-takes and new material. Pudovkin was under pressure to complete the film fast, such that it could be marketed abroad.[19] By 1931, he had started work on *The Deserter*. *Kino* complained that Pudovkin had already made and re-made *Life is Very Good* to no good purpose. After such vast expenditure of time and funds, Mezhrabpom-Film, although pleading compliance with Pudovkin's wishes, should, says *Kino*, be required to release the film immediately. Furthermore, it is said, Pudovkin should heed the comments of the worker critics of the film, in order that his forthcoming production be of 'a high ideological standard'.[20]

Viktor Shklovsky had commented upon the deficiencies of Rzheshevsky's scenario as early as 1929, comparing it unfavourably with the previous collaborations with Zarkhi.[21] In April 1932 he submitted a list of amendments for Pudovkin's attention, to add to the seven pages of detailed corrections supplied following his official interview.[22] In December, the film was re-released under the new title *A Simple Case*, but, again, the reviews were unfavourable. Fevralsky, writing for the Red Army paper, *Krasnaia zvezda*, praises the cinematography and the actors' performances but says that it is all the more to be lamented that such achievements cannot disguise the film's basic flaws. Again, the reviewer routinely cites Pudovkin's past credentials as a measure of his failure. Liadov, in the Moscow evening paper, *Vecherniaia Moskva*, says that individual frames are beautifully composed but that the film is not well constructed as a whole and that it fails to convey 'the pathos of the epoch of socialist reconstruction':

> Another misfortune for Pudovkin: a regrettable choice of scenario. The scenario's author and the author of the production speak in different languages. The lyricism and romantic psychologism of Rzheshevsky is apparently totally alien to the director of the monumental epics, *The End of St. Petersburg* and *The Heir to Genghis Khan*.
> Reaching for an historical-literary analogy, it is as if Stendhal suddenly began to write in the manner of Châteaubriand . . .
> We shall look forward to some new success, which will completely compensate for the time wasted on such a hopeless enterprise.[23]

A Simple Case (Life is Very Good) is an odd film scarred by its original flaws and forced revisions. For Pudovkin it marked a radical move away from the 'hard skeletal' structure with which he had worked hitherto with Zarkhi and Doller, in favour of an emotional, symbolic scenario. Meanwhile, Zarkhi returned to the theatre.[24] On theother hand, there is much in the imagery which is familiar from previous films although here (as critics were quick to point out)the 'poetic' elements were frequently poorly integrated with thesubject. For instance, the opening of the film recalls the depiction of the Volga landscape at the beginning of *The End of St. Petersburg*: a man stands with his back to camera in a field, the furrows running diagonally top left to bottom right of frame, with his shadow caststrongly right to left; there is a close-up of the man's hand turning slowly then of the man in profile. 'A common story of the civil war . . . five years of hard living and of struggle . . .'. His slow walk across frame is cut against a woman running through woods, the shadows of the trees casting swiftly

The hero returns to his first wife

changing patterns on her face, the woman then shown in the distance on a long winding path, rushing to greet the man.

Often *A Simple Case* uses overlays, as in *The Mother* and in *The Living Corpse*, sometimes combining image with text, so that visual continuity and flow is not disrupted, sometimes using the sizing and setting of type as a visual element. There is an abundance of imagery drawn from nature, reminiscent of Pudovkin's own *Storm over Asia* and of Dovzhenko's *Earth* [Zemlia, 1930]:[25] rocks are split asunder, waters are turbulent and fruit shrivels ... but then life renews itself, the ground erupts into life and the fruit swells. Pudovkin uses a sequence of iron lattices and grilles moving horizontally across screen to show the train carrying Mashenka speeding away (akin to the vertical ascent of the lift shaft in *The End of St. Petersburg*).

A Simple Case (Life is Very Good) is also of interest technically, for Pudovkin's development of his notion of 'Close-Ups in Time'. In his essay of this title of 1931, he describes this as a means of guiding the attention of the spectator to a particular purpose, akin to shifts in the size of object in the frame, or to masking of areas of the frame:

> When the director shoots a scene, he changes the position of the camera, now approaching it to the actor, now taking it farther away from him, according to the subject of his concentration of the spectator's attention – either some general movements or else some particularity, perhaps the features of an individual. This is the way he controls the spatial construction of the scene. Why should he not do precisely the same with the temporal? Why should not a given detail be momentarily emphasisedd by retarding it on the screen, and rendering it by this means particularly outstanding and unprecedently clear?
> A short-length shot in 'slow-motion' can be placed between two longer normal-speeded shots, concentrating the attention of the spectator at the desired point for a moment. 'Slow-motion' in editing is not a distortion of an actual process. It is a portrayal more profound and precise, a conscious guidance of the attention of the spectator.[26]

In *Storm over Asia*, the withdrawal of the Mongol, the gathering of his strength before he strikes the white man, is fast-cranked and decelerated for the viewer, the blow itself appears accelerated in force within the context of the sequence; the movement is performed whole, partially mechanically intensified thereafter. In *The End of St. Petersburg*, clouds speed over the city, heightening the pace towards its downfall. Before the train leaves in *A Simple Case*, there is a shot of legs, rushing along the pavement: one pedestrian is sent skidding. After the sequence of lattices and grilles there is an intertitle, 'Three minutes ago...' and feet are shown in mid-shot, rushing down a flight of steps. Then there is another title, '...the long-distance train moves away' (and the same shot is repeated, slowed-down) then '...through Kiev, Kazatin, Zhmerinku' (and the shot of feet is shown again, even slower). Similarly, Pudovkin uses a repetition of shots (possibly under the influence of *October*) to indicate Fedia's trepidation as he arrives at the woman's apartment: he fears that his friend and comrade at arms, Pavel Langovoi, has accepted her invitation and betrayed Mashenka. Fedia knocks on the door and the door is shown swinging open three times, delaying what Fedia and the viewer sees. He looks severely around the room and is told that Pavel has gone. The door quickly swings tight shut. But Pavel comes out of another room and sees Fedia leaving.

For Iezuitov, this was a period for Pudovkin of 'experiment and diversion'. He says that Pudovkin initially intended to make *A Simple Case (Life is Very Good)* as a sound film, putting into practice his theory of asynchronisation, outlined in the 1929 *Kino i kul tura* article 'On the Principle of Sound in Film' and developed further in 1934 in 'Asynchronisation as a Principle of Sound Film'.[27] The plan was not realised, but Iezuitov describes certain sequences in detail:

> Here is how he hoped to construct the scene in which Langovoi and Mashenka say goodbye, before the departure of the heroine to the countryside. In the frame: the motionless train, standing at the platform. Mashenka's face is visible in the carriage window. 'I want to tell you something', she says to Langovoi. At this moment there is the sound of a train moving and the accelerated chugging of its wheels, whereas the picture shows the train motionless as previously. 'What, then, what?', Langovoi asks, to the accompaniment of shifting carriages. 'I've forgotten'. And these words of Mashenka are barely audible in the midst of the feverish thundering of the wheels. The train on the soundtrack picks up speed and we hear the end of the sentence, '... you are taller than me...'. Then the sound of the moving train breaks in. And on the screen, with the separation of the couple Mashenka and Langovoi, the actual train leaves. In this scene the sound track ran ahead of the image. For what purpose? In order to create a greater strain in the scene of departure, in order to summon up disturbance and agitation in the viewer towards the fate of the heroine. From this we may draw the chief conclusion that, in combining sensations of time, time is not necessarily just as it is actually recorded but that we may feel that it stretches to the final second, that we can pack into it the experience of months.[28]

The Deserter

Nor was *The Deserter* completed entirely as planned. A co-production between the German company Prometheus and Mezhrabpom-Film, it was originally intended to be made in a Russian and a German version: in practice, although the script for the latter survives, only the former was realised.[29] Other joint enterprises included Piscator's *The Fishermen s Revolt* [Aufstand der Fischer, 1934, but not shown in Germany until 1960]. However, the production was fraught with difficulties: Hanns Eisler, originally appointed as composer, received no information from Piscator and returned to Germany; the greater part of Erdman's script was rejected; Piscator proved a maverick and costs rose exponentially.[30] Pudovkin and others praised the film for its realism and for its pathos in the depiction of a revolutionary theme, defending it against criticisms in *Kino* and elsewhere.[31]

In spite of Pudovkin's hopes for *A Simple Case*, outlined by Iezuitov, Pudovkin describes *The Deserter* as his first sound film and it is discussed as such by his contemporaries. It represents Pudovkin's own thinking on sound perspective and asynchronisation but may also be compared (and sometimes contrasted) with Eisler's work with Brecht and Dudow on *Kuhle Wampe* [Germany, 1932] and Eisler's later formulation with Adorno of a theory of an appropriate Marxist practice in sound film: 'The rhythm of films', they comment, 'results from the structure and proportion of the the formal elements, as in musical compositions ... but this rhythmical structure of the motion picture is neither necessarily complementary nor parallel to its musical structure'; the soundtrack, says Pudovkin, 'should pursue its own line'.[32] When in *The Deserter* the German delegates leave Hamburg, a triumphant chorus links the soundtrack over black leader to their arrival at the May Day parade; as Renn travels by train back to Gemany, there are unlinked snatches of music which recall the life he has left.

After the obscurity of *A Simple Case*, *The Deserter* marked a return to a clear theme and a positive hero. Even so, reports Iezuitov, some commentators descended like hawks upon the film, seizing upon mere snatches of dialogue, and failed to apprehend the devlopment of the hero's actions through the events of the film, to appreciate the film as a coherent whole.[33] But it restored Pudovkin's reputation, with some critics, at least: 'Pudovkin reveals his mastery in this film', says the reviewer for *Vecherniaia Moskva*, 'to be precise, in the desertion of the hero he portrays not the private psychology of an individual but rather he consciously propagates a great socialist theme'.[34]

Pudovkin worked again with Golovnia and Kozlovsky, yet again with Ivan Chuvelev (from *The Mother* and *The End of St. Petersburg*) and Chistiakov (here as Fritz) and, for the first time, with the Moscow Art Theatre actor Boris Livanov as the docker Karl Renn.[35] Although Livanov had worked previously in silent cinema, his roles, even by his own account, had proved unremarkable and it was *The Deserter* which initiated his film career proper.[36] Renn is at first at best attached to the

Communist cause only half-heartedly, although the conditions of labour are shown to be hard: dockers queue at the gate for work and the infirm and the old (men over 40 and women over 25) are rejected, in favour of children as young as 13. Pudovkin plays a docker struggling to carry a tea-chest on-board. He collapses under the strain and his place is immediately taken by someone from the queue. When Grete tells Renn of the coming of the strike breakers to Hamburg, he is reluctant to rouse himself, then he arrives late at the strikers' meeting and listens to the leaders' speeches impatiently. He is dismissive of Fritz, the Communist leader. But he is nevertheless (or, rather, is strategically) chosen as a delegate to Moscow.

Here Renn encounters a set-piece demonstration of Soviet achievement (documented by Golovnia in May and November): a parade, shot from above, of floats, smiling marching Pioneers, soldiers, sailors and athletes. A formation fly-past completes the spectacle, accompanied by a triumphant chorus. A similar display serves as the grand finale to Alexandrov's *The Circus* [Tsirk, 1936]. As Eugene Lyons describes the experience from the ground in the mid '30s:

> ...the military display unrolled across the square, two and a half hours of men, horses, cannon, machinery, uniforms ... fifty abreast under clouds of red, singing, hurrahing ... this is the world's most unique parade [the only one] in which there are no spectators. Everybody marches ... in Red Square parades are the substance of history.[37]

Renn spends three months working in a diesel factory and discovers at first hand the dedication of Soviet workers. They set themselves the task of fulfilling in 36 days the supply of light to the metal plant, but in only 30 days of intensive work and 30 nights of constant vigil the task is accomplished. There is a long sequence conveying the final concentrated effort: finally the perfectly regular rhythm of the sound track indicates that all is well. Renn has become more calm and more earnest. He is duly elected to the Presidium and is met with a thunderous ovation (the children in the brigades clap so hard that their hands sting and they spit on their palms; when the best workers are named the Komsomol leader smiles in spite of himself).

When Renn returns to Germany, the city is as before, the same policeman in white gloves conducting traffic, still fawning to the bourgeoisie packed into their cars. But now Renn marches at the front of the crowd of strikers: 'Defend the USSR', reads a banner, 'the fatherland of workers throughout the world'. There is heroic music (cymbals and so forth) in spite of the strikers being shown blooded and beaten as they clash with the police, echoing but superseding the kettle drums which previously announced the arrival of the strike breakers. Similarly, in *Kuhle Wampe* the slum district is shown to accompanying music which is 'brisk, sharp', 'contrasted with the loose structure of the scenes, this acts as a shock deliberately aimed at arousing resistance rather than sentimental sympathy'.[38] The intention with the march in *The Deserter*, says Pudovkin, was to render 'the subjective attitude to be adopted by the spectator towards the content of the events in the image. Marxists know that in every defeat of the workers lies hidden a further step towards victory'. He and Shaporin decided to render the soundtrack in music only:

> The score was written, played and recorded for the whole of the sequence as a single-purposed unity, a workers' march tune with constantly running through it the note of stern and confident victory, firmly and uninterruptedly rising in strength from beginning to end...
>
> By the time the banner of the demonstration appears, the music has grown more and more definite, its significance is clear to the spectator, and it drags him into step with the workers' mass now firmly marching along the wide, suddenly emptied streets.
>
> The police hurl themselves at the demonstrators, the battle begins, but the brave music informed with the revolutionary spirit that moves the workers and links them to spectator continues to grow. The banner falls, but the music rises to a crescendo...

The banner is handed down the line to Grete. Like the Mother before her, she is finally knocked down by mounted policemen ... but the banner is still waving aloft:

> The demonstration is beaten, the hero perishes, but the music grows ... And suddenly, at the very last moment, the banner that blazes up above the crowd synchronises in the finale with a maximum strength of emotional intensity in a musical phrase crowning in one topmost flight of sound the whole sequence and the whole picture

> ... It has been clear to me that the arousal of spectators cannot be attributed to the component elements separately, such as the skilful editing of the image or the high quality of Shaporin's score. Ultimately, the crux of the matter is ... that the emotion derives from far deeper elements integrated as a result of the combination of the two lines – the objective representation of reality in the image and the revelation of the profound inner content of reality in the sound.[39]

For all that this was a new venture for Pudovkin, his first sound film, there is much which bears comparison with the work of the '20s. Indeed, says Iezuitov, writing in 1938, in the early years of sound the idea of montage still held sway, sometimes 'preventing on screen the representation of living, human characters' (a stock phrase, indeed, of Pudovkin's own *The Actor in Film*). The chief concern was to direct dialogue in such a way that it did not become merely theatrical.[40] Sometimes, he says, the audience experienced such a conflict between montage and performance as an impression of instability and uncertainty: in *The Deserter*, viewers only just managed to grasp a sense, from the tangle of montage, of the hero's aspirations and of his 'transparent reality'.

Just as *The End of St. Petersburg* and *Storm over Asia* began by establishing the environment of their characters, *The Deserter* opens with concrete images (aural and visual) of a commercial and industrial city. There is much which is familiar from the Big City films of, for instance, Kaufman, Vertov and Ruttmann: crowds, streets, trams, machines and the mechanisation of labour, the sounds of hammers and factory sirens (see chapter four, above). While the dockers queue for a day's work, an illuminated bill-board announces 'Miss Detroit has won the Beauty Contest'. A series of images is projected with increasing speed, eventually overlapping.

The Deserter shows the comedy and tragedy of capitalism under Social Democracy. There is the recurring image of a white-gloved flunkey, a finial on a pedestal, who conducts the traffic to the strains of a palm-court orchestra, a slow waltz with a heavy tuba bass line. There is a held shot of a waiter bowing (as if in perpetuity) to a man sleeping in a chair, who then wakes momentarily to place his order. But, at night, one man is beaten up by the police and another decides to end it all: he throws himself into the river and, in slow motion, is swallowed

A policeman conducting traffic

Fritz defies the tanks

up by the water. Tanks are sent in, even after the strikers have decided to return to work. As they flee (running left to right of frame) Fritz runs back to save his comrade, Strauss. Fritz, too, is shot down and the tank's gun barrel clicks up, smartly, as though the job is now done ... but the moaning of the wounded left lying in the street (like the agonising death in the trenches in *The End of St. Petersburg*) continues then continues.

Konstantin Stanislavsky and *The Actor in Film*

In 1934, Pudovkin published the series of lectures which he had given the previous year at the State Institute of Cinematography. In the 1920s, the subject of the actor in film had frequently appeared in books and journals, either as an aspect of film schooling or in its own right: one thinks, for instance, of Petrov's *What the Cinema Actor Needs to Know*, Turkin's *The Film Actor*, Derzhavin's 'The Actor or the Model?', Sokolov's 'The Education of the Film Actor' and Khersonsky's ' On dramatic techinique in the Role of the Actor', as well as Pudovkin's own 'Types instead of Actors' (1929) and his remarks in *The Film Director and Film Material* (1926). Theoretical questions about the mastery of acting in film, about the interrelation of theatre and film and the stage actor and the actor on screen, are, says Iezuitov in the introduction to *The Actor in Film*, of pressing concern, '... the problems of acting culture in cinematography are always vital'. Pudovkin's observations, he says, result directly from his own experiences with actors: 'It is especially opportune and useful now to set forth such practical propositions, when the call for the creation of living, real and heroic images in our own remarkable contemporary cinema of necessity coincides with the growing art of film acting'.[41]

By 1931, Pudovkin was renouncing publicly the earlier devotion to montage as obsessive and 'obsolete when considered in relation to the rapid growth of Soviet film technique'.[42] His acknowledgement of a preoccupation with formal issues, at the expense of character and plot development, appears to endorse the position adopted by Dinamov (and later Shumiatsky) and the leaders of the Central Committee who had condemned Eisenstein, Dovzhenko and Vertov for barren intellectual aestheticism. 'The overvaluation of montage', said Shumiatsky, chairman of the central Soviet film organisation from 1930, 'represents the primacy of form over content, the isolation of aesthetics from politics'.[43] In 1929 Pudovkin joined the Communist Party and in 1935 it was he, and not Eisenstein, who was decorated as the doyen of cinematography.[44] Judged by the self-proclaimed progressivist (but arguably romantic and utopian) agenda set by the 1920s avant-garde, does Pudovkin betray an artistic cause by his complicity with the regime? Conversely, can Pudovkin's espousal of Stanislavsky be deemed opportune and progressive, in as much as the holism of the System appears to render it amenable to work with speaking actors and sound, superseding techniques specific to or concomitant with silent film? The System presents itself as a useful tool for the actor and director faced with the exigencies of standard production procedure (shooting out of sequence, multiple takes); the emphasis under Shumiatsky on characterisation centred the director's attention upon the actor and required the skills of professionals.

Set against the agenda of the early 1920s, Pudovkin's espousal of Stanislavsky can be deemed regressive, in that it returns to a model derived from the theatre, that art from which the 'new' cinema most vehemently sought to distance itself and, more especially, from a form of theatre regarded as outmoded. 'All the younger generation and all the innovators were on our side then', recalls Eisenstein in 1927, 'including the Futurists Meyerhold and Mayakovsky: ranged in bitter opposition against us were Stanislavsky the traditionalist and Tairov the opportunist'.[45] In the mid 1920s, Stanislavsky was out of favour with avant-garde artists and often with the state authorities: his 1927 production of Beaumarchais' *The Marriage of Figaro* was slated for his equivocally empathetic handling of the Count Almaviva.[46] The innovators were equally disdainful of pre-revolutionary 'Film d'Art' cinema, for achieving nothing more than the mechanical recording of the 'art of the actor'. 'The film remained', says Pudovkin in *The Film Director and Film Material*, 'but living photography. Art did not enter into the work of him who made it'.[47]

The antipathy between cinema and theatre had been reinforced originally by common academic and critical hostility, and Stanislavsky's own denial of cinema's unique artistic status and scepticism as to the possibility of the cinema becoming anything other than ancillary to the legitimate stage. In 1912 he had written:

> Theatre and cinema belong to different spheres and things by which the theatre excites, attracts and charms us can never be provided by

> cinema ... Theatre lives by the exchange of spiritual energy which goes continually back and forth between audience and actor; that contact of feeling that can unite actor and audience ... That will never and can never occur in the cinema where the living actor is absent, where the flow of spiritual motions is effected by mechanical means.[48]

Meyerhold too had expressed resistance initially towards film.[49] However, Kuleshov, Pudovkin and the FEKS directors readily credited Foregger and more significantly Meyerhold and his pupil Eisenstein with innovative and experimental work from which cinema drew its own lessons or found complementary. Writing in 1934, on the occasion of Meyerhold's sixtieth birthday, Pudovkin says that he 'brought theatre just to the limit beyond which cinema immediately began'.[50] Kuleshov defers to the precedence of Eisenstein's episodic presentation of *Enough Simplicity*. . . .[51] Osip Brik, in his 1926 *Sovetskii ekran* article 'Cinema in the Theatre of Meyerhold' (illustrated with pictures of Igor Ilinsky as Arkashy in Ostrovsky's *The Forest*) says that the new theatre takes the theme and spirit of a play and not necessarily the entirety of the literary scenario; the play is conveyed by means of gesture, mime and intonation and is pieced together from separate episodes as is a film on the editing table.[52] In contrast, Pudovkin in *The Actor in Film* seems content to lift wholesale Stanislavsky's quotations in *My Life in Art* from the old stage masters Coquelin and Karatigin.[53] Pudovkin's advocacy of Stanislavsky cites his famous rehearsal of Turgenev's *A Month in the Country* under trees with Olga Knipper, experiments conducted in the Pushkino barn and the Moscow Art Studio before the Revolution and quotes from the System as it was taking shape in the 1920s rather than from Stanislavsky's subsequent retractions and revisions:

> Owing to the closeness of the public and cast [in 'The Loss of "The Hope" '] all exaggeration and gesture and intonation had to go and every half-tone and subtle nuance acquired extreme importance. The unusually intimate association between actor and spectator produced a feeling of particular sincerity and directness ... it revealed to Stanislavsky new possibilities of altering existing theatrical forms and transforming the stage performance into a more direct reflection of real life.[54]

The sensation of the audience in the cinema of proximity encouraged a similar tendency in the film actor, says Pudovkin.[55]

Ultimately, are the terms regressive and progressive useful towards an understanding of Pudovkin's work? Can the influence of Stanislavsky and Kuleshov upon Pudovkin be respectively, decisively thus represented or is this merely to repeat a prejudice rooted in an avant-garde hagiography? Is the tacit conflation of political and artistic credibility no more than a simplistic interpolation of Lenin's insistence on the necessity of the Party as the vanguard of the Revolution (see introduction, above)? Does the division between two camps presume as unbreachable the contesting claims of the various Soviet factions and deny the number of possible positions that could be (and were) held with equal sincerity? My contention here is that, while Pudovkin may align himself theoretically on different occasions with one faction or another, in practice he is something of a hybrid.

James Naremore, in *Acting in the Cinema*, consistently casts Pudovkin as Stanislavsky's 'most ardent disciple'.[56] Pudovkin maintains that the relationship was more one of convergence than conversion. Indeed, his claim that his position has been arived at gradually, through trial and error and reflection upon personal experience suggests a mode of development of which Stanislavsky himself would approve whole-heartedly. Pudovkin called upon his experience not only as a director but also as an actor (with Perestiani, Gardin, Kuleshov, Trauberg and Kozintsev and Otsep). In *Ivan the Terrible*, says Eisenstein, Pudovkin committed himself to his role so thoroughly that he made himself ill.[57] Inkizhinov says that, although a poor actor himself, Pudovkin worked by demonstration.[58] 'Refracting theory through the prism of experience', Stanislavsky and Pudovkin become similar in tone as much as in content.

Pudovkin retains his belief as to what constitutes the aims of art but apparently changes his mind about how this is to be best achieved. For Pudovkin, writing in 1926, 'the highest valuation of a work of art is the experience of a real emotion'. that is to say, it is to be evaluated according to its subjective effect.[59] Montage is recognised by Pudovkin as a powerful means towards this end: 'editing is not merely a method of linking separate scenes or pieces but is a method that controls the "psychological guidance" of the spectator'.[60] Pudovkin continues in the 1920s to acknowledge the observations of Kuleshov on specific functions fundamental to their art, but begins to regard that which had previously been uniquely celebrated as now deleterious to the aims of that art. Pudovkin acknowledges that montage can effectively create a fictive, purposeful geography or temporal unity (see chapter one, above) and acknowledges also that film montage allows the director to construct the appearance of an entirely new human being who does not exist in reality, by assembling a sum of parts shot in close-up (creative anatomy). It is these individual shots which confirm Kuleshov in his attachment to reality. Pudovkin acknowledges that the performance of an actor can be rendered effectively (in Kuleshov's terms, with speed and economy) by its differentiation into essential elements taken separately and by their subsequent selective re-integration:

> Between the natural event and its appearance on screen there is a marked difference. It is exactly this difference that makes the film an art. Guided by the director, the camera assumes the task of removing every superfluity and directing the attention of the spectator in such a way that he shall see only that which is significant and characteristic ... The will of the director transforms and subdues reality in order to assemble the work out of it.[61]

In 1929, speaking to a foreign audience, Pudovkin stresses that the exploration of montage is a course along which one might still usefully proceed.[62] However, in practice he had moved away from Kuleshov's example even if he had not yet wholly transferred his allegiance elsewhere.

By 1934 and the publication of *The Actor in Film*, Pudovkin is placing the unity of an actor's performance, the reality and integrity of the event, as a priority over efficiency. His respect for the 'whole and life-like image' requires that technical obstacles to the rendition of an actor's performance as a whole be as far as possible counteracted. Stanislavsky's method is advocated as a means of achieving unity and integrity of performance, of overcoming procedural interruptions which correspondingly threaten an impression of wholeness in the audience. Montage constitutes dismemberment of reality, Pudovkin adheres to the totality. In 1934, Pudovkin writes: 'The realism of a representation increases as its approach to the complexity of an actual object and as its deepening by detail, but at the same time it must portray the object as part of a whole'.[63] For Pudovkin, the actor acquires new significance and thereby priority as that unity through which emotion is at one and the same time conveyed and aroused. The actor becomes a figure of communion, of 'spiritual exchange'. Performance is accorded the creative prerogative in the realisation of the scenario, rather than editorial construction. Pudovkin criticises the earlier de-valuation of the actor to the status of a mere shot-sign:

> The actor became, so to say, shuffled, sorted out, used in effect, like an aeroplane, a motor car, or a tree. The director, in searching for the right methods of constructing a performance cinematographically, failed to understand that to get the fullest value in a performance, cinematographic or otherwise, by a living human being, that living person must not only not be eliminated in the process of shooting, not only preserved but revealed; and if not accomplished in a realistic manner, that is to say, not unified and alive, in the end the person in the film would be a great deal more lifeless than the aeroplane and the motor car (which, it has to be said, is precisely what did happen in the films of some directors).[64]

Pudovkin finds in cinema the fullest means of realising and validating the intentions of Stanislavsky. It is as though Stanislavsky had been frustrated and encumbered in his intentions rather than of his own volition had elected to not use cinema, not to see in it the potential recognised by Pudovkin. Pudovkin finds that the cinema close-up maximises empathy between performance and audience; montage eye-line matches, rather than being no more than a particular instance of editorial concinnity, achieve the psychological communion and intensity of Stanislavsky's ensemble on stage.

Pudovkin records that his reservations had been expressed, and his shift in position had been arrived at independently in practice, before they became codified in the later paean to Stanislavsky. Vera Baranovskaia remembered the trepidation with which she approached her work on *The Mother*, unaccustomed as she was to the procedures of its director (see chapter three, above). She identifies the difficulty in film acting of overcoming its practical exigencies, shooting a role in separate pieces and out of sequence, and says that the craft of the professional actor is that which enables him or her to master 'mosaic work'. Pudovkin in 1934 repeats her formulation:

> In the cinema, exactly as in the theatre, we immediately come right up against the problem posed by the discontinuity of the actor's

> work being in direct contradiction with his need for a continuous creative 'living into' [vzhivanie] and embodiment of the image played.[65]

In *The Path of Artistic Cinema*, Iezuitov maps a history which, in 1934, proves fortuitous for Pudovkin. The terms of the comparison with Eisenstein are simplistic but nevertheless favour Pudovkin (see chapter three, above):

> In those years, when the school of intellectual cinema was on the rise, the school of Pudovkin also firmly established itself. In relation to Eisenstein it adopted a distinct position. If Eisenstein renounced the subject, Pudovkin made subjective construction the fundamental principle of his craft. Eisenstein made films of mass action, Pudovkin of the activities of the hero. Eisenstein hardly ever resorted to the assistance of the actors, orientating himself towards typage, but Pudovkin could not conceive of a picture without the participation of actors. ..It was natural for Eisenstein to renounce the representation of the psychology of a person but with Pudovkin this was affirmed. The films of Eisenstein were therefore akin to to physiology whereas Pudovkin's films were more emotional. The difference between the two directors extends to technique. Eisenstein made use of montage as the basis of his work, that is to say, the collision of pictures. Pudovkin coupled them together. In resolving the problems of film language, Eisenstein preferred blatant metaphors, Pudovkin liked much more metaphors which were concealed ... The dispute between these two schools, the school of Eisenstein and the school of Pudovkin, was similar to that which pertained between the system of Meyerhold and that of Stanislavsky, between the literary art of Mayakovsky and, for instance, the art of Fadeev.[66]

The early writings of Kuleshov and Pudovkin can be said to be products of a scientistic 'Zeitgeist' (see chapter one and chapter two, above). 'Our exercises, our training', says Kuleshov, 'were conceived according to fundamental laws extracted from the analysis of the structure of film, the camera and the human mechanism of the actor'.[67] In such an atmosphere the writing of theoretical works was itself construed as a practical, productive activity engaged in by the artist as worker. In order to enhance his credibility, Pudovkin stakes a similar claim for Stanislavsky, forcing a comparison with the methods of Pavlov in physiology and of Michurin in biology:

> Before Stanislavsky ... the majority had been content either to depict personal emotions or to formulate general principles of a poetic rather than scientific character ... Stanislavsky's great merit lies in the fact that the results of his theatrical analysis, scrupulously verified by experiment, have produced a number of objective principles which can serve every actor and every producer as a basis for methodical work...[68]

Ironically, Pudovkin urges the case much further than Stanislavsky ever did on his own behalf: Stanislavsky's identification of the pressing need for a *grammar* governing the actor's work is reminiscent rather of the ambiance of a previous age. Unlike Meyerhold, he concerns himself with the actor rather than a systemitisation of the entire dramatic event or experience (for instance, Meyerhold's $N=A^1 + A^2$). Indeed, he often felt the dichotomy himself between himself in a role and himself as his own director. Equally, Stanislavsky is concerned that acting finds itself distinguished from music and painting in the absence of a codified technique, but is prompted more by a perceived lack in professional standing than by an endeavour to find some universal principle underpinning all the arts collectively. On his own behalf, Stanislavsky says in *My Life in Art*:

> In a series of variegated exercises I tried to develop ... the inner rhythm of that unseen energy which calls out movement and action ... These are purely practical methods and theses ... it would be a mistake to look in them for any scientific bases from which I feel myself to be very far.[69]

He is wont to stress that his initiation into the mysteries of his art has developed with profound introspection and soul-searching:

> The super-conscious is ruled by inspiration ... is that miracle without which there can be no true art and which is served by the conscious technique of the actor which I tried to establish ... My system does good only when it becomes second nature of the actor,

when he stops thinking of it consciously, when it begins to appear natural as of itself...'[70]

Stanislavsky's final legacy to Pudovkin rests in his almost lyrical exposition of the place of the film actor himself as a living breathing human being. For an audience the experience of watching a film should become, says Pudovkin in 1934, more like watching everyday, ordinary behaviour. 'the final object of the actor and his performance is to convey to the spectator a real person, or at least a person who could conceivably exist in reality'.[71] This is to say, that performance should be judged by its mimetic authenticity and credibility, in reference to something which resides outside the experience of the film. Pudovkin suggests also that the 'magic IF' of Stanislavsky is a means whereby the actor can counteract the ruptures imposed upon the unity and integrity of his performance by shooting out of sequence and by successive takes. Significantly enough, he never suggests a radical change in the procedures responsible for the disruption. However, by the time that Pudovkin writes *The Actor in Film*, it is as though the entire institution is to be reproached for its removal from another 'everyday' life. Pudovkin quotes the Diderot paradox. By the time that Pudovkin writes *The Actor in Film*, his theoretical concerns appear to have shifted from the act to the actor. When Pudovkin says that it is crucial that the director have a proper understanding of '...the living individual, a human being as a person, with his own profundity and complexity', he refers surely less to a role as an external given which the actor is required to characterise than to the actor himself.[72]

Notes

1 see 'Muzyka v kino', *Kino*, October–December 1923, p. 19; L. Sabaneev, 'Kino i muzyka', *Sovetskoe kino* 2–3, May–June 1925, pp. 29–32 and Vladimir Messman, 'Muzyka v kino', *Sovetskoe kino* 6–7, 1926; Khristanf Khersonskii, 'Muzyka v kino' and Sergei Budoslavskii, 'Metody postroeniia kino-muzykal'noi kompozitsii', *Kino-zhurnal ARK* 3, 1925 p. 17 and pp. 18–19; Evgenii Mandel, 'Muzykal'naia illiustratsiia k fil'me', *Kino-zhurnal* 9, 1925; see also Aleksandr Pergament, 'Kino i muzyka', *Art-ekran* 4, 1923, p. 5

2 IM/BFI/SM item 89; there is a quantity of correspondence in the archive indicating the size of orchestra which the Film Society employed, the length of rehearsal time and its (often disputed) fee ... but little information as to the scores

3 Jean and Luda Schnitzer, *Cinema in Revolution*, tr. D. Robinson, London 1974, p. 141; see also Eisenstein, *Selected Works* I, ed. Richard Taylor, London 1988, p. 188 re 'correction' of the religious dance sequence in *Storm over Asia* by its musical accompaniment

4 *Pages from the Life of Dmitri Shostakovich*, tr. Hobbs and Midgley, London 1981, p. 54

5 Dmitri Shostakovich, 'O muzyke k "Novomu Vavilonu"', *Sovetskii ekran* 12 March 1929, p. 5; compare Eisenstein's discussion of Prokofiev's score for *Alexander Nevsky* [Aleksandr Nevskii, 1938] in 'Vertical Montage', Richard Taylor, ed. *Selected Works* II, London 1991

6 'Budushchee zvukovoi fil'my. Zaiavka' *Sovetskii ekran* 32, 1928, *Zhizn iskusstva* 5 August 1928, tr. Taylor, *FF*

7 Pudovkin, 'Vyrazitel'noe dvizhenie', *Kinorezhisser i kinomaterial*, *SS* I, p. 121

8 Pudovkin, 'Asinkhronnost' kak printsip zvukovogo kino', *SS* I, p. 158

9 Jean and Luda Schnitzer, *Cinema in Revolution*, London 1974, p. 190

10 Pudovkin, 'Apparat zastavliaet zritelia videt' tak, kak etogo khochet rezhisser', *Kinorezhisser i kinomaterial*, *SS* I, p. 126

11 Pudovkin, 'Ekrannyi obraz', *Kinorezhisser i kinomaterial*, *SS* I, p. 110 and 'S. M. Eisenstein (ot "Potemkina" k "Oktiabriu")', *SS* II, p. 122; Galvano della Volpe, *Critique of Taste*, tr. M. Caesar, London 1978, p. 223

12 Eisenstein, 'The Music of Landscape', *Nonindifferent Nature*, tr. Herbert Marshall, Cambridge 1987, p. 314

13 Pudovkin, 'Priemy', *Kinostsenarii*, *SS* I, p. 71; he tacitly quotes William James, *Psychology*, London 1892, pp. 277–279

14 Pudovkin, 'Naturshchik vmesto aktera', *SS* I, p. 184

15 see *FF*, pp. 208–215; Aleksandr Karaganov, *Vsevolod Pudovkin*, Moscow 1973, p. 117 For an excellent discussion of the subsequent application of this directive under Boris Shumiatsky, see Richard Taylor in *Inside the Film Factory*, London 1991, pp. 193–216

16 VGIK Kabinet kinovedeniia 2955 and 5528; Pudovkin, 'O iazyke stsenariia', *Sovetskii ekran* 48, 27 November 1928 pp. 6–7; see also 'Nasha kartina' [1929], *SS* II, pp. 64–66

17 VGIK Kabinet kinovedeniia 695

18 Gosfil'mofond 759/2/1; see also 'Vystuplenie na obsuzhdenii fil'ma "Prostoi sluchai" na zarode "Manometr"', *SS* III, pp. 27–32

19 letter from Mezhrabpom – fil'm to Glavrepertkom, January 1931, Gosfil'mofond 759/2/1

21 see Viktor Shklovskii, 'Beregites' muzyki', *Sovetskii ekran* 1 January 1929 and 'Laboratoriia stsenariia', *Kino i zhizn*' 17, 1930 tr. Richard Taylor, *FF*, pp. 252 and 294; Valérie Posener says that Rzheshevskii's fate was finally sealed by the hullabaloo over Eisenstein's *Bezhin Meadow*: Valérie Posener and Aïcha Kherroubi, eds. *Le Studio Mejrabpom*, Paris 1996, p. 80

22 Gosfil'mofond 759/2/1, 23 April 1931; 'Prakticheskie predlozheniia po peredelki kartine "Ochen' khorosho zhivetsia"', 28 April 1931

23 VGIK Kabinet kinovedeniia 1711: A. Fevral'skii, 'Rasskaz o prostom

sluchae', *Krasnaia zvezda* 16 December 1932; N. Liadov, 'Sluchai s Pudovkinom', *Vecherniaia Moskva* 9 December 1932

24 RGALI 2003/1/84 'Pochemu ia pereshel iz kino v teatr' 1932; for Zarkhi's thoughts on the sound film scenario see RGALI 2003/1/82 'Rozhdenie zvukovogo fil'ma' and 'O teorii i praktike zvukovogo stsenariia' 1930; Iezuitov says that Pudovkin's 'classic' films should more properly understood as the joint work of Pudovkin and Zarkhi together: *Pudovkin*, Moscow 1937, p. 203

25 for Pudovkin's thoughts on *Zemlia* see 'Put' Dovzhenko – pravil'nyi put'' [1932] , *SS* II, p. 139

26 Pudovkin, *Film Technique*, tr. I. Montagu, New York 1949, pp. 148 and 153; see also 'Vremia krupnym planom', *Proletarskoe kino* 1, 1932, pp. 30–32. Pudovkin tacitly refers here to the explosion sequences in *A Simple Case.*

27 Pudovkin, 'K voprosu zvukovogo nachala v fil'me' and ' Asinkhronnost' kak printsip zvukovogo kino', *SS* I

28 Nikolai Iezuitov, *Pudovkin*, Moscow 1937, pp. 174–175

29 RGALI 2060/1/4: this script is incomplete but is of great interest for Pudovkin's annotated sketches of the camera plan and choreography for the mass scenes in the film

30 Oksana Bulgakova, 'Les rapports avec l'Allemagne' in Valérie Posener and Aïcha Kherroubi, eds. *Le studio Mejrabpom*, Paris 1996, p. 113

31 Pudovkin, Barnet, et. al., '*Aufstand der Fischer*' in Tatiana Zapasnik and Adi Petrovich, *Die Zeit in Grossaufnahme*, Berlin 1983, p. 560; for Osip Brik's criticism see *Kino*, 22 October 1934

32 Theodor Adorno and Hanns Eisler, *Composing for the Films* [1947], London 1994, p. 68

33 Nikolai Iezuitov, *Aktery MKhAT v kino*, Moscow 1938, p. 91; on the classic attributes of the positive hero, 'his dryness, hardness and freedom from sentimentality', see Rufus W. Mathewson *The Positive Hero in Russian Literature*, Stanford 1975

34 VGIK 429, 'Vplenu chastnogo sluchaia', *Vecherniaia Moskva*, 10 June 1933

35 for Golovnia's thoughts on embarking on work on the film see 'Okno v zhizn'', *Kino-Moskva*, 30 September 1932 and in *Svet v iskusstve operatora*, Moscow 1945

36 Nikolai Iezuitov, *Aktery MKhAT v kino*, Moscow 1938, p. 90

37 Eugene Lyons, *Modern Moscow*, London 1935, p. 212; see also Rosalind Sartori, 'Stalinism and Carnival: Organisation and Aesthetics of Political Holidays' in Hans Günther, ed. *The Culture of the Stalin Period*, London 1990

38 Theodor Adorno and Hanns Eisler, *Composing for the Films*, London 1994, p. 26

39 Pudovkin, 'Dvoinoi ritm zvuka i izobrazheniia', *Akter v fil me*, *SS* I, pp. 216–217 (where Pudovkin refers to Berlin although the shooting script, and Montagu's translation, locate the action in Hamburg); see also 'Problema ritma v moem pervom zvukovom fil'me', *SS* I, pp. 163–166 and 'Zvuk i obraz', *SS* II, p. 67; on Pudovkin's experiments with sound in *The*

Deserter, see also Ian Christie in *Inside the Film Factory*, London 1991, pp. 176–192 and Kristin Thompson, 'Early Sound Counterpoint', *Yale French Studies* 60, 1980, pp. 115–140

40 Nikolai Iezuitov, *Aktery MKhAT v kino*, p. 90

41 Pudovkin, *Akter v fil'me*, Leningrad 1934, pp. 5–6

42 Pudovkin, 'Scenario and Direction, *Experimental Cinema* 1.3, February 1931, p. 16

43 Richard Taylor, *Inside the Film Factory*, p. 196

44 Richard Taylor, *Film Propaganda*, London 1979, p. 91

45 Eisenstein, *Selected Works* I, ed. Richard Taylor, London 1988, p. 74

46 Jean Benedetti, *Stanislavski*, London 1988, p. 276

47 Pudovkin, 'Osobennosti kinomateriala', *Kinorezhisser i kinomaterial, SS*, p. 95

48 Stanislavskii, qu. Benedetti, *Stanislavski*, London 1988, p. 193

49 Edward Braun, *Meyerhold on Theatre*, London 1969, p. 134

50 Pudovkin, 'Meierkhol'd', *Sovetskoe iskusstvo* 6, 5 February 1934

51 Ronald Levaco, ed. *Kuleshov on Film*, Berkeley 1974, p. 164

52 Osip Brik, 'Kino v teatre Meierkhol'da', *Sovetskii ekran* 20, 18 May 1926, p. 6

53 Pudovkin, 'Realizm akterskogo obraza', *Akter v fil me, SS* I, p. 224; compare Konstantin Stanislavskii, *Moia zhizn v iskusstve* [1926], Moscow 1962, pp. 66–67

54 see Jean Benedetti, *Stanislavski*, London 1982, p. 63; Pudovkin, 'Rabota aktera v kino i "sistema" Stanislavskogo', *Izbrannye stat'i*, Moscow 1955, p. 207; *The Loss of 'The Hope'* was first performed in the studio in 1913

55 Pudovkin, *Akter v fil'me, SS* I, p. 220; for Eisenstein's memory of the studio on Skobolevskaia, see François Albera and Naum Kleiman, eds. *Eisenstein: le mouvement de l'art*, Paris 1986, p. 83; pictures of the studio survive in the MKhAT archive in Moscow

56 James Naremore, *Acting in the Cinema*, Berkeley 1988, pp. 39 and 72

57 Eisenstein, *Selected Works IV, Beyond the Star* ed. Richard Taylor, London 1995, p. 236

58 Valeri Inkizhinov, 'Les Souvenirs d'Inkijinoff', *Cinéma*, June 1972, p. 123

59 Pudovkin, 'Material kino', *Kinorezhisser i kinomaterial, SS* I, p. 100

60 Pudovkin, 'Montazh kak orudie vpechatleniia', *Kinostsenarii, SS* I, p. 72

61 Pudovkin, 'Metod kino', *Kinorezhisser i kinomaterial, SS* I, p. 98

62 Pudovkin, 'Naturshchik vmesto aktera', *SS* I,

63 Pudovkin, 'Realizm akterskogo obraza', *Akter v fil me, SS* I, p. 222

64 Pudovkin, 'Preryvnost' akterskoi raboty v kino', *Akter v fil me, SS* I, p. 195

65 Pudovkin, 'Preryvnost' akterskoi raboty v kino', *Akter v fil me, SS* I, p. 193

66 Nikolai Iezuitov, *Puti khudozhestvennogo fil'ma*, Moscow 1934, pp. 82 and 89

67 Ronald Levaco, ed. *Kuleshov on Film*, Berkeley 1974, p. 100

68 Pudovkin, 'Rabota aktera v kino i "sistema" Stanislavskogo', *Izbrannye stat i*, Moscow 1955, p. 210

69 Konstantin Stanislavskii, *My Life in Art*, tr. J. J. Robins, London 1948, pp. 561; see also Eisenstein, regretting that these exercises prove so

*un*systematic, comparing them unfavourably with the spiritual exercises of such 'mystics' as Loyola and Xavier

70 Konstantin Stanislavskii, *My Life in Art*, p. 483 and 528; see also Mikhail Bulgakov's satire on the method in action, in *Black Snow* [1965], London 1991, pp. 87 and 162: 'Tell Veshnyakova', Toropetzkaia read out, 'that I have solved the problem of the part of Xenia ... I was standing with Praskovia Fyodorovna on the bank of the Ganges and it came to me: the answer is that Veshnyakova should not enter through the big double doors centre stage, but from the side, near the piano. She shouldn't forget that she has recently lost her husband and in her state of mind nothing would induce her to come in by the centre doors. She should walk like a nun, looking down at the floor and holding a little bunch of marguerites: so appropriate for a widow...' 'God, how true! How profound!' cried Veshnyakova. It's true! Somehow I felt wrong coming through the big doors' ... Ivan Vasilievich, after fifty five years of work as a director, had invented his famous "method", universally regarded as a creation of genius, which prescribes how an actor should prepare himself to play a part. I don't doubt for a moment that the method really is a work of genius, but the practical application of it reduced me to despair'.

71 Pudovkin, 'Protivorechiia v rabote aktera', *Akter v fil'me, SS* I, p. 190

72 Pudovkin, 'Preryvnost' akterskoi raboty v kino', *Akter v fil'me, SS* I, p. 195

7. The Eisenstein/Pudovkin Controversy

Léon Moussinac, surveying the Soviet scene in situ in 1928, famously drew a comparison between Eisenstein and Pudovkin: 'A film by Eisenstein resembles a shout; a film by Pudovkin evokes a song'.[1] The intention here is to investigate any distinct principles underpinning their evident stylistic differences and their reputed 'feud'; to enquire whether Pudovkin's pronouncements on theoretical issues amount to an independent theoretical stance (see chapter one, above); to examine what was required of theories of film-making and film reception in the context of the scientistic climate in which their own writings were produced (see chapter two).

However, this task can be undertaken only with caution. To match the literary output of Eisenstein with that of Pudovkin is hardly to compare quantitatively like with like. In 1962, writing in the foreword to Nizhny's memoir, Ivor Montagu speaks of the available published work of Eisenstein as 'an iceberg-above-water fragment of the whole he left behind'; in 1993, confessing his own less than complete knowledge of Eisenstein's writings, David Bordwell refers to the entire oeuvre as 'a baggy monster'.[2] The six published volumes alone of the Selected Works (1964–1971) run to more than five hundred pages apiece. Against this, we have Pudovkin's 'basic primers' (*The Film Scenario [The Theory of the Scenario]* and *The Film Director and Film Material* and the later *The Actor in Film*) together with the various and sporadic articles and lectures concerned with these themes and with specific films, originally published in journals and some collected in the Russian anthologies. Even the best-known of these works are not necessarily (nor even intentionally) theoretically well-considered; much of this material is anecdotal. It seems worth repeating the suggestion, made in an earlier chapter, that this paucity is a measure of Pudovkin's reluctance to commit himself to paper, especially in a politically harsh and unpredictable climate. There is in Eisenstein a marked tendency, an impetus, an enthusiasm for theorising per se (even if the results are not always wholly satisfying as theory). Pudovkin seemed increasingly simply to lack the stomach for it. And all too readily he is prepared to consign the work of a film to the fate of its maker:

> Everything said here regarding simple methods of taking shots has certainly only information value. What particular method of shooting is to be used, only his own taste and his own finer feelings can tell the scenarist. Here are no rules; the field for new invention and combination is wide.[3]

Pudovkin and Eisenstein devoted themselves in the 1920s to the furtherance of the revolutionary cause. Pudovkin, before Eisenstein, became a member of the Communist Party and stood as a Party candidate.[4] They share the Marxist belief that experience may be rationally directed by means of theory, but both defend themselves against its fossilisation into dogma; indeed, the zeal which Eisenstein invests in his theoretical work actively resists such a fate. They dedicated their film-making talents to propagandistic and consciousness-raising subject matter (the work, Lenin said, of professional agitators) and sought, although by different means, to address a wide and popular audience; their writing, similarly, is directed towards utilitarian ends. 'The purpose of this study', says Pudovkin of *The Film Scenario*, 'is to communicate what is, it is true, a very elementary knowledge of the basic principles of directorial work'.[5] Both were concerned with the training of personnel to work in film and Eisenstein, especially, conceived plans for the better organisation of the industry as a whole.[6] Pudovkin, especially, is given to acknowledge how much the final product owes to to the collaborative nature of its making. Pudovkin wrote of the need to educate the public at large in film literacy, to make of the film spectator 'the ideal perspicuous observer' [ideal'nyi, ostreishii nabliodatel']. Eisenstein became aware, to his cost, that different audiences receive films differently. However, their engagement with less pragmatic theoretical issues was also recognised as a necessary contribution. Far from being regarded as an idle indulgence (idle speculation is a reprehensible bourgeois occupation, says Eisenstein) this constructive work was equally valued and valid:[7]

> Let us quote Engels' remarks ... on the question of the significance of theory in the social-democratic movement. Engels recognised not two forms of great struggle (political and economic), as is the fashion among us, but three, placing the theoretical struggle on a par with the first two.[8]

A polemical tone was adopted to fuel debate between various theoretical factions, sometimes against major foreign theoreticians (Pudovkin's *Kino-zhurnal ARK* article 'Fotogeniia' was written in response to Delluc; Eisenstein's 1926 'Béla Forgets the Scissors' was written in response to a lecture given by Béla Balázs), sometimes against compatriots. Eisenstein persistently introduced Pudovkin into the argument as the butt of criticism, both as a director and as presumed theoretician, in order to illustrate his own case more forcibly. He accused him, for instance, of using hackneyed images dependent upon verbal metaphors in Otsep's *The Living Corpse*, contributed to the hostile reception of *Storm over Asia* and, even in the late 1930s, can be found volunteering improvements to *The Mother*.[9] Certainly, there were genuine differences between them, but Pudovkin nevertheless admired Eisenstein enormously. In the 1920s he acknowledged that watching *The Battleship Potemkin* had been an inspiration and even in the late 1940s still proclaimed it to be one of the greatest silent films.[10] In turn, Eisenstein, in 1928, praised *The End of St. Petersburg* as 'the first epic from an individual psychological theme of the past ... A hit in every way'.[11]

Although Lenin's pronouncement sanctioned theory writing as a worthwhile endeavour, Pudovkin locates his own contribution within narrow limits. He accepts his place in the struggle as the given condition of his film-making activity but does not take issue with, nor interrogate the necessity of, this circumstance: nor does he establish this as a theoretical prerequisite for his own film writing. Whereas Eisenstein perpetually cites Marx, Plekhanov and Lenin (and, furthermore, the precursors in a materialist intellectual and scientific tradition in which Marxism was founded) there is in Pudovkin no evidence of a close familiarity with these sources. Indeed, even the term 'dialectic' is a license taken in the English translation, *Film Technique*, not present in the 1926 originals.[12] Eisenstein's citations seem to serve as an appeal to a readership equally erudite and politicised, aware of the skill with which the intellectual 'tour de force' has been accomplished; simultaneously their unimpeachability lends weight and support to his arguments. They contribute to the ranks of great names against which Eisenstein pits himself and to which he is intent upon proving himself a good match (as Jacques Aumont observes), if not their master.[13] In spite of the esteem in which Pudovkin was held as a practitioner he never seems to have sought to present himself as a philosopher or 'grand savant'. Pudovkin, referring in public somewhat scathingly to the 'galaxy' of star names with which an Eisenstein paper was littered, may well have been, with some justification, intimidated and overawed by the scope of the master's enterprise.[14] It may also be worth suggesting that, although not entirely exempt from official criticism himself, Pudovkin's more modest intellectual ambition rendered him of more immediate service as a Soviet cultural delegate under Stalin. Nevertheless, while Eisenstein, like Pudovkin, is keen to foster that area of practice which ultimately lies beyond the capacity of scientistic theorising or regulation, Pudovkin's romantic position was one which he was also prepared to defend politically: film production plans must be 'carried out by living people as a free development of creative individuality and not as the execution of an order or commission'.[15]

The writings of the early 1920s of Pudovkin and Eisenstein are based upon the observation of imported films and on reports of films which had yet to be released. Consistently they seek to distance themselves from any of the theatrical practices associated with the pre-revolutionary 'Film d'Art' movement. Pudovkin mentions films on which he served his apprenticeship with Vladimir Gardin (*Locksmith and Chancellor* and *Hammer and Sickle*), but he makes no significant claim that the work of this old-school director extended any great influence upon him and instead reserves public acknowledgement for Kuleshov (see chapter one, above). Eisenstein later contrived analyses of his own films to illustrate conscious devices and constructs. Sometimes this serves to give the impression that, in retrospect, Eisenstein was in the artistic vanguard of correct thinking. Eisenstein acknowledges the success of American stunt films with audiences and the supremacy of Chaplin. Pudovkin credited the Americans with the vitalisation of the camera: 'It acquired the faculty of movement on its own, and transformed itself from a spectator to an active observer. Henceforward the camera, controlled by the director, could not merely enable the spectator to see the object shot, but could induce him to apprehend it'.[16] Pudovkin similarly praises Chaplin, as much as director as performer. Pudovkin and Eisenstein draw their students' attention to popular American cinema (for instance *Tol able David*, *Daddy*, *Saturday Night* and *Woman of Paris*) even though Eisenstein, in particular, was dismissive of their romantic and politically incorrect content.[17] Eisenstein complains that Pudovkin is unduly attached to the example of Griffith; certainly Pudovkin finds in Griffith a combination of 'the inner dramatic content of the action and a masterly employment of external effort (dynamic tension)', certainly the breaking ice floes in *The Mother* owe something to *Way Down East*, but Pudovkin concedes that Griffith is far from infallible – only the last part of *Intolerance* is considered worthy, its 'ponderousness and tiredness effaced its effect for the most part'.[18] Eisenstein also accuses Pudovkin of continuing unthinkingly in the footsteps of his erstwhile teacher, although Pudovkin himself does not find Kuleshov's films entirely beyond reproach.[19] Eisenstein considered that it was not sufficient to progress by piecemeal adjustments in practice and criticises Pudovkin for failing to advance theoretically Kuleshov's concept of montage: by 1929, he says, 'thoroughly outmoded'.[20] It could be suggested that Pudovkin's primer contents itself with the codification of current practice, seeking to extract from it a number of cogent principles which it is assumed to contain. Pudovkin's project, it could be suggested, grounds itself conservatively in the normative acceptance of practical conventions; a film is, for instance, assumed to be a certain length, consisting of a given number of reels projected at a given speed (see chapter five, above). While never proscriptive ('Here are no rules; the field for new invention and combination is wide'), Pudovkin rarely risks a definite comprehensive hypothesis beyond the limits of individual experiments.

Both Pudovkin and Eisenstein defended film's artistic status. Pudovkin rejected Vertov's denunciation of film as art; Eisenstein accused him of making mischief in his manifestos against art.[21] Eisenstein and Pudovkin, along with Kuleshov, Timoshenko, Eikhenbaum and others, agreed that montage was the specific property by which film art was to be defined, governed and evaluated: 'editing is the basic creative force', says Pudovkin, at the opening of the German edition of *The Film Director and Film Material*, 'the foundation of film art'.[22] 'Because of its methodology, shot and montage are the basic elements of film ... To determine the essence of montage is to solve the problem of film as such', says Eisenstein , in 1929.[23] For both, art is inextricably bound to craft. But Eisenstein often judged the methods employed by Pudovkin and found his art somewhat wanting:

> What then characterises montage and, consequently, its embryo, the shot?
> Collision. Conflict between two neighbouring fragments. Conflict. Collision.
> Before me lies a crumpled yellowing sheet of paper.
> On it there is a mysterious note:
> 'Series-P' and 'Collision-E'.
> This is a material trace of the heated battle on the subject of montage between E (myself) and P (Pudovkin) six months ago.
> We have already got into a habit: at regular intervals he comes to see me late at night and, behind closed doors, we wrangle over matters of principle.
> So it is in this instance. A graduate of the Kuleshov school, he zealously defends the concept of montage as a series of fragments. In a chain. 'Bricks'.
> Bricks that expound an idea serially. I opposed him with my view of montage as a collision, my view that the collision of two factors gives rise to an idea.
> In my view a series is merely one possible particular case.
> Remember that physics is aware of an infinite number of combinations arising from the impact (collision) between spheres. Depending on whether they are elastic, non-elastic or a mixture of the two. Among these combinations is one where the collision is reduced to a uniform movement of both in the same direction.
> That corresponds to Pudovkin's view.
> Not long ago we had another discussion. Now he holds the view that I held then. In the meantime he has of course had the chance to familiarise himself with the set of lectures that I have given at the GTK since then.
> So, montage is conflict.[24]

It does not suit Eisenstein's purpose here to mention the number of possible exceptions in Pudovkin's practice from the stance in which Eisenstein represents him – for instance, where movement initiated in one shot is not continued into the next (during the prison escape in *The*

End of St. Petersburg) or where an image is ironically paired with a title (heralding the infant lama in *Storm over Asia*). This is to say, even before his feud with Eisenstein in 1929 and his supposed change of heart (supposed, this is, by 'E' and not confirmed explicitly by 'P'). Pudovkin's work is not entirely consistent nor commensurate. Significantly enough, Eisenstein does not re-examine the primers for contradictions in this stance nor does he identify past points of contact between Pudovkin and himself. For instance, although Eisenstein later retracts, both he and Pudovkin had used the analogy of a shot performing in sequence as a word serves in a sentence.[25]

Eisenstein's notion of montage as conflict applies to film a principle derived from and extensible elsewhere: Eisenstein thereby appropriates for his theoretical position a measure of ideological credibility and approval:

> In the realm of art this dialectical principle of the dynamic is embodied in
> CONFLICT
> as the essential basic principle of the existence of every work of art and every form.
> FOR ART IS ALWAYS CONFLICT:
> 1. because of its social mission
> 2. because of its nature
> 3. because of its methodology.[26]

Eisenstein considers conflict not only as a mode of construction between separate shots and the overall structure of a film but also as an antagonistic mode of address to the spectator: 'In our conception a work of art ... is first and foremost a tractor ploughing over the audience's psyche in a particular class context'.[27] One is reminded of Bukharin's declaration of intent with regard to the intelligentsia, 'ideologically conditioned in a definite way. Yes, we will put our stamp on intellectuals, we will work them over as in a factory'.[28] In 'The Montage of Film Attractions', Eisenstein advocates that the audience be subjected to 'a series of blows to the consciousness and emotions'. He here invokes Pavlov: 'The method of agitation through spectacle consists in the creation of a new chain of conditioned reflexes by associating selected phenomena with the unconditioned reflexes they produce'.[29] For Eisenstein, the ordering of images does not of necessity correspond to a logical exposition of a pre-ordained plot pre-existent in the director's imagination nor should it correspond to a latent expectation in the viewer.

By contrast, Pudovkin is altogether more mild and amenable, more temperate and conciliatory and foregoes the model offered by physiology. He speaks of the 'psychological guidance' of the spectator. Already in his account of the making of *The Mechanics of the Brain* Pudovkin presumes that the spectator's interest in a simple narrative or exposition will naturally follow a given course (natural, that is, in the sense of the observation of a comparable everyday event) and that it is to this potential, intentional view of an imaginary ideal observer that, as a rule of thumb, the editing plan should correspond.[30] For the most part, Pudovkin suggests, the director concedes to and complies with the presumed expectation and does not seek to disrupt it; montage is a means of easing its course by the elimination of superfluous detail and 'insignificances that fulfil only a transitional function':

> Imagine yourself observing a scene unfolded in front of you, thus: a man stands near the wall of a house and turns his head to the left; there appears another man slinking cautiously through the gate. The two are fairly widely distant from one another – they stop. The first takes some object and shows it to the other, mocking him. The latter clenches his fists in a rage and throws himself at the former. At this moment a woman looks out of a window on the third floor and calls, 'Police!' The antagonists run off in oppposite directions. Now, how would this have been observed?
>
> 1. The observer looks at the first man. He turns his head.
>
> 2. What is he looking at? The observer turns his glance in the same direction and sees the man entering the gate. The latter stops.
>
> 3. How does the first react to the appearance on the scene of the second? A new turn by the observer; the first takes out an object and mocks the second.
>
> 4. How does the second react? Another turn; he clenches his fists and throws himself on his opponent.
>
> 5. The observer draws aside to watch how both opponents roll about fighting.
>
> 6. A shout from above. The observer lowers his head and sees the result of the warning – the antagonists running off in opposite

> directions ... Here we have approached closely the basic significance of editing. Its object is the showing of the development of the scene in relief, as it were, by guiding the attention of the spectator now to one, now to the other separate element.[31]

As with Kuleshov, it is important not only that the episode is broken down for the sufficient assembly of a logical sequence but also that this sequence can be adequately constructed from individual, independent bits shot in isolation; economical construction is advocated, the minimum (in terms of number of shots) is promoted as the optimum. Also like Kuleshov, it seems significant that the example locates an external observer, apportioning his interest between active protagonists.[32] Elsewhere, Pudovkin suggests that the camera may also be located in the scene subjectively, to considerable effect, to identify one or another protagonist's point of view. The montage is again dependent upon narrative logic and diegetic contiguity.

Pudovkin sometimes speaks of montage as a more positively interventionist and constructive procedure, obliging the spectator to become 'the ideal perspicuous observer': these methods he summarily lists as contrast, parallel, symbolic, simultaneous or reiterative montage.[33] Pudovkin here asserts that it is incumbent upon the director, in his selection of shots and their assembly, their subject matter and manner of cutting, to construct a non-naturalistic reality, 'not as everyone sees it'; montage specifically enables the bringing together of elements which are not of necessity spatially or temporally contiguous:

> The lens of the camera is the eye of the spectator. He sees and remarks only that which the director desires to show him, or, more correctly put, that which the director himself sees in the action concerned.[34]
>
> One must learn to understand that editing is in actual fact a compulsory and deliberate guidance of the thoughts and and associations of the spectator ... If the editing be co-ordinated according to a definitely selected course of events or conceptual line, either agitated or calm, it will either excite or soothe the spectator.[35]

But even where the content of a shot is not unambiguously predicated by the content of its precursor, Pudovkin seems to suggest that there is a thematic or formal movement, a definite motivation for transferral of attention and that this impetus effects the serial connection which Eisenstein seeks to shatter and replace with collision.

> *Contrast* – Suppose it be our task to tell of the miserable situation of a starving man; the story will impress the more vividly if associated with mention of the senseless gluttony of a well-to-do man ... On the screen the impression of this contrast is yet increased, for it is possible not only to relate the starving sequence to the gluttony sequence, but also to relate scenes and even separate shots of the scenes to one another, thus ... forcing the spectator to compare the two actions ... one strengthening the other...[36]

In Pudovkin's example of contrast, the idea of poverty is connotated in the first series of shots; the second series exaggerates the first connotation, throws it into relief, but nothing new is posited, no new idea is produced spontaneously by the juxtaposition; the juxtaposition is not theoretically presented as a union of opposites, it is not deemed to effect a synthesis with antithesis.

Certainly, even though the experience of watching a Pudovkin film can prove conspicuously physically bombarding (Eisenstein's example of perfect metric montage, the patriotic parade in *The End of St. Petersburg*), Pudovkin urges constraint upon the director and is anxious that film watching is an aesthetically pleasing and constrained activity – the film should not be inordinately long; tensions should be balanced such that the spectator is not exhausted before the thematic climax; undue use of certain technical devices (irises and shutters) should be judiciously avoided for fear of trying the viewer; Pudovkin advocates novelty as a phatic element, reviving and retaining attention rather than forcibly shocking or 'ploughing over the psyche': 'the spectator should be preserved for maximum tension at the end'.[37]

In the same year of the reputed feud, Eisenstein wrote:

> According to Kuleshov's definition (which Pudovkin also shares as a theorist) montage is the means of unrolling an idea through simple shots (the 'epic' principle).
>
> But in my view montage is not an idea composed of successive shots stuck together but an idea that DERIVES from the collision between two shots that are independent of one another (the 'dramatic' principle).[38]

Neither in principle nor by method does Pudovkin allow of shots which are independent: 'In this preliminary paperwork must be created that style, that unity, which conditions the value of any work of art'.[39] Pudovkin is never indifferent to the pre-filmic event which the shot preserves and there is always intentionality in the selection of material and of the shot: the film shown to the audience corresponds to the idea of the film from which the editing plan is drawn and the film staged and shot. When Pudovkin speaks of editing as creative he speaks as much of the painstaking initial analysis into basic units (camera angles) as the later synthesis of the whole. Eisenstein implies in his writing in the period 1922–1926 that the film is not known before the final process, that the film as material art object and as idea does not exist until it reaches the editing table; by the 1930s his teaching implies that the initial process is equally significant. Pudovkin sticks firmly throughout to his triadic principle, which suited well his practice and his ideal of film-making as a collaborative venture, one in which all participants fully comprehend the needs and tasks of their colleagues. For Pudovkin, the creative work lies as much with the scenarist and the director of the mise-en-scène, holding the established idea of the film in their heads as they proceed, as it does with the editor. Through this series of montage processes the film is rigorously built, but the idea of the film is conceived beforehand.

Pudovkin's pronounced position with regard to montage changes with time. In the early 1930s he obligingly endorses official censure of a past preoccupation with montage. Although he is, as ever, disapointingly imprecise in his terminology, in this instance he may be understood to mean the fast cutting for which Soviet silent cinema was known abroad (Eisenstein averages less than 1.7 seconds per shot, Pudovkin 2.5 seconds, Dovzhenko 3.5–4.5 seconds and Hollywood 5–6 seconds, says Bordwell).[40] He intends also to identify a film-making practice in which the editing process takes creative precedence over all else, or, yet worse, a purely formal and autonomous exercise which disregards the representational content of the image. Pudovkin's procedural principle allowed him to adapt relatively comfortably to the new emphasis on the actor's performance, a position at which he had arrived, he maintains, through his work with artists from the Moscow Art Theatre. Indeed, Eisenstein coincidentally corroborates Pudovkin's claim by saying that in 1924–1925 (that is, even in the silent period) there was a prevailing trend 'that living man could only be shown in film in long dramatic scenes. And that cutting (montage) would destroy the idea of real man'[41] (see chapter three, above). In *The Actor in Film* Pudovkin is keen to stress that film preserves the real time in which an actor's performance was delivered before the camera; he emphasises that the actor's performance engages a fully psychologised 'real lived experience', a commodity which Eisenstein was wont to despise. 'The discontinuity of the actor's work', says Pudovkin, 'must never be ignored but always treated as a difficulty to be overcome'.[42] The ideological shift of the 1930s towards individual consciousness and effort, a turn away from the earlier determinism for which Pavlov had seemingly lent support, met with official directives for films with naturalistic characters and linear plot development.

At this time, Pudovkin urges Ivor Montagu not to republish the 'basic primers' in the absence of an apologia accounting for the milieu in which they had been written (see introduction, above). 'Types instead of Actors' proves embarrasssingly incompatible with the tenets of 'The Actor in Film'; Pudovkin now wishes to stress that editing is the foundation of film art but that art is not constituted by montage alone.[43] By the 1940s, Pudovkin is making cursory additional references to 'dialectical thinking' and appears to have extended the connections which he finds acceptable in principle to include those which he had himself effected in practice (thereby resolving some of the earlier anomalies); but essentially he repeats the examples of correct logical construction given previously:

> A myriad of methods of connection may exist between the highly ideophilosophical connection and the externally-formal connection, but all of them must be present in the shots being joined in order that montage create an action on screen which develops without interruption, is understandable and is completely meaningful. Two shots cannot be joined together if one of them in some manner or aspect does not continue the other. This of course must be understood to include the widest range of possible forms of connection including sharp contrast or contradiction, which are sometimes the best ways of joining two or more shots in a continuous development of a single idea.[44]

Essentially, this is mere tinkering. One has little sense of Pudovkin's engagement with theoretical issues consolidating or developing with time, with changing technical opportunities or with the vicissitudes of the political climate, beyond his reappraisal of the actor. Here I think, is where the real difference with Eisenstein lies; if one is the hedgehog (P) then the other is the fox (E). Pudovkin logs his sound experiments on *A Simple Case* and *The Deserter* but there is nothing comparable to the thoroughness of Eisenstein's commentary on *Nevsky*. For Eisenstein, montage serves as a 'fulcrum of analysis' much as the reflex serves Bekhterev and Pavlov. It is his consistent attachment to montage as a theoretical key (to art, to nature, to social progress) which bestows upon his writing the considerable coherence it commands over its vast surface. Montage provides the hypothesis in which Eisenstein sets out to prove an equivalence between film-making and viewing: variation in one function is matched with a corresponding reformulation in the other. For Eisenstein, theorising is the means of perceiving reality more closely, more astutely, more correctly. Pudovkin presents a number of worked examples rather than an attempt at theory. Pudovkin's classifications are fuzzy (albeit not as unsatisfactory as some critics, to suit their own agenda, have suggested) and his thinking sadly vague;[45] Eisenstein's categorisation and recategorisation and cross-referencing has real intellectual status and force even where it tends towards pedantry. Sometimes the structure in place allows him to accommodate, integrate and exploit new technologies of production: undaunted by the advent of sound and in spite of the well-founded fears of the 1928 manifesto, Eisenstein's 'The Fourth Dimension in Cinema' develops ideas expounded in 1924. He recognises crucially that in sound cinema the focus of attention reverts centripetally into the shot rather than concentrating on the connections between them. The theory develops towards collision within the shot (hidden editing) such that in his discussion of *Crime and Punishment* with Nizhny he argues for a method hitherto considered 'unfilmic'.[46] Montage provides the means whereby Eisenstein reconciles himself theoretically to the official revival of Stanislavsky and the methods of the Moscow Art Theatre (my erstwhile 'deadly enemy').[47] Certainly these shifts and turns were opportune (Eisenstein had often openly declared his hostility to naturalistic performance and psychologism hitherto) but there is more at stake than personal vindication, I think.

Amongst the 'galaxy of stars' referred to by Eisenstein there are numerous eminent scientists. He is familiar with contemporary research and its historical and theoretical context; he apprehends Marxism, too, as a science which, as such, can be dismantled to discover fundamental laws of matter beyond the confines of the discipline. Eisenstein seemingly appreciates the full force of J. B. S. Haldane's definition of correct methodology: 'the dialectical method in science is to push a theory to its logical conclusion and show that it negates itself';[48] this is to say, he appreciates Marxism as science but also recognises what might be required of a science thoroughly informed by Marxism. Marxism as a discipline ('referring to systematic scholarship offering a coherent interpretation of a set of phenomena'), grounds itself as much in natural science and a science of cognition as in philosophy. To Marx and Engels, Darwin's theory of evolution was a vindication of the dialectical process: 'to Marx and Engels, Darwin's theory of evolution was an important illustration of the principle of transition of quantity into quality'.[49] Lenin reproached Plekhanov for deviating from the materialism of Marx and Engels in positing his notion of the 'hieroglyph'. In *Materialism and Empirio-Criticism* he asserted the primacy of matter and that this view is scientifically corroborated; 'natural science instinctively adheres to the materialist theory of knowledge'.[50] But Eisenstein's extensive and eclectic reading includes not only scientists working in the approved materialist tradition, but also those often disparaged by later Soviet commentators as idealist or bourgeois (or simply foreign). Freud (whose writings were translated and widely available by this date), was a source of inspiration for Eisenstein's writing in the 1930s and contributed to a teaching syllabus at VGIK which included also Pavlov, William James, Helmholtz and Darwin.[51] The course structure suggests that he found something of use in all of them. Eisenstein was familiar with the early treatises of Bekhterev and often couches his theorising in language redolent of reflexology. This, too, develops with time away from the basic mechanistic model of the early 1920s: in 'Perspectives' (1929), he speaks of:

> A complex of conditioned reflexes grown wise with experience. And the direct passion of conditioned reflexes.
> In the crucible of the dialectic a new fact in construction has been smelted.
> A new social life has been forged.

Or again:

> There is no way in which we can produce within ourselves a

> revision of our perception of the act of 'cognition' as an act with immediate effects. Even though reflexology has adequately demonstrated that the process of cognition means an increase in the quantity of conditional stimulants that provoke an active reflex reaction from a particular subject
> Which means that, even in the actual mechanics of the process, there is something active and not passive.[52]

In 'Beyond the Shot' Eisenstein turns to the psychologist Luria for support for an argument that the close-up affords an exceptional magnification, equivalent to the scale of its significance in the mental image of an event.[53] 'A new trend in Soviet psychology became discernible by the end of the 1920s', says Loren Graham, 'this stemmed from the realisation that with the defeat of subjectivism and introspection ... the greatest danger was now from militant materialists who hoped to swallow up psychology in a purely physiological understanding of mental activity. The defenders of psychology rallied around the concepts of psyche and consciousness'.[54] However, it seems to me that David Bordwell over-simplifies the situation and exaggerates his own case when he designates a shift in Eisenstein's epistemology (and hence his theorising) between an early period influenced by Pavlov's mechanism and a later period, in which Pavlov had fallen from official favour, which sought to accommodate the work of Luria's master, Vygotsky. Ben Brewster and Trevor Whittock cast doubt on this thesis; Aumont and Taylor argue persuasively for consistency and coherence over shift.[55] In any case, Vygotsky likewise did not enjoy official approval and remained unpublished until the 1960s.[56]

It seems to me that Eisenstein seeks rather to identify points at which the extant theoretical structure can expand to incorporate the new material, and that, again, this indicates development rather than rupture. Eisenstein engages with potential moments of negation, rather than avoiding or ignoring them.

'Science has its "ions" its its "electrons" its "neutrons". Art will have – attractions!', writes Eisenstein in 1945.[57] Pudovkin drew an analogy between the methods of his film practice and the process of calculus, one with which, as a chemist, he was very familiar: 'For every event a process has to be carried out comparable to ... "differentiation" – that is to say, dissection into parts or elements ... there follows ... a combination of the discovered separate elements into a whole – the so-called "integration"'.[58] The process welcomed a recasting by ideologues (Lenin not least among them) in dialectical mode; Pudovkin does not make this easy manoeuvre.[59] Again, unlike Eisenstein, he does not assert the ideological correctness of his formal practice before applying it to the affirmation of a particular political reality, even though, in the 1930s, he of necessity opens lectures by declaring the political allegiance: 'We, as Marxists...'.[60] Indeed, the absence of a conspicuous self-examination may have helped Pudovkin's 'basic primers' to the success which they enjoyed abroad. Lewis Jacobs' appraisal of their reception in the United States is confirmed by Steiner and Hurwitz:

> It did not concern itself with basic dramatic principles common to all the theatrical arts. We made the error of overlooking the fact that Pudovkin was presupposing this base and we considered it a Bible of film principle rather than a series of collected essays on film technique.[61]

Even more remarkable, it seems to me, given Eisenstein's patent and fashionable enthusiasms, is the absence in Pudovkin's writing of the 1920s of any acknowledged reference to current scientific research; the 1926 publications, *The Film Scenario* and *The Film Director and Film Material*, appeared without footnotes to support any such attachment. Although Pudovkin occasionally mentions, anecdotally, his work on *The Mechanics of the Brain*, he never seeks to underpin whatever principles of film and cinema he presents by extrapolating from what he evidently understood well, from first principles, of Pavlov's work on higher nervous activity, even though it might have lent considerable ideological buttressing and credibility to his own position. Unfashionably, in an article of 1938, Pudovkin mentions in passing Pavlov's hypothesis of language as a second order function (see chapter two, above), in support of his own thesis of gesture as the primary form of expression. But neither in *Mechanics,* nor in his writing about this film, nor in his writing about film principles in general does Pudovkin allow himself the holistic indulgence of Eisenstein. Equally, given Pavlov's own resistance to misinterpretation by those who sought to extract political and ideological capital from his work, the comparative reticence of *The Mechanics* and of Pudovkin's account of it thereafter, may well have contributed to Pavlov's own eventual reconciliation to the project. As a constructive model for film and cinema principle, Pudovkin is more concerned with the procedures whereby the experiments are conducted and the proof effected than by the cognitive ramifications of Pavlov's results. Pudovkin states that montage both corresponds normatively to naturally motivated observation and that, as a rhythmic mode, it can serve a conducive auxiliary function (it 'soothes or excites') or that its content can function to form an impression (either emotional or intellectual) – but he is far from explicit as to the distinct physiological and psychological bases of his suppositions. He provides his reader with the vaguest and most general of references:

> There is a law in psychology that lays it down that if an emotion gives birth to a certain movement, by imitation of this movement the corresponding emotion can be called forth.[62]

The urgency with which Eisenstein perpetually wills himself to classify and identify discrete qualitative processes (by 1929, defined as metric, rhythmic, tonal and overtonal montage) was directed towards an ambitious project, the creation of a cinema in which the distinct elements of his enquiry eventually would be resolved:

> Intellectual cinema will be the cinema that resolves the conflicting combination of physiological overtones and intellectual overtones, creating an unheard of form of cinema which inculcates the Revolution into the general history of culture creating a synthesis of science, art and militant class consciousness.[63]

This revised thesis of cinema integrates a re-formulation of the viewer along with a developed, more complex notion of film-making. The utilitarian agenda had required film-makers to examine the reception of their films with a general audience, both in terms of the thematic content, the types and characters represented, and the formal effects employed. The first edition of *Sovetskoe kino* includes an article on observation exhorting film personnel to watch audiences assiduously and Eisenstein reports the reception of the Kerensky sequence in *October* and cites the exacting efforts of the research laboratory for audience psycho-physiology: the construction of the Soviet new man and woman was dependent upon a formulaic quantitative and qualitative appraisal of the base material.[64] Eisenstein, together with many commentators in film journals, very soon discovered that audiences were not homogenous nor consistent in their reactions and that the viewer could not be equated as a tabula rasa on which the film simply operated. The butchering sequence in *The Strike* made no impression upon rural audiences; provincial audiences found it harder to follow fast and complex montage than their metropolitan counterparts, more accustomed to film viewing:

> . . . on a worker audience the slaughter did not have a 'bloody' effect for the simple reason that the worker associates a bull's blood above all with the processing plants near a slaughter-house!
> While on a peasant, used to slaughtering his own cattle, there will be no effect at all.[65]

Pudovkin's description of 'audience' is more generalised in the primers and this address more generalist. Pudovkin's characteristic relative taciturnity and caution as an ideologue and theoretician proved politically fortuitous; but this still does not imply that the intellectual gymnastics by which Eisenstein re-articulated his position were politically motivated, even if they were nevertheless advisable.

Soviet doctrine dedicated itself to the improvement of society but recognised that this would be achieved only through the fabrication of the new Soviet citizen, by educating the citizen's awareness of his or her position in Nature, Labour and Society.[66] Pudovkin's appeal for education in film literacy is situated alongside this wider campaign for basic schooling. Cinema was pressed into service as a tool of enormous significance in the pedagogic project. In their films, Eisenstein seems more determined upon didacticism than Pudovkin (the gods and Napoleon sequences in *October*, for instance). Pudovkin was, indeed, amongst those who, when circumstances required a condemnation, found Eisenstein guilty of pitching his films above the heads of his audiences:

> Young Eisenstein produced *The Strike* . . . filled with mere formal tricks. Instead of showing a serious and important stage in the history of the Russian labour movement, the formalistic freaks of the author led spectators away from real life, confused and sometimes distorted the link of the film with actual historical reality.[67]

Pudovkin speaks of ‘compulsion’, of the director ‘infallibly leading’ the viewer, but thematically Pudovkin’s major films re-affirm a known course. He is concerned for and achieves an effectively orchestrated conceptual and emotional appeal to the audience. However, he is less than eloquent theoretically as to how this reaction is articulated in the mind of the viewer. It is for elucidation and support on precisely such issues that Eisenstein turns to Luria and Freud and to classic treatises on aesthetics such as Schopenhauer and Christiansen. Eisenstein is keen to understand the various theories advanced of cognitive and psychological mechanisms and development in order that film may be employed all the better to affect and impress his audience, to manufacture a newly receptive, newly aware audience in the process of film viewing. Here again, Pudovkin’s position seems more conservative. He seems rather to accept his film audience as a given, the ‘literacy’ being accomplished preparatory to the viewing. The audience of a Pudovkin film may be roused, inspired to undertake great deeds but Pudovkin does not postulate that the experience of film viewing *itself* can effect an organic change in the viewer.

> Engels believed that the unity of theory and practice was connected with the problem of cognition ... the most telling evidence against idealistic epistemologies was that man’s knowledge of nature resulted in practical benefits, man’s theories of matter ‘worked’ in the sense that they yielded products for his use.[68]

Theoretical writing aspired to be scientific in its concerns with social utility and also in the methodology which it attempted to espouse. This confidence in the beneficent workings of science was not unique to the Soviet Union, but it received there a particular impetus, aptly paraphrased by Lenin: ‘communism equals Soviet power plus the electrification of the entire country’.[69] Soviet theorising was equally scientific in the inductive model it adopted for itself. It could not afford to entertain any suggestion that its theses were not empirically verifiable.[70] Hence the frequent occurrence of syllogisms, intrinsic to theories of a totalising aspect: Eisenstein demonstrates his theses by recourse to constructions which already consciously employ the terms of his proof. The interest and use lies in the process, in the working-out.

Pudovkin is broadly attached to the notion that Marxism is demonstrably socially progressive and adopts this as the major theme or 'supra artistic concept' of his films. Marx believed himself to be labouring in accordance with scientific precedence; producers of Marxist of art frequently imitated what they understood of a more strictly correct scientific method and perception. Here again, Pudovkin is curiously out of vogue. His early publications neither affect the jargon nor the scientistic typography familiar in such as Punin, Meyerhold, Timoshenko and (occasionally) Eisenstein, presenting their theses as tables or mathematical equations or diagrams.[71] He does not assume Eisenstein's somewhat forced pose, employing his own films as an exemplary objective test case for his own hypotheses (for instance, in 'The Dramaturgy of Film Form'). Pudovkin equally lacks Eisenstein's attentive identification of differences, his taxonomy of distinct entities as a means of analysing phenomena clearly and recognising process. He also is less willing to explore I think, the cinematic relationship between the film and its audience. Pudovkin's efforts are directed at calculating the product which he delivers in respect of given common sense appraisals of reception. Even where Eisenstein's writing is wildly unsystematic and eclectic, unable to confine itself to the matter of a particular discipline, there is an urge towards rational explanation and the discovery of a rational direction in experience. Not only is Eisenstein fond of locating his own

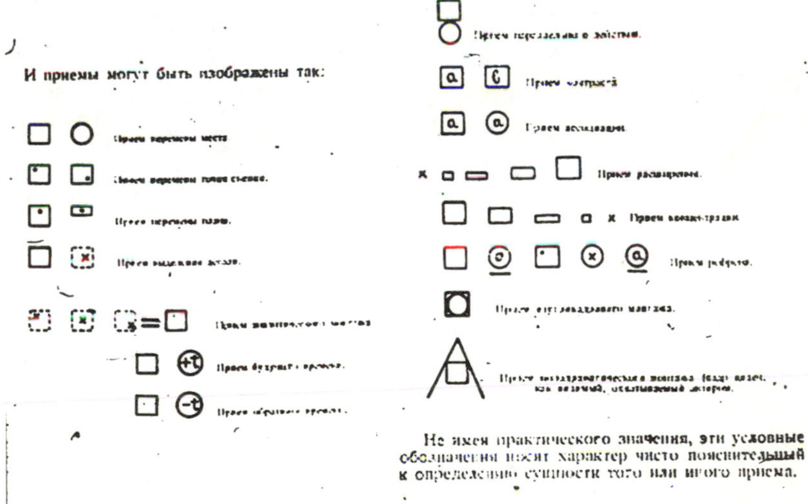

Timoshenko's diagrammatic rendition of Kuleshov

practice and theory metaphysically, he also relishes historical systems which have striven for all-encompassing totality. He cites the pure number ratios of Pythagoras, the visual and acoustic harmonies of the Golden Section and censures Pudovkin for his neglect of such universal truths:

> This sort of work has a very special effect on the person who contemplates it – not only because it raises itself to the level of natural phenomena, but also because the law which governs those who contemplate the work, to the extent that they themselves are part of organic nature – the contemplator feels himself organically bound to a work of this type, united, conmingled with it, exactly as he feels himself united and conmingled with the surrounding organic milieu and with nature.[72]

Eisenstein not only recognises the urgency of his political circumstances but also acknowledges an explicit ideological structure as the context within which he works: 'these concepts are not tools', observes Jacques Aumont, 'they are completely inseparable from the very way in which they are formulated'.[73]

Certainly Pudovkin advances his case more by commonplace assumption and in answer to immediate social and political demands made of him and his fellow Soviet film workers, than by rigorous proof of such connections. But he is equally less attached to a logical theoretical structure per se than is Eisenstein; significantly again, the shifts and piecemeal adjustments in Pudovkin's theorising are justified in his own reckoning by his gains in practical experience, rather than in a theoretical recognition of problems as yet unaccounted for, or in any attempt to consolidate ontological, epistemological and aesthetic propositions. Pudovkin is little interested in theory for its own sake. Pudovkin's basic primers provide a manual which appears of more immediate practical use (he was in his own practice notoriously methodical), and which has predictive power only in as much as his axioms endorse convention and rely on the equilibrium of the viewer with the film; he allows for change in practice and perception in the most general terms but offers little indication as to how its course can or should be determined. The themes which concern Pudovkin (the centrality of the actor; the material, spatial and temporal means specific to cinema; cinema and didacticism) are shared with contemporaneous film commentators in Russia and elsewhere. Pudovkin did not initiate the subjects of debate which his writings address and often his contributions are not original nor unique; sometimes he contributes simply a codification of current means and ends. Pudovkin's theorising is very much the circumspect product of a particular set of historical circumstances, to which he responds pragmatically and expediently. Eisenstein, however, endeavours to provide the foundations of an ambitiously inclusive theory of cinema which accounts for qualitative transformation: that is to say, a truly revolutionary theory.

Pudovkin's writing may fail to fulfil satisfactorily some of the criteria one might reasonably level at a consolidated film theory, but this is not to say that the writing is of no theoretical or utilitarian value. Rather than censuring Pudovkin for the objective incoherence of his theory and the inconsistency between his theory and his practice, it seems to me to be worth recognising the specific historical circumstances in which it was produced. Theory, for Pudovkin, proved itself useful as a contingent resource, and his theory and practice were mutually informing rather than immediately correspondent. Pudovkin's 'theory', at any given time, is perhaps never more than a provisional hypothesis. Pudovkin's strength, it seems to me, lies rather in the films themselves and in the example which they continue to afford as experiments in the manipulation and ordering of material, spatial and temporal means.

Notes

1 L. Moussinac, *Le Cinéma soviétique*, Paris 1928, p. 161
2 Vladimir Nizhny, *Lessons with Eisenstein*, London 1962, p. xi; David Bordwell, *The Cinema of Eisenstein*, London 1993, p. xiii
3 Pudovkin: 'Prosteishie spetsial'nye priemy s'emki', *Kinostsenarii*, *SS* I, p. 69
4 Richard Taylor, *Film Propaganda*, London 1979, p. 91
5 Pudovkin: 'Predislovie', *Kinostsenarii*, *SS* I, p. 53
6 see, for instance, 'Give us a State Plan' 1927 and 'The Twelfth Year' 1928 in Eisenstein, *Selected Works* I, ed. Richard Taylor, London 1988
7 Eisenstein, *Selected Works* I, p. 61
8 V.I. Lenin, *What is to be Done?,* tr. Robert Service, Harmondsworth 1988, p. 93
9 Eisenstein, *Selected Works* I, p. 177 and II, London 1991, p. 264
10 see Pudovkin: 'Ekrannyi obraz', *Kino rezhisser i kino material*, *SS* I, p. 110 also, Pudovkin and Smirnova, *Puti razvitiia sovetskoi khudozhestvennoi kinematografii*, Moscow 1950, p. 8

11 Eisenstein, *Selected Works* I, p. 112
12 IM/BFI/SM, translator's note; by 1934, Pudovkin is employing the approved terminology: 'Naturalism, idealism and realism in art stand in the same relation to one another as do mechanism, idealism and dialectical materalism in philosophy' Pudovkin, *Akter v fil'me, SS* I, p. 224
13 J. Aumont, *Montage Eisenstein*, tr. Hildreth, London 1987, p. 12
14 actually, Eisenstein can often be caught out in his references; it seems that his erudition was sometimes more affected than real but that he certainly liked to convey the impression of being well-informed and thoroughly au courant
15 Babitsky and Rimberg, *The Soviet Film Industry*, New York 1955, p. 316
16 Pudovkin, 'Metod kino', *Kinorezhisser i kinomaterial, SS* I, p. 96
17 for Eisenstein's thoughts on *Woman of Paris* (a much discussed film in Russia in the mid '20s) see Eisenstein, *Selected Works* I and for Pudovkin's original and revised views see *Kinostsenarii* and *Akter v fil'me*; for Eisenstein's teaching from *Tol able David* and for Pudovkin on this, *Daddy* and *Saturday Night* (and its 'slight content') see also V. Kepley jr. 'Pudovkin and the Classical Hollywood Tradition', *Wide Angle* 7.3 (1985)
18 Pudovkin, 'Tema', *Kinostsenarii, SS* I, p. 55
19 Pudovkin, 'Siuzhetnoe oformlenie temy', *Kinostsenarii, SS* I, p. 60: 'the dynamically saturated earlier reels are easy to look at and grip the spectator with ever-increasing excitement. But after the end of the third reel, where the cowboy's adventures came to an unexpected end, the spectator experiences a natural reaction, and the continuation, in spite of the excellent directorial treatment, is watched with much diminished interest'.
20 Eisenstein, *Selected Works* I, p. 163
21 Eisenstein, *Selected Works* I, p. 62
22 Pudovkin: *Film Technique*, tr, Montagu, pp. xiii and xv; 'Predislovie' [1928], *SS* I, p. 131
23 Eisenstein, *Selected Works* I, p. 163
24 Eisenstein, *Selected Works* I, p. 144; for Pudovkin's response in 1930 to a direct question about his differences over a question of montage, see 'Lektsia na rezhisserskom fakul'tete GIKa', *SS* III, p. 205
25 Eisenstein, *Selected Works* I, p. 46
26 Eisenstein, *Selected Works* I, p. 161
27 Eisenstein, *Selected Works* I, p. 62
28 qu. Sheila Fitzpatrick, *Education and Social Mobility*, Cambridge 1979, p. 84
29 Eisenstein, *Selected Works* I, p. 45; Eisenstein later suggests that he did not know of Pavlov at this date; see 'How I became a film director' 1945 in *Selected Works* III, p. 289 and in *Izbrannie proizvedeniia* I, p. 104: 'Thus was born the term "the montage of attractions". If I had known of Pavlov at that time I would have called the montage of attractions" "the theory of artistic irritants" [teoriia khudozhestvennykh razdrazhitelei].'
30 see Noël Burch, ' Film's Institutional Mode and the Soviet Response', *October* 11 (1979) pp. 86–87

31 Pudovkin, 'Priemy obrabotki materiala', *Kinostsenarii, SS* I, p. 70
32 Pudovkin's example corresponds to an 'experiment' of Kuleshov, shown at the Pordenone festival in 1996, in which a man crawls up to a balustrade and is watched by another man.
33 Pudovkin, 'Montazh kak orudie vpechatleniia (montazh sopostavliaiushchii)', *Kinostsenarii, SS* I, pp. 72–74
34 Pudovkin, 'Material kino', *Kinorezhisser i kinomaterial, SS* I, p. 100
35 Pudovkin, 'Priemy obrabotki materiala', *Kinostsenarii, SS* I, p. 71
36 Pudovkin, 'Montazh kak orudie vpechatleniia', *Kinostsenarii, SS* I, p. 73
37 Pudovkin, 'Priemy', *Kinostsenarii, SS* I, p. 72
38 Eisenstein, *Selected Works* I, p. 163
39 Pudovkin, 'Predislovie', *Kinostsenarii, SS* I, p. 53
40 Bordwell, *Eisenstein,* p.46; see also Bryher, *Film Problems of Soviet Russia,* Territet 1929, p.15 and Barry Salt, *Film Style and Technology*, London 1992, pp. 172–173 for further comparison
41 Eisenstein, *Selected Works* I, p. 178
42 Eisenstein, *Selected Works* I, p. 47; Pudovkin: 'Protivorechiia v rabote aktera', *Akter v fil'me, SS* I, p. 191; see also the discussion of Mae Marsh's hands in *Intolerance* (chapter four, above)
43 V. I. Pudovkin, 'Film Acting: Two Phases', *Theatre Workshop* 1.1 (1936) pp. 53–67, in which Pudovkin volunteers criticisms of Kuleshov's films and procedures, including the rehearsal of films without film
44 qu. Peter Dart, *Pudovkin s Films and Film Theory*, New York 1974, p. 163, taken from 'O montazhe', *Izbrannye stat'i*, Moscow 1955 (this article dates from after 1945)
45 for instance, see Rudolf Arnheim, *Film as Art*, London 1958 p. 82 and fn. 33 above; it seems clear to me that Pudovkin refers to events simultaneous in the course of the dramatic action in the class 'parallelism' and not simply to a method of cutting insufficiently distinct from 'contrast'. Arnheim cursorily summarises Pudovkin and Timoshenko before volunteering his own new, improved schema
46 Nizhny, p. 97
47 Eisenstein, *Selected Works* I, p. 74
48 J. B. S. Haldane, 'Beyond Darwin' [1939], *On Being the Right Size*, Oxford 1985, p. 13
49 Loren R. Graham, *Science and Philosophy in the Soviet Union*, London 1973, pp. 52 and 54
50 V. I. Lenin, *Materialism and Empirio-Criticism* [1908], London 1952, p. 37
51 Nizhny, p. 154 and Marie Seton, *Sergei M. Eisenstein*, London 1952, p. 483
52 Eisenstein, *Selected Works* I, p. 155; see also 'Overtonal Montage' (1929)
53 Eisenstein, *Selected Works* I, p. 141
54 Graham, p. 365; this shift was not peculiar to the U.S.S.R.
55 see Ben Brewster's reply to Bordwell's 'Eisenstein's Epistemological Shift' in *Screen* 15.4 (1974–1975) and Trevor Whittock, *Metaphor and Film*, Cambridge 1990, p. 102

56 Graham, p. 368 re Vygotsky's 1934 'Thought and Language'; also David Joravsky, *Russian Psychology: A Critical History*, Oxford 1989
57 Eisenstein, *Selected Works* III, p. 289
58 Pudovkin, 'Analiz', *Kinorezhisser i kinomaterial*, *SS* I, p. 102
59 V. I. Lenin, *On the Question of Dialectics* [1915], Moscow 1980, p. 10
60 for explicit reference, see for instance, Pudovkin, 'Dvoinoi ritm zvuka i izobrazheniia', *Akter v fil'me*, *SS* I, p. 217
61 Lewis Jacobs in Pudovkin, *Film Technique*, New York 1949, p. iv; Steiner and Hurwitz, qu. Vlada Petrić, 'Soviet Revolutionary Films in America', Ph. D. thesis, New York University, 1973, p. 459
62 Pudovkin, 'Priemy', *Kinostsenarii*, *SS* I, p. 71; Pudovkin tacitly quotes William James: see *Psychology*, London 1892, pp. 277–279
63 Eisenstein, *Selected Works* I, p. 194
64 Eisenstein, *Selected Works* I, p. 125
65 Eisenstein, *Selected Works* I, pp. 65 and 201; see also Viktor Shklovskii, 'K voprosu ob izuchenii zritelia', *Sovetskii ekran* 50, 11 December 1928, p. 6
66 Sheila Fitzpatrick, *Education and Social Mobility in the Soviet Union*, Cambridge 1979, p. 20
67 Pudovkin, Aleksandrov, Pirev, *Soviet Films: Principle Stages of Development*, Bombay 1951, p. 6
68 Graham, p. 62
69 a much quoted phrase, quoted by Richard Stites, *Revolutionary Dreams*, Oxford 1989, p. 49
70 see Karl Popper, *The Logic of Scientific Discovery*, London 1972, p. 40, presenting an argument against induction: '... inference to theories from singular statements which are "verified by experience" ... is logically inadmissable. Theories are therefore never empirically verifiable ... I shall certainly admit a system as empirical or scientific only if it is capable of being tested by experience. These considerations suggest that not the verifiability but the falsifiability of a system is to be taken as a criterion of demarcation ... it must be possible for an empirical scientific system to be refuted'.
71 see, for instance, Edward Braun, *Meyerhold on Theatre*, London 1969, p. 50: '$N=A^1+A^2$ (where N= the actor; A^1= the artist who conceives the ideas and issues the instructions necessary for its execution; A^2= the executant who executes the conception of A^1; see also Punin's 'First Cycle of Lectures'. John E. Bowlt, ed. *Russian Art of the Avant-Garde*, London 1988, p. 171: S(Pi+Pii+Piii+ ... P#)Y=T,where S = sum of principles (P), Y=intuition, T=artistic creation
72 qu. Aumont, p. 64 and Eisenstein, *Selected Works* I, p. 187
73 Aumont, p. 25

Bibliography

Archival Sources

Material has been consulted in the following collections: the Russian State Archive of Literature and Art, Moscow (RGALI); the State Institute of Cinematography, Moscow (VGIK); the Cinema Museum, Moscow (Muzei kino); Gosfilmofond, Moscow; the British Film Institue, London (BFI)

Books

Adams-Sitney, Paul, *Modernist Montage* (New York, Columbia UP, 1990)

Adorno, Theodor and Eisler, Hanns, *Composing for the Films* [1947] (ed.) Graham McCann, (London, Athlone Press, 1994)

Albera, François, (ed.) *Vers une théorie de l acteur* (Lausanne, L'Age d'Homme, 1990)

and Ekaterina Khoklova and Valérie Posener, (eds.) *Kouléchov et les siens* (Locarno, Editions du Festival du Film de Locarno, 1990)

and Naum Kleiman, (eds.) *Eisenstein: le mouvement de l art* (Paris, Éditions du Cerf, 1986)

Aldridge, Alexandra, *The Scientific World View in Dystopia* (Michigan, Ann Arbor, 1984)

Amar, Jules, *Le Moteur humain et les bases scientifiques du travail* (Paris, n.p., 1914)

Amengual, Barthélémy, *V. I. Poudovkine* (Lyon, Serdoc, 1968)

Arnaud, Angélique, *Delsarte, ses cours, sa méthode* (Paris, Pentu, 1859)

Frańcois Delsarte, ses découvertes en esthétique, sa méthode (Paris, Delagrive, 1882)

Arnheim, Rudolf, *Film as Art* (London, Faber, 1958)

Ash, M. G. and Woodward, W. R., *The Problematic Science: Psychology in Nineteenth Century Thought* (New York, Praeger, 1982)

Psychology in Twentieth Century Thought and Society (Cambridge, CUP, 1987)

Attwood, Lynne, (ed.) *Red Women on the Silver Screen* (London, Pandora, 1993)

Aumont, Jacques, *Montage Eisenstein*, tr. Hildreth, Penley, Ross (London, BFI, 1987)

Babitsky, Boris and Rimberg, John, *The Soviet Film Industry* (New York, Praeger, 1955)

Bablet, Denis, *Collage et montage* (Lausanne, L'Age d'Homme, 1978)

Baer, Nancy van Norman, *Theatre in Revolution* (London, Thames and Hudson, 1991)

Bakshy, Alexander, *The Path of the Modern Russian Stage* (London, Cecil Palmer and Hayward, 1916)

Balázs, Béla, *Theory of the Film*, tr. Bone (London, Dennis Dobson, 1952)

Bann, Stephen, (ed.) *The Tradition of Constructivism* (London, Thames and Hudson, 1974)

Barbaro, Umberto, *Il film e il risarcimento marxista dell arte* (Rome, Editori Riuniti, 1961)

La settima arte: Pudovkin (Rome, Editori Riuniti, 1961)

Barkhatova, Elena, *Russian Constructivist Posters* (Paris, Flammarion, 1993)

Barron, Stéphanie and Tuchman, Maurice, (eds.) *The Avant-Garde in Russia 1910–1930* (Cambridge Mass., MIT Press, 1980)

Bazin, André, *Qu est-ce-que-le cinéma?* (Paris, Editions du Cerf, 1958–1962)

Bekhterev, Vladimir, *General Principles of Reflexology* [1923], tr. E. and W. Murphy (London, Jarrolds, 1933)

Belyi, Andrei, *Petersburg* [1913], tr. J. Cournos (London, Weidenfeld and Nicholson, 1960)

Benedetti, Jean, *Stanislavski* (London, Methuen, 1982)

Stanislavski (London, Methuen, 1988)

Bergson, Henri, *Creative Evolution* [1907], tr. A. Mitchell (London, Macmillan, 1911)

Birkos, Alexander S., *Soviet Cinema* (Hamden, Archon Books, 1978)

Bochow, Jörg, *Das Theater Meyerhold und die Biomechanik*, (Berlin, Mime Centrum, 1997)

Bordwell, David, *Eisenstein* (Cambridge Mass., Harvard UP, 1993)

Bowlt, John E., (ed.) *Russian Art of the Avant-Garde* (London, Thames and Hudson, 1988)

Bradley, John, *Allied Intervention in Russia* (London, Weidenfeld and Nicholson, 1968)

Braun, Edward, *Meyerhold on Theatre* (London, Methuen, 1969)

The Theatre of Meyerhold: Revolution on the Modern Stage (London, Methuen, 1979)

Meyerhold: A Revolution in Theatre (London, Methuen, 1995)

Brooks, Jeffrey, *When Russia Learned to Read* (Princeton, Princeton UP, 1984)

Bryher (Winifred Ellermann), *Film Problems of Soviet Russia* (Territet, Pool, 1929)

Bulgakov, Mikhail, *Black Snow* [1965], tr. M. Glenny (London, Harvill, 1991)

The Heart of a Dog [1987], tr. M. Glenny (London, Harvill, 1989)

Burch, Noël, *Theory of Film Practice*, tr. H. R. Lane (London, Secker and Warburg, 1973)

Carter, Huntley, *The New Theatre and Cinema of Soviet Russia* (London, Chapman and Dodd, 1924)

The New Spirit in the Cinema (London, Harold Shaylor, 1930)

Cartwright, Lisa, *Screening the Body*, (Minneapolis, Minnesota UP, 1995)

Cherniavsky, Michael, *Tsar and People: Studies in Russian Myths* (New Haven, Yale UP, 1969)

Christie, Ian and Gillett, John, (eds.) *Formalism, Futurism, FEKS*, (London, BFI, 1978)

and Graffy, Julian, *Iakov Protazanov: The Continuity of Russian Cinema* (London, BFI, 1993)

Clark, Katerina, *The Soviet Novel: History as Ritual* (London, Chicago UP, 1985)

Petersburg, Crucible of Cultural Revolution (Cambridge, Mass., Harvard UP, 1996)

Cohen, Louis Harris, *The Cultural-Political Traditions and Developments of the Soviet Cinema 1917–1972* (New York, Arno, 1974)

Compton, Susan, *Russian Avant-Garde Books, 1917–1934* (London, British Museum, 1992)

Constantine, M. and Fern, A., *Revolutionary Soviet Film Posters* (Baltimore, Johns Hopkins UP, 1974)

Cuny, Hilaire, *Ivan Pavlov*, tr. P. Evans (London, Souvenir Press, 1964)

Dart, Peter, *Pudovkin s Films and Film Theory* (New York, Arno Press, 1974)

Darwin, Charles, *The Expression of the Emotions in Man and Animals* [1872] (Chicago, Chicago UP, 1965)

della Volpe, Galvano, *Critique of Taste*, tr. M. Caesar (London, NLB, 1978)

Delluc, Louis, *Ecrits cinématographiques* (Paris, Cinémathèque Française, 1990)

Dickinson, Thorold and de la Roche, Catherine, *Soviet Cinema* (London, Falcon Press, 1948)

Eagle, Herbert, *Russian Formalist Film Theory* (Michigan, Michigan Slavic Publications, 1981)

Edwards, Christine, *The Stanislavski Heritage*, London, Peter Owen, 1966

Eisenstein, S.M., *Izbrannie proizvedeniia*, 6 vols., (Moscow, Iskusstvo, 1964–1971)

The Film Sense tr. Jay Leyda (London, Faber, 1968)

Nonindifferent Nature tr. Herbert Marshall (Cambridge, CUP, 1987)

Selected Works ed. Richard Taylor (London, BFI, I 1988, II 1991, III 1996, IV 1995)

Elliott, David, (ed.) *Alexander Rodchenko* (Oxford, MOMA, 1979)

Mayakovsky: Twenty Years of Work (Oxford, MOMA, 1982)

New Worlds: Russian Art and Society 1900–1937 (London, Thames and Hudson, 1986)

(ed.) *Eisenstein at 90* (Oxford, MOMA, 1988)

(ed.) *Photography in Russia* 1840–1940 (London, Thames and Hudson, 1992)

Elliott, Eric, *Anatomy of Motion Picture Art* (Territet, Pool, 1928)

Elsaesser, Thomas, (ed.) *Early Cinema: Space Frame Narrative* (London, BFI, 1990)

Erenburg, I., *Materializatsiia fantastiki* (Moscow, Kinopechat', 1927)
Erlich, Victor, *Russian Formalism: History Doctrine* (The Hague, Mouton, 1965)
Figes, Orlando, *Peasant Russia, Civil War* (Oxford, Clarendon Press, 1989)
A People s Tragedy (London, Pimlico, 1997)
Fischer, Louis, *The Soviets in World Affairs* (London, Jonathan Cape, 1930)
Fitzpatrick, Sheila, *The Commissariat of Enlightenment* (Cambridge, CUP, 1970)
Education and Social Mobility in the Soviet Union (Cambridge, CUP, 1979)
(ed.) *Cultural Revolution in Russia* (Bloomington, Indiana UP, 1984)
Fortescue, Stephen, *The Communist Party and Soviet Science* (London, Macmillan, 1986)
Frolov, Y. P., *Pavlov and his School* [1938] (London, Johnson, 1970)
Fülöp-Miller, René, *The Mind and Face of Bolshevism*, tr. Flint and Tait (London, G. P. Putnam's Sons, 1927)
Gardin, V. R., *Vospominaniia*, 2 vols. (Moscow, Goskinoizdat, 1949–1952)
de George, Richard T., *Patterns of Soviet Thought* (Michigan, Ann Arbor, 1966)
Glagoleva, Nina, *Vsevolod Pudovkin: Slovo o Pudovkine*, (Moscow, Gosfil'mofond, 1968)
Mat (Moscow, Iskusstvo, 1975)
Golovnia, Anatolii, *Svet v iskusstve operatora* (Moscow, Goskinoizdat, 1945)
Gorkii, Maxim, *The Mother*, tr. I. Schneider (Secaucus, Citadel Press, 1977)
My Universities [1921], tr. R. Wilks (Harmondworth, Penguin, 1981)
Graham, Loren R., *Science and Philosophy in the Soviet Union* (London, Allen Lane, 1971)
Science and the Soviet Social Order (London, Harvard UP, 1990)
Gray, Camilla, *The Russian Experiment in Art* (London, Thames and Hudson, 1986)
Gray, Jeffrey A., *Pavlov s Typology* (Oxford, OUP, 1964)
Pavlov (Brighton, Harvester Press, 1979)
Gregory, Richard, *Eye and Brain* (London, Weidenfeld and Nicolson, 1990)
Grierson, Roderick, (ed.) *Gates of Mystery* (Cambridge, Lutterworth Press, 1993)
Groys, Boris, *The Total Art of Stalinism* (Princeton, Princeton UP, 1992)
Günther, Hans, (ed.) *The Culture of the Stalin Period* (London, Macmillan, 1990)
Haldane, J. B. S., *Daedalus or Science and the Future* (London, Kegan Paul Trench Trubner, 1924)
On Being the Right Size (Oxford, OUP, 1985)
Halperin, Charles J., *Russia and the Golden Horde* (London I. B. Tauris, 1987)
Hamon-Sirejols, Christine, *Le Constructivisme au théatre* (Paris, CNRS, 1992)
Hapgood, E. Reynolds, *Stanislavski s Legacy* (London, Eyre Methuen, 1968)
Hardy, Forsyth, (ed.) *Grierson on Documentary* (London, Faber & Faber, 1979)
Harms, Rudolf, *Philosophie des Films* [1926] (Zurich, Verlag Hans Rohr, 1970)
Heath, Stephen and de Lauretis, Teresa, (eds.) *Questions of Cinema* (London, Macmillan, 1981)
Herwitz, Daniel, *Making Theory/Constructing Art: on the authority of the avant garde* (Chicago, Chicago UP, 1993)
Hobbs, G. and Midgeley, C., (eds.) *Pages from the life of Dmitri Shostakovitch* (London, Robert Hale, 1981)

Hoover, Marjorie C., *Meyerhold: the Art of Conscious Theater* (Amherst, Mass. UP, 1974)

Horton, Andrew, (ed.) *Inside Soviet Film Satire* (Cambridge, CUP, 1993)

Hosking, Geoffrey, *A History of the Soviet Union* (London, William Collins, 1990)

Iezuitov, Nikolai, *Puti khudozhestvennogo fil ma* (Moscow, Kinofotoizdat, 1934)

Pudovkin (Moscow, Iskusstvo, 1937)

Aktery MKhAT v kino (Moscow, Goskinoizdat, 1938)

Gardin XL let (Moscow, Goskinoizdat, 1940)

Ivanits, Linda J., *Russian Folk Belief* (New York, M. E. Sharpe, 1992)

James, William, *Psychology* (London, Macmillan, 1892)

Johansson, Kurt, *Gastev: Proletarian Bard* (Stockholm, Almqvist and Wiksell, 1983)

Joravsky, David, *Soviet Marxism and Natural Science* (London, Routledge, 1961)

Russian Psychology: A Critical History (Oxford, OUP, 1989)

Kaganov, Grigorii, *Images of Space: St. Petersburg in the Visual and Verbal Arts*, tr. S. Monas (Stanford, Stanford UP, 1997)

Karaganov, Aleksandr, *Vsevolod Pudovkin* (Moscow, Iskusstvo, 1973)

Kenez, Peter, *Cinema and Soviet Society* (Cambridge, CUP, 1992)

Kerr, Alfred, *russische Filmkunst* (Berlin, Ernst Pollak, 1927)

Khan-Magomedov, Selim, *Rodchenko* (London, Thames and Hudson, 1986)

Kleberg, Lars, *Theatre as Action*, (Basingstoke, Macmillan, 1993)

and Lövgren, H., (eds.) *Eisenstein Revisited* (Stockholm, Almqvist and Wiksell, 1987)

Koch, Sigmund and Leary, David, (eds.) *A Century of Psychology as Science* (New York, McGraw Hill, 1985)

Kretschmer, Ernst, *Physique and Character* [1936] (New York, Cooper Square, 1970)

Kuleshov, Lev *Praktika kinorezhissery* (Moscow, Khudozhestvennaia literatura, 1935)

Selected Works, tr. Dmitri Agrachev and Nina Belenkaia, (Raduga, Moscow, 1987)

Laing, Dave, *The Marxist Theory of Art* (Hassocks, Harvester Press, 1978)

Lawton, Anna, (ed.) *The Red Screen* (London, Routledge, 1992)

Leach, Robert, *Revolutionary Theatre* (London, Routledge, 1994)

Léger, Fernand, *Functions of Painting*, tr. Edward Fry (London, Thames and Hudson, 1973)

Lemmeremier, Doris, *Literaturverfilmung im sowjetischen Stummfilm* (Vienna, Otto Harrassowitz, 1989)

Levaco, Ronald, (ed.) *Kuleshov on Film* (Berkeley, Calif. UP, 1974)

Lewes, George Henry, *The Physiology of Common Life* (London, George Allen & Unwin, 1860)

Leyda, Jay, *Kino: A History of the Soviet and Russian Film* (London, George Allen & Unwin, 1960)

Likhachev, B. S., *Istoriia kino v Rossii 1896–1913* (Leningrad, Academia, 1927)

Lindgren, Ernst, *The Art of the Film*, (London, George Allen & Unwin, 1950)

Lodder, Christina, *Russian Constructivism*, (New Haven, Yale UP, 1963)

London, Kurt, *The Seven Soviet Arts* (London, Faber & Faber, 1937)

Luckett, Richard, *The White Generals* (Harlow, Longman, 1971)

Lukács, Georg, *The Historical Novel* (London, Merlin, 1962)

Lunacharskii, Anatolii, *Kino na zapade i u nas* (Moscow, Tea-Kino-Pechat', 1928)

Lunacharskii o kino (Moscow, Iskusstvo, 1963)

Lunn, Eugene, *Modernism and Marxism* (London, Verso, 1985)

Lyons, Eugene, *Modern Moscow*, (London, Hurst & Blackett, 1935)

Mach, Ernst, *The Science of Mechanics*, tr. T. J. McCormack (London, Open Court, 1919)

Maiakovskii, V. V., *The Complete Plays*, tr. G. Daniels (New York, Simon Schuster, 1971)

How are Verses Made?, tr. G. M. Hyde (Bristol, Bristol Classical Press, 1990)

Manvell, Roger, (ed.) *Experiment in the Film* (London, Grey Walls Press, 1949)

Marchand, René and Weinstein, Pierre, *L'Art dans la Russia nouvelle: le cinéma* (Paris, Editions Rieder, 1927)

Mar'iamov, A. *Vsevolod Pudovkin* (Moscow, Goskinoizdat, 1951)

Masi, Stefano, *V. I. Pudovkin* (Florence, La Nuova Italia, 1985)

Mathews, Tom Dewe, *Censored* (London, Chatto & Windus, 1994)

Mathewson, Rufus, *The Positive Hero in Russian Literature* (Stanford, Stanford UP, 1975)

Mayne, Judith, *Kino and the Woman Question* (Ohio, Ohio State UP, 1989)

Michelson, Annette, (ed.) *Kino-Eye: the writings of Dziga Vertov*, tr. O'Brien (London, Pluto Press, 1984)

Moholy-Nagy, Laszlo, *Vision in Motion* (Chicago, Chicago UP, 1956)

Painting Photography Film [1925], tr. J. Seligman (London, Lund Humphries, 1969)

Mondrian, Piet, *Plastic Art and Pure Plastic Art*, (New York, Wittenborn, 1945)

Moussinac, Léon, *La Naissance du cinéma* (Paris, Librairie Gallimard, 1925)

Le Cinéma soviétique, (Paris, Librairie Gallimard, 1928)

Münsterberg, Hugo, *The Film: A Psychological Study* [1916] (New York, Dover, 1970)

Naremore, James, *Acting in the Cinema*, (Berkeley, California UP, 1988)

Nilsen, Vladimir, *Lessons with Eisenstein*, tr. J. Leyda and I. Montagu (London, George Allen & Unwin, 1962)

Pack, Susan, *Film Posters of the Russian Avant-Garde*, (Cologne, Taschen, 1995)

Panofsky, Erwin, *Idea*, (London, Harper & Row, 1968)

Passuth, Krisztina, *Moholy-Nagy* (London, Thames & Hudson, 1987)

Pavlov, Ivan, *Conditioned Reflexes: An Investigation of the Physiological Activity of the Cerebral Cortex*, tr. G.V. Anrep (Oxford, OUP, 1927)

Lectures on Conditioned Reflexes, tr. W. Horsley-Gantt (London: Martin Lawrence, 1928)

Selected Works (Moscow, Foreign Languages Publishing House, n.d.)

Petrić, Vlada, *Constructivism in Film: The Man with the Movie Camera* (Cambridge, CUP, 1987)

Petrov, A. and Sozont'ev, G., *Radio i derevnia* (Moscow, Gosudarstvennoe tekhnicheskoe izdatel'stvo, 1926)
Picon-Vallin, Béatrice, (ed.) *Meyerhold: Ecrits sur le théâtre* III (Paris, L'Age d'Homme, 1980)
Meyerhold (Paris, CNRS, 1990)
Pike, Chris, (ed.) *The Futurists, the Formalists and the Marxist Critique* (London, Ink Links, 1979)
Poggioli, Renato, *The Theory of the Avant-Garde* (Cambridge, CUP, 1970)
Polo, Marco, *The Travels*, tr. R. Latham (Harmondsworth, Penguin, 1979)
Popper, Frank, *Origins and Development of Kinetic Art* (London, Studio Vista, 1968)
Posener, Valérie and Kherroubi, Aïcha, *Le studio Mejrabpom* (Paris, Réunion des Musées Nationaux, 1996)
Plekhanov, G. V., *The Role of the Individual in History* [1898] (London, Lawrence & Wishart, 1940)
Art and Social Life [1912], tr. A. Fineberg, (London, Lawrence & Wishart, n.d.)
Selected Philosophical Works, tr. J. Katzer (Moscow, Progress Publishers, 1976)
Propp, Vladimir, *Theory and History of Folklore* (Manchester, MUP, 1984)
Pudovkin, Vsevelod, *Kinostenarii (teoriia stsenariia)* (Moscow, Kinoizdatel'stvo RSFSR, 1926)
Kino rezhisser i kino material (Moscow, Kinopechat', 1926)
Akter v fil me (Leningrad, Gosudarstvennaia akademia iskusstvoznaniia, 1934)
Film Technique and Film Acting, tr. I. Montagu (New York, Lear, 1949)
Film Technique and Film Acting, tr. I. Montagu (London, Vision Press, 1954)
Film Technique and Film Acting, tr. I. Montagu (London, Vision Press, 1968)
Izbrannye stat i (Moscow, Iskusstvo, 1955)
Sobranie sochinenii 3 vols., eds. T. Zapasnik and A. Petrovich, (Moscow, Iskusstvo, 1974–77)
Pudovkin, Vsevelod and Smirnova, Elizaveta, *Puti razvitiia sovetskoi khudozhestvennoi kinematografii* (Moscow, Pravda, 1950)
Pudovkin, Aleksandrov, Pirev, *Soviet Cinema: Principal Stages of Development* (Bombay, 1951)
Ransome, Arthur, *Six Weeks in Russia* (London, George Allen & Unwin, 1919)
Reed, John, *Ten Days that Shook the World* [1926] (Harmondsworth, Penguin, 1982)
Riordan, James, *Sport in Soviet Society* (Cambridge, CUP, 1977)
Robertson, James C., *The Hidden Cinema* (London, Routledge, 1993)
Rotha, Paul, *The Film Till Now* (London, Vision Press, 1951)
Rudnitsky, Konstantin, *Russian and Soviet Theatre: Tradition and the Avant-Garde* (London, Thames & Hudson, 1988)
Rusanov, L., *Vsevolod Pudovkin* (Moscow, Goskinoizdat, 1939)
Sadoul, Georges, *L'Histoire du cinéma* IV (Paris, Denoël, 1952)
Recherches soviétiques (Paris, Agence Littéraire et Artistique, 1956)
Salt, Barry, *Film Style and Technology* (London, Starwood, 1992)
Scharf, Aaron, *Art and Photography* (Harmondsworth, Penguin, 1974)
Schmidt, Paul, *Meyerhold at Work* (Austin, Texas UP, 1980)

Schneider, Ilya, *Isadora Duncan: The Russian Years*, tr. D. Magarshack (London, Macdonald, 1968)

Schnitzer, Jean and Luda, *Poudovkine* (Paris, Seghers, 1966)

Cinema in Revolution, tr. D. Robinson (London, Secker & Warburg, 1973)

Segel, Harold B., *Twentieth Century Russian Drama* (London, Johns Hopkins UP, 1993)

Seton, Marie, *Sergei M. Eisenstein, a Biography* [1952] (London, Bodley Head, 1978)

Shaw, George Bernard, *Everybody's Political What s What?* (London, Constable & Co., 1944)

Shklovskii, Viktor, *Za sorok let* (Moscow, Iskusstvo, 1965)

Shlapentokh, Dmitri and Vladimir, *Soviet Cinematography* (New York, Aldine de Gruyter, 1993)

Sorlin, Pierre, *The Film in History* (Oxford, OUP, 1980)

Sorrell, Tom, *Scientism: Philosophy and the Infatuation with Science* (London, Routledge, 1991)

Spencer, Herbert, *The Principles of Psychology* (London, Longman, Brown, Green, Longmans, 1855)

Stanislavskii, Konstantin, *Moia zhizn' v iskusstve* [1926] (Moscow, Iskusstvo, 1962)

My Life in Art, tr. E. Reynolds Hapgood, (London, Geoffrey Bles, 1948)

Stites, Richard, *Revolutionary Dreams* (Oxford, OUP, 1989)

Russian Popular Culture (Cambridge, CUP, 1992)

Swettenham, John, *Allied Intervention in Russia* (London, Allen & Unwin, 1967)

Talbot, D., (ed.) *Film: An Anthology* (Berkeley, California UP, 1967)

Tariol, Marcel, *Louis Delluc* (Paris, Seghers, 1965)

Tarkovsky, Andrey, *Sculpting in Time*, tr. K. Hunter-Blair (London, Bodley Head, 1986)

Taylor, F. W., *The Principles of Scientific Management* [1911] (New York, Harper, 1947)

Taylor, Richard, *The Politics of the Soviet Cinema* (Cambridge, CUP, 1979)

Film Propaganda (London, Croom Helm, 1979, 2nd edn, London, IBTauris, 1998)

(ed.) *The Poetics of Cinema* (Oxford, RPT Publications, 1982)

and Christie, Ian, (eds.) *The Film Factory* (London, Routledge, 1988)

and Christie, Ian, (eds.) *Inside the Film Factory* (London, Routledge, 1991)

and Christie, Ian, (eds.) *Eisenstein Rediscovered* (London, Routledge, 1992)

and Derek Spring, (eds.) *Stalinism and Soviet Cinema* (London, Routledge, 1993)

Timoshenko, S., *Iskusstvo kino i montazh fil'ma* (Leningrad, Academia, 1926)

Tolstoy, V., Bibikova I., Cooke, C., *Street Art of the Revolution* (London, Thames & Hudson, 1984)

Trotskii, Leon, *Literature and Revolution* [1924] (Ann Arbor, Michigan UP, 1960)

Tsivian, Yuri, *Early Cinema in Russia and its Cultural Reception* (London, Routledge, 1994)

and Cherchi Usai, Paolo, *Silent Witnesses* (London, BFI, 1989)

Turkin, Valentin, *Kino-iskusstvo, Kino-akter, Kino-shkola* (Moscow, Kino-izdatel'stvo RSFSR, 1925)
Kino-Akter (Moscow, Tea-Kino-Pechat', 1929)
Ullman, Richard H., *Britain and the Russian Civil War* (Princeton, Princeton UP, 1968)
von Geldern, James, *Bolshevik Festivals 1917–1920* (London, California UP, 1993)
Vucinich, Alexander, *Science in Russian Culture 1861–1917* (Stanford, Stanford UP, 1970)
Wells, H. G., 'Russia in the Shadows', *The Works of H. G. Wells* (Atlantic Edition, London, 1927)
Worrall, Nick, *Modernism to Realism on the Soviet Stage* (Cambridge, CUP, 1989)
Willemen, Paul, *Looks and Frictions* (Bloomington, Indiana UP, 1994)
Williams, Linda, (ed.) *Viewing Positions* (New Brunswick, Rutgers UP, 1995)
Williams, Raymond and Orrom, Michael, *Preface to Film* (London, Film Drama Limited, 1954)
Youngblood, Denise J., *Soviet Cinema in the Silent Era* (Ann Arbor, Michigan UP, 1985)
Movies for the Masses (Cambridge, CUP, 1992)
The Magic Mirror (Wisconsin, Wisconsin UP, 1999)
Zak, Mark, *Rasskaz o Pudovkine* (Moscow, Biuro propagandy kinoiskusstva, 1970)
Zamiatin, Evgenii, *We* [1920–21], tr. C. Brown (Harmondsworth, Penguin, 1993)
Zapasnik, Tatiana and Petrovich, Adi, (eds.) *Pudovkin v vospominiiakh sovremennikov* (Moscow, Iskusstvo, 1989)
Wsewolod Pudowkin, die Zeit in Grossaufnahme (Berlin, Henschelverlag, 1983)

Journal Articles and Theses

Alpers, Boris, 'Pudovkin', *Kino i zhizn'* 5, 1929
Aristarco, Guido, 'Teoria di Pudovkin', *Bianco e Nero* 9.5, July 1948
Bailes, K. E., 'Alexei Gastev and the Soviet Controversy over Taylorism', *Soviet Studies* XXIX.3, 1977
Baranovskaia, Vera, 'Akter dramy v kino', *Sovetskoe kino* 38, 21 September 1926
Bordwell, David,'Eisenstein's Epistemological Shift', *Screen* 15.4, 5 1974–75
Brik, Osip, 'Kino v teatre Meierkhol'da', *Sovetskii ekran* 20, 18 May 1926
'From the Theory and Practice of a Script Writer', *Screen* 15.3 Autumn 1974
Bryher (Winifred Ellermann), 'Pudovkin's "Mechanics of the Brain"', *Close-Up*, 3.4, 1928
Burch, Noël, 'Film's Institutional Mode and the Soviet Response', *October*, Winter 1979
Burns, Paul E., 'Linkage: Pudovkin's Classics Revisited', *Journal of Popular Film and Television*, 9.2, Summer 1981
Derzhavin, Konstantin, 'Akter ili naturshchik?', *Art-ekran* 4, 1923
Devidov, Mikhail, 'Naschet geroev v kino i v literature', *Sovetskii ekran* 50, 11 December 1928

Fefer, Boris, 'Povedenie cheloveka', *Sovetskoe kino* 1, 1 February 1926
Golovnia, Anatolii, 'S"emki kartiny "Povedenie cheloveka"', *Sovetskii ekran* 40, 5 October 1926
'Osnovy operatorskoi raboty', *Sovetskii ekran* 44, 1 November 1927
'Okno v zhizn"', *Kino-Moskva* 30 September 1932
Gordon, Mel, 'Meyerhold's Biomechanics', *Drama Review* 18.3 September 1974
Guthrie, E. R., 'Pavlov's Theory of Conditioning', *The Psychological Review* 41 1934
Halperin, Charles J., 'George Vernadsky, Eurasianism, the Mongols and Russia', *Slavic Review* 41.3 1982
Horowitz, Irving Louis, 'The Politics of Physiological Psychology', *Integrative Physiological and Behavioural Science* 28.2 1993
Inkhizhinov, Valerii, 'Les Souvenirs d'Inkijinoff', *Cinéma* 167 1972
'Bair i ia', *Sovetskii ekran* 33, 14 August 1928
Kepley, Vance Jr. and Betty, '*Intolerance* and the Soviets', *Wide Angle* 3.1 1979
'Foreign Films on the Soviet Screen', *Quarterly Review of Film Studies* 4.4 1979
'W. I. R. and the Cinema of the Left', *Cinema Journal* 23.1 1983
'Pudovkin and the Classical Hollywood Tradition', *Wide Angle* 7.3 1985
'Pudovkin and the Continuity Style: Problems of Space and Narration' *Discourse* 17.3 1995
'Pudovkin, Socialist Realism and the Classical Hollywood Style', *Journal of Film and Video* 47.4 1995–96
Khersonskii, Khrisanf, 'Mat"', *Pravda* 21 October 1926
'O dramaturgicheskoi tekhnike amplua aktera', *Kino-zhurnal ARK* 6–7 1925
Kleiman, Naum, 'Kak Eizenshtein rabotal s akterami', *Iskusstvo kino* 1 1968
Pavlov, Ivan 'On Communist Dogmatism', Gantt transcript, *Integrative Physiology and Behavioural Science* 27.3 1992
Petrić, Vlada, 'Soviet Revolutionary Films in the USA', Ph. D., New York University, 1973
Potamkin, Harry Alan, 'The Personality of the Player', *Close-Up* 6.4 1930
Pudovkin, Vsevolod, 'Fotogeniia', *Kino-zhurnal ARK* 4–5, 1925
'Montazh nauchnoi fil'my', *Kino-zhurnal ARK* 9, 1925
'Kak delaetsia kul'turfil'ma', *Sovetskoe kino* 1, 1927
'Film Direction and Film Manuscript', *Experimental Cinema* 1.1 (February 1930), 1.2 (June 1930)
'Vremia krupnym planom', *Proletarskoe kino* 1, 1932
'Film Acting: Two Phases', *Theatre Workshop* 1.1 (October 1936)
Rakhmanova, O., 'O metode vospitaniia aktera', *Kino-zhurnal ARK* 6–7, 1925
Shostakovich, Dmitri, 'O muz'yke k "Novomu Vavilonu"', *Sovetskii ekran* 12 March 1929
Sokolov, Ippolit, 'Vospitanie kino-aktera', *Proletskoe kino* (Moscow, Proletkino, 1925)
Tait, A. L., 'The Literary Works of A. V. Lunacharskii', Ph.D., Cambridge University, 1971

Taylor, Richard, et. al., 'Russian and Soviet Cinema: Continuity and Change', *Historical Journal of Film, Radio and Television* II.2, 1991

Todes, Daniel P., 'From Radicalism to Scientific Convention', Ph.D., Michigan U, 1981

Tsivian, Yuri, 'In the Land of the Soviets', *Griffithiana* 55–56, 1996

Thompson, Kristin, 'Early Sound Counterpoint', *Yale French Studies* 60, 1980

Index

Actor in Film, The, x, xvi, xxv, 74, 139, 153–4, 155, 157, 179
Adventures of Mr. West in the Land of the Bolsheviks, The (Kuleshov), 2, 12, 14, 16
Alexander Nevsky (Eisenstein), 124, 180
Arhheim, Rudolf, xxi, 17, 24, 73
Arsenal, The (Dovzhenko), 92

Balázs, Béla, 9, 57, 97, 100, 170
Ballet mécanique, Le (Léger), 100
Baranovsaia, Vera, x, xvi, xxv, 17, 59, 69, 70, 74–76, 160
Barnet, Boris, 11, 12, 17
Batalov, Nikolai, xvi, xxv, 17, 72, 74
Battleship Potemkin, The (Eisenstein), xii, 59, 76, 142–3
Bazin, André, xxv, xxvi, 20, 105
Bekhterev, Vladimir, 39, 43, 47, 81–84, 129–30, 180–81
Bergson, Henri, 84–85
Berlin: Symphony of a Great City (Ruttmann), xxii, 96, 168
Brik, Osip, xv, 118, 158
Bukharin, Nikolai, 30, 166
Burch, Noël, viii, 21, 103

Chapaev (Vasilievs), 114
Chess Fever, 14, 17–9, 20
Chernyshevsky, Nikolai, 32, 62
Chistiakov, Alexander, 10, 74, 150
Christie, Ian, xiii

Darwin, Charles, 11, 33, 45, 47, 111, 181
Death Ray, The (Kuleshov), xvi, 4, 16
della Volpe, Galvano, xiv, 143
Delluc, Louis, 4, 88, 89, 170
Delsarte, François, xvii, 4, 15
Deserter, The, xxiv, 4, 74, 145, 149–55, 180
Diderot, Denis, 13, 163
Doller, Mikhail, xxv, 146
Dovzhenko, Alexander, xxiv, xxvii, 155
Dura Lex (By the Law) (Kuleshov), 101

Eggert, Konstantin, 20
Eikhenbaum, Boris, 9, 20, 23, 172
Eisenstein, Sergei, xiv, xxi, xxiv, xxvii, 17, 23, 58–9, 89, 155; and typage, 126, 128 and sound, 141; and montage, 169–189
End of St. Petersburg, The, x, xx, 17, 19, 37, 87–106, 131, 146, 153, 170, 174, 177
Engineer Prait s Project (Kuleshov), 4, 17
Eye of Glass, The (Lily Brik), xxii

Fairbanks, Douglas, xiii, 18, 105
FEKS (Factory of the Eccentric Actor: Kozintsev and Trauberg), xvii, 11, 15, 157
Film Director and Film Material, The, xv, xxi, xxv, 2, 21, 48, 56–7, 97, 172, 183
Film Scenario, The, xv, xxv, 2, 20, 21, 48, 57, 183
Fogel, Vladimir, 17
Forty-First, The (Protazanov), 113
Freud, Sigmund, 34, 38, 43, 181, 186

Gardin, Vladimir, xiii, 1, 11, 62, 92
Gastev, Alexei, 14
Gay Canary, The (Kuleshov), 3
Golovnia, Anatoli, x, xxii, xxv, 36, 59, 90, 95, 106, 115–6, 125, 151
Gorky, Maxim, 61–64, 67–70, 113, 117, 124

Griffith, David Wark, viii, x, xxv, 9, 57, 71–2
Groys, Boris, xii, xiv

Hammer and Sickle, The (Gardin), 1, 2
Harvest, The, xxiii
Hunger... Hunger... Hunger (Gardin), 2, 92

Iezuitov, Nikolai, ix, 2, 40
Iampolsky, Mikhail, 15
Inkizhinov, Valeri, xvi, xxv, 17, 76, 125–6
Intolerance (Griffith), 1, 76, 93
Iutkevich, Sergei, xxiv
Ivan the Terrible (Eisenstein), xxiv, 158

James, William, 33, 44, 83, 181

Kepley Jr., Vance, 98
Khokhlova, Alexandra, 3, 5, 14, 15, 16
Kerensky, Alexander, 119
Kiss of Mary Pickford, The (Komarov), 18
Kuleshov, Lev, i, xv–xvii, 2–20, 23, 47, 57, 91, 100, 101, 161
Kuhle Wampe (Dudow), 150, 152

Lenin, Vladimir, xii, 30, 32, 35, 82–3, 119, 169, 181, 183
Life is Very Good (A Simple Case), xxiv, 22, 74, 114, 139–147, 180
Living Corpse, The, xvi, xxiv–v, 9, 74, 142–43, 144, 170
Locksmith and Chancellor (Gardin), 1, 92
Lunacharsky, Anatoli, 30, 35, 72–3, 85, 117, 125

Mariamov, A. M., ix, 36, 38, 63
Man With a Movie Camera, The (Vertov), 97–8
Mayakovsky, Vladimir, xx, xxiii, 22, 61, 120, 128, 156
Mechanics of the Brain, The, x, 2, 18, 22, 29–49, 127, 175, 183
Meyerhold, Vsevolod, x, 13, 14, 56–8, 86, 156, 161–2, 187
Montagu, Ivor, xv–xix, 37, 74, 105
Moscow in October (Barnet), x, xx
Mother, The, xiv, xxiv, 37, 55–77, 92, 96, 113, 120, 121, 142–3, 147
Moussinac, Léon, i, xiv, 4, 11, 36
Mozzhukhin, Ivan, 6

Münsterberg, Hugo, 43, 55

Admiral Nakhimov, xxiii, 4, 29
Nanook (Flaherty), 130–31
New Babylon, The (Kozintsev and Trauberg), 113, 120, 140–1
Nilsen, Vladimir, xxi

October (Eisenstein), x, xx, 128, 148, 184

Pavlov, Ivan, 8, 29–49, 81, 98, 174, 180–2
Perestiani Ivan, 1
Piotrovsky, Adrian, viii, 71–2
Plekhanov, Georgi, 111, 131–9, 170, 181
Podobed, P. A., 4, 13, 17
Poggioli, Renato, xi, xii
Preobrazhenskaia, Olga, 1, 124
Protazanov, Iakov, xiii, 4, 17, 20, 62, 124
Pudovkin, Vsevolod: as an actor, xvi, xxiv, 1, 3, 9, 17, 74–5;
  on acting, x, 2, 11, 12, 16, 17, 104, 125, 127, 142, 153–5, 159;
  on non–actors, 4, 17, 74, 126–7;
  and montage, xxii, xxvi, 1, 2, 5, 21, 24, 44–47, 58-9, 87–92, 98–9, 142-4, 158, 168–89; Kuleshov experiment, 6–10

Razumny, Alexander, 8, 63, 66, 73
Rodchenko, Alexander, xxii, 14, 101, 103
Romm, Mikhail, 35, 142
Rotha, Paul, xxiv, 36
Ruttmann, Walter, xxii

Sadoul, Georges, ix, xxiii
Sechenov, I. M., 31–35
Shipulinsky, Feofan, 1, 9, 20
Shklovsky, Viktor, xiii, xiv, 60, 63, 72, 105, 145
Shpikovsky, Nikolai, 18, 20
Shutko, Kirill, 23
Simple Case, A (see *Life is Very Good*)
Soviet Toys (Vertov), 125
Stalin, Joseph, xii, xiv, xxiv, 119, 171
Stanislavsky, Konstantin, xvii, 2, 13, 18, 74–75, 156–62, 180
Stenberg brothers, xxii
Storm over Asia, xi, xxiv, 18, 37, 58, 70, 111–38, 174
Strike, The (Eisenstein), xvii, 57, 129, 142, 185

Suvorov, xxiii, xxiv, 29

Taylor, F. W. and Taylorism, 13
Taylor, Richard, xiii, 182
Timoshenko, Semion, 187
Ten Years (Shub), xx
Tisse, Edouard, 2
Tolstoy, Lev, 58, 61–4, 72, 76
Trotsky, Lev, 65
Tsivian, Yuri, 9, 96
Turkin, Valentin, xv

Vachnadze, Nata, 9
Vertov, Dziga, xiv, xxi–xxiv, 45, 60, 97, 120, 155–6, 172

Woman of Paris (Chaplin), 95, 172

Zamiatin, Evgeny, 12, 33
Zarkhi, Natan, x, 2, 62, 65–70, 88, 145–6
Zemtsova, Anna, 14, 15, 29
Zavattini, Cesare, xxvii